THE HISTORY OF AL-ṬABARĪ

AN ANNOTATED TRANSLATION

VOLUME IV

The Ancient Kingdoms

The History of al-Ṭabarī

Editorial Board

Ihsan Abbas, University of Jordan, Amman

C. E. Bosworth, The University of Manchester

Jacob Lassner, Wayne State University, Detroit

Franz Rosenthal, Yale University

Ehsan Yar-Shater, Columbia University (*General Editor*)

SUNY

SERIES IN NEAR EASTERN STUDIES

Said Amir Arjomand, Editor

Bibliotheca Persica
Edited by Ehsan Yar-Shater

The History of al-Ṭabarī

(Ta'rīkh al-rusul wa'l-mulūk)

VOLUME IV

The Ancient Kingdoms

translated and annotated
by

Moshe Perlmann

University of California, Los Angeles

annotations of Iranian names and terms
by Shaul Shaked
Hebrew University of Jerusalem

State University of New York Press

The preparation of this volume was made possible by a grant from the Program for Research Tools and Reference Works of the National Endowment for the Humanities, an independent federal agency; and in part by the Persian Heritage Foundation.

Published by
State University of New York Press, Albany

Printed in the United States of America

For information, address the State University of New York Press, 90 State Street, Suite 700, Albany, NY 12207
Library of Congress Cataloging in Publication Data

Tabarī, 838?–923.
The ancient kingdoms.

Bibliotheca Persica (SUNY series in Near Eastern studies) (The history of al-Tabari = Ta'rīkh al-rusul wa'l-mulūk; v. 4)
Translation of extracts from: Ta'rikh al-rusul wa'l-mulūk; v. 4)
Bibliography: p.
Includes index.
1. Iran—History—To 640. 2. Jews—History. 3. Arabs—History—To 662. 4. Legends, Jewish. 5. Legends, Christian. I. Perlmann, Moshe. II. Title. III. Title: Ta'rīkh al-rusul wa'l-muluk. IV. Series: Bibliotheca Persica (Albany, N.Y.) V. Series: SUNY series in Near Eastern studies. VI. Series: Ṭabarī, 838?–923. Ta'rīkh al-rusul wa-al-muluk. English; v. 4.
DS275.T332513 1987 935 85-17282
ISBN 0-87706-181-8
ISBN 0-88706-182-6 (pbk.)

Acknowledgements

In 1971 the General Editor proposed to the UNESCO to include a translation of al-Ṭabarī's *History* in its Collection of Representative Works. UNESCO agreed, but the Commission in charge of Arabic works favored other priorities. Deeming the project worthy, the Iranian Institute of Translation and Publication, which collaborated with UNESCO, agreed to undertake the task. After the upheavals of 1979, assistance was sought from the National Endowment for the Humanities. The invaluable encouragement and support of the Endowment is here gratefully acknowledged.

The General Editor wishes to thank sincerely also the participating scholars, who have made the realization of this project possible; the Board of Editors for their selfless assistance; Professor Franz Rosenthal for his many helpful suggestions in the formulation and application of the editorial policy; Professor Jacob Lassner for his painstaking and meticulous editing; and Dr. Susan Mango of the National Endowment for the Humanities for her genuine interest in the project and her advocacy of it.

Preface

THE HISTORY OF PROPHETS AND KINGS (*Ta'rīkh al-rusul wa'l-mulūk*) by Abū Jaʿfar Muḥammad b. Jarīr al-Ṭabarī (839–923), here rendered as the *History of al-Ṭabarī*, is by common consent the most important universal history produced in the world of Islam. It has been translated here in its entirety for the first time for the benefit of non-Arabists, with historical and philological notes for those interested in the particulars of the text.

Ṭabarī's monumental work explores the history of the ancient nations, with special emphasis on biblical peoples and prophets, the legendary and factual history of ancient Iran, and, in great detail, the rise of Islam, the life of the Prophet Muḥammad, and the history of the Islamic world down to the year 915. The first volume of this translation will contain a biography of al-Ṭabarī and a discussion of the method, scope, and value of his work. It will also provide information on some of the technical considerations that have guided the work of the translators.

The *History* has been divided here into 38 volumes, each of which covers about two hundred pages of the original Arabic text in the Leiden edition. An attempt has been made to draw the dividing lines between the individual volumes in such a way that each is to some degree independent and can be read as such. The page numbers of the original in the Leiden edition appear on the margins of the translated volumes.

Each volume has an index of proper names. A general index volume will follow the publication of the translation volumes.

Al-Ṭabarī very often quotes his sources verbatim and traces the chain of transmission (*isnād*) to an original source. The chains of transmitters are, for the sake of brevity, rendered by only a dash (—) between the individual links in the chain. Thus, According to Ibn Ḥumayd—Salamah—Ibn Isḥāq means that al-Ṭabarī received the report from Ibn Ḥumayd who said that he was told by Salamah, who said that he was told by Ibn Isḥāq, and so on. The numerous subtle and important differences in the original Arabic wording have been disregarded.

The table of contents at the beginning of each volume gives a brief survey of the topics dealt with in that particular volume. It also includes the headings and subheadings as they appear in al-Ṭabarī's text, as well as those occasionally introduced by the translators.

Well-known place-names, such as, for instance, Mecca, Baghdad, Jerusalem, Damascus, and the Yemen, are given in their English spellings, Less common place-names, which are the vast majority, are transliterated. Biblical figures appear in the accepted English spelling. Iranian names are usually transcribed according to their Arabic forms, and the presumed Iranian forms are often discussed in the footnotes.

Technical terms have been translated wherever possible, but some, such as dirham and imām, have been retained in Arabic forms. Others that cannot be translated with sufficient precision have been retained and italicized as well as footnoted.

The annotation aims chiefly at clarifying difficult passages, identifying individuals and place-names, and discussing textual difficulties. Much leeway has been left to the translators to include in the footnotes whatever they consider necessary and helpful.

The bibliographies list all the sources mentioned in the annotation.

The index in each volume contains all the names of persons and places referred to in the text, as well as those mentioned in the notes as far as they refer to the medieval period. It does not include the names of modern scholars. A general index, it is hoped, will appear after all the volumes have been published.

Ehsan Yar-Shater

Contents

Translator's Foreword

The events of the present volume revolve around two major subjects: Iran, and the Hebrews after Solomon. Both of these subjects include data on the past of the Arabs (Anbār, Ḥīrah and the Jews in the Hijāz). Judaeo-Christian lore (Christ, the Seven Sleepers, Saint George, Jonah, Samson) is set in the period of the obscure princelings who ruled between Alexander the Great and the rise of the Sasanian Empire. Not only does Ṭabarī combine Arab and Iranian themes, but he attempts to synchronize them with the body of Judaeo-Christian lore. For information concerning the latter, the author relied on early Islamic authors, principally, Ibn al-Kalbī and Wahb b. Munabbih. Much of his data is derived from the Alexander Romance on the one hand, and on the other hand from a cycle of legend and tradition that was later given artistic shape by Daqīqī and Firdawsī who flourished within a half century of his death.

M. P.

Los Angeles, California

An Account of the Persian Kings who Ruled the Region of Babylonia and the East After Kayqubādh.

Kayqubādh b. Zāgh b. Būjbāh was followed by Kayqāwus[1] b. Kayabiwah[2] b. Kayqubādh the king. It is reported that on the day he became king he said, "God accorded us the earth and whatever is in it that we might proceed upon it in obedience to Him." Report has it also that he slew a number of the powerful men of the lands around him; that he thwarted any infringement upon his land and subjects by the enemies around them; and that he lived in Balkh.[3] A uniquely beautiful and perfectly [598]

---

1. The second part of this name is derived from ancient Iranian Kavi Usan, giving Qāwūs which sometimes occurs in Arabic and Persian sources as Qābūs, with an additional and superfluous Kay. The latter is again derived from ancient Iranian Kavi, added in these cases as a title. For the title Kay, from the ancient form Kavi. The Arabic orthography of these names is retained throughout the translation. See Christensen, *Kayanides*, 43. On the person mentioned here see EI^2, s.v. Kay Ḳā'ūs, and Christensen, *Kayanides*, 73ff., 108ff., where an analysis of the various ancient Iranian traditions reflected in Ṭabarī's account will be found. A connected narrative of these legends, based mostly on the *Shāhnāmah*, may be seen in Spiegel, *Eranische Alterthumskunde*, I, 584ff.

2. See Justi, *Iran Nb*, 19f., s.v. Aipiwaṅhu.

3. A late form of the name of ancient Bactria. See EI^2, s.v. Balkh.

formed son was born to him, and was named Siyāwakhsh.[4] The king assigned and entrusted his son's training to Rustam[5] al-Shadīd b. Dastān b. Brāmān b. Hawarbak b. Karshāsb b. Athrat b. Sahm b. Narīmān, who was governor (*isbahbadh*) of Sijistān[6] and the adjacent territory to the south. Rustam took charge of the prince, and they proceeded to Sijistān, with the prince remaining under his tutelage. Rustam assembled selected nurses and maids for the infant until he developed. Following that, Rustam selected teachers to instruct the child until he mastered horseback riding, and then to teach him chivalry until he became expert in the art. Finally, he brought him as an accomplished young man to Kayqāwus, who examined him and found him efficient, nay outstanding, in every respect. The father rejoiced.

Kayqāwus is said to have married the daughter of Frāsiyāt,[7] the king of the Turks;[8] others say she was the daughter of the king of the Yaman.[9] Her name was Sūdhābah,[10] and she was a sorceress. She became enamored of Siyāwakhsh and made overtures to him, but he did not respond—it would take too long to relate the story of these two. But finally, as I was told, when Sūdhābah saw that Siyāwakhsh was firm in his re-

---

4. Siyāwakhsh, Siyāwush: Some references will be found in *EI*[1], s.v. Kai-Ḳā'ūs. See also Christensen, *Kayanides*, 79, 111f.

5. Rustam is derived from Middle Iranian Rōd-stahm. See Markwart, *ZDMG*, 49 (1895), 642; Christensen, *Kayanides*, 121ff., 130ff.

6. Sijistān is ancient Sakastāna, the land of the Saka tribes, also known in the Islamic period as Sistan. See *EI*[1], IV, 456ff., and G. Gnoli, *Richerche storiche sul Sistan*.

7. Frāsiyāt is a corruption of Frāsiyāb (sometimes written Afrāsiyāb), which in its turn is a late derivative of the ancient name Frangrasyan. See Christensen, *Kayanides*, 43, 61ff., 85ff.; *EI*[2], s.v. Afrāsiyāb; *Enc. Iran.*, I, 570ff., s.v. Afrāsiāb.

8. According to the original legend he was a Turanian king, and therefore an enemy of Iran. Later, the early designation Turan was replaced anachronistically by a reference to the Turks.

9. This remark contains an allusion to another story, according to which Su'dah, the daughter of the king of the Yaman, was married to Kay Qāwūs after the latter had suffered defeat by the Yemenite king, but was rescued by Rustam. See Christensen, *Kayanides*, 110.

10. Sudhābah is perhaps a derivative of Middle Persian Sudhābag. See Christensen, *Kayanides*, 62ff., 110ff. The name Sudhāba could conceivably be an Iranized form of Su'da (which seems somewhat more likely in the present context).

fusal to comply with her wish that he commit adultery with his father's spouse, she made him hateful to his father. Siyāwakhsh then asked Rustam to plead with his father to send him to fight Frāsiyāt because the latter withheld certain gifts (that had been) stipulated when he gave away his daughter in marriage to Kayqāwus and concluded a peace between the two realms. Siyāwakhsh thus intended to keep away from his father, Kayqāwus, and the intrigue of his wife Sūdhābah. Rustam, indeed, acted accordingly and asked Kayqāwus to consent. [599]

A substantial force was assigned to the son who then proceeded to the land of the Turks to meet Frāsiyāt. When Siyāwakhsh reached him, a truce was concluded between them. Siyāwakhsh reported to his father about the truce, but the father ordered him to oppose Frāsiyāt and do combat with him, unless the latter submitted by fulfilling the previous stipulations. Siyāwakhsh, however, considered that to follow his father's command and fight Frāsiyāt, after a truce and peace had been concluded and scrupulously observed by Frāsiyāt, would be dishonorable, vicious and sinful. He therefore refrained from implementing his father's order in this matter. He was also apprehensive lest he again be approached by his father's spouse who had urged him to be with her, and whom he had spurned. He was inclined to flee from his father, so he sent a message to Frāsiyāt asking for a guarantee of safe-conduct to enable him to leave his father and join Frāsiyāt, whereupon the latter agreed. It is said that the legate between them was Fīrān b.[11] Wīsaghān, a Turk of great standing. When Siyāwakhsh did this, he was abandoned by the men of his father's army who set out to return to Kayqāwus. [600]

When Siyāwakhsh reached Frāsiyāt, the latter received him with honor and gave him in marriage one of his daughters, Wisfāfarīd,[12] the mother of Kaykhusrawanh.[13] Not only was Siyā-

11. The Iranian form of this name is Pīrān, of the family of Wisag. See Christensen, *Kayanides*, 111; Markwart, *Wehrot*, 58n.

12. Wisfāfarīd is a corruption of Wispān-friya, which means "Beloved by all." See Christensen, *Kayanides*, 111 and n. 2. An alternative interpretation of the meaning of this name could be Middle Persian Wisp-āfrīd, which would mean either "Blessed by all [the deities]" or "[Worshiper of God,] the Creator of all."

wakshs held in esteem, but his training and good sense, his expertness, and his chilvary and bravery made such an impact on Frāsiyāt that he became apprehensive concerning his own kingship. This alienated him from Siyāwakhsh, especially as two sons of Frāsiyāt and a brother of his, Kīdar[14] b. Fashinjān,[15] became envious and apprehensive for their kingdom. Finally Frāsiyāt allowed them to kill Siyāwakhsh.

A long story is told concerning the cause of their decision to kill him. In any case, they killed him and mutilated him while his spouse, the daughter of Frāsiyāt, was pregnant with his son
[601] Kaykhasrawanh. They also sought a way to induce an abortion but did not succeed.

Fīrān, who brought about the peace between Frāsiyāt and Siyāwakhsh, learned that Frāsiyāt had caused Siyāwahkhsh's assassination, and he disapproved of it. He threatened Frāsiyāt with the consequences of his treachery, and warned him that Kayqāwus and Rustam would avenge the death of Siyāwakhsh. He urged Frāsiyāt to hand over his daughter Wisfāfarid, so that she might stay with him until her child was born and slain; whereupon Frāsiyāt complied. But when she gave birth to the child, Fīrān had pity on her and the newborn child. He failed to slay the infant and concealed the matter until the child grew up. Kayqāwus is said to have sent Bayy[16] b. Jūdharz[17] to the land of the Turks to inquire about the child born to the spouse of his son Siyāwakhsh and, if successful in his inquiry, to bring the child (back with him). Bayy appeared (in the land of the Turks) for that purpose. Incognito, he continued inquiring into the matter for some time without obtaining any information or

---

In some sources this name occurs as Farangīs. See further Justis *IranNb*, 371, s.v. Wispān-friya; *Enc. Iran.*, I, 573b.

13. Kay-Khusraw is intended. His name, Haosravah, is spelled here in an archaizing manner. See Christensen, *Kayanides*, 90ff.; *EI²*, s.v. Kay-Khusraw.

14. Kīdar is a corruption of Kēdan. See Christensen, *Kayanides*, 111. His other name was Karsēwaz.

15. Fashinjān, the father of Kēdan and of Frāsiyāb, was Pashang. See Christensen, *Kayanides*, 85; *Enc. Iran.*, I, 571.

16. The ancient form of this name is Wēw. A common form which occurs in the texts is Geēw. See Markwart, *ZDMG*, 49 (1895), 642; Christensen, *Kayanides*, 59, 112, and index under Gēw.

17. The Iranian form of the name is Gōdarz. See references in the preceding note.

leads from anybody. But later he found out about the child, and by a ruse he succeeded in getting both mother and child out of the land of the Turks to Kayqāwus. They say that when Kayqāwus learned of the assassination of his son, he summoned a number of his leading warchiefs, among them Rustam b. Dastān al-Shadīd and Ṭūs[18] b. Nawdharān.[19] These two were men of vigor and valor.

The Persians exhausted the Turks by slaying and capturing them, while engaging Frāsiyāt in intense combat. Rustam personally killed Shahr and Shahrah,[20] the two sons of Frāsiyāt, while Ṭūs with his own hand killed Kīdar, Frāsiyāt's brother. They say that the devils were at the service of Kayqāwus. Some scholars well versed in the history of the ancients assert that the devils who were subservient to him submitted to him by the order of Solomon the son of David, and that Kayqāwus ordered the devils to build a city which he named Kaykadar or Qayqadūr. It was, they contend, eight hundred *farsakh* (4800km) in length.[21] By his order they set up around it a series of walls made of yellow brass, brass, copper, fired clay, silver and gold. The devils carried it between heaven and earth, with all the animals, treasures, wealth and people that it contained. [602]

They mention that Kayqāwus would not talk while he ate and drank.[22] Later, Almighty God sent to the city that Kayqāwus had thus built, someone who would destroy it. Kayqāwus ordered his devils to prevent the man from destroying the city but they were unable to do so. When Kayqāwus saw that the devils were unable to protect the city, he turned against them, and slew their chieftains. Kayqāwus was victorious over any king who opposed him. So it went until he became worried about the glory and the kingship granted to him, and he no

18. Tōs is the Avestan Tusa. Christensen, *Kayanides*, 58f.
19. On this name see below, n. 105.
20. The name of Frāsiyāb's son according to the *Shāhnāmah* is Surkhah. See *Enc. Iran.*, I, 573b; Justi, *Iran Nb*, 293, s.v. Šēdah, suggests that this name should be emended to read Shēdah. However, Ṭabarī, 615, reports that the latter survived the attacks of Frāsiyāt.
21. One *farsakh* equals three *mīl* or approximately six kms. See *EI*[2], s.v. farsakh.
22. This behavior conforms to the precepts of Zoroastrianism.

longer partook of anything unless it reached him by ascent to heaven.

[603] Hishām b. Muḥammad related:[23] Kayqāwus arrived in Babylon from Khurāsān[24] and said, "The whole earth is in my possession; now I must learn about heaven and the planets and what is beyond them." God granted him strength to rise in the air with his retinue until they reached the clouds; then God deprived them of that strength, and they fell downwards and perished, and the king alone escaped. Thus a new stage began, and his kingship went awry. The earth was torn among many kings on the fringes, and raids by and against him followed; sometimes he was victorious, at other times he was defeated.

Kayqāwus attacked the land of the Yaman[25] which was ruled in those days by Dhū al-Adhʿār b. Abrahah Dhū al-Manār b. al-Rā'ish.[26] When Kayqāwus arrived in the Yaman, Dhū al-Adhʿār b. Abrahah marched against him. He had been struck by semiparalysis, and was not in the habit of leading a raid in person before that. But when Kayqāwus advanced against Dhū al-Adhʿār and plundered his land, the latter personally marched out (against him) with a force of the Ḥimyar and the descendents of Qaḥṭān.[27] He defeated Kayqāwus and took him prisoner, while destroying his army. He kept him imprisoned in an encased well.

Hishām also reports that a powerful man named Rustam had come out of Sijistān with his cohort. The Persians asserted that he had attacked the Yaman and extricated Qabūs, that is Kayqāwus, from his prison. The people of the Yaman assert that when word reached Dhū al-Adhʿār that Rustam was approaching, he marched against him with his forces and equipment. Each side established a defensive perimeter around its camp.
[604] Both leaders were worried about the fate of their respective armies, and feared that if they clashed no one would survive.

---

23. See *EI*², s.v. Hishām b. Muḥammad al-Kalbī, and al-Kalbī.

24. See *EI*², s.v. Khurāsān. The term was used rather generally for the eastern regions of Iran. The original meaning of the term is "land of the rising sun."

25. See *EI*¹, s.v. al-Yaman.

26. On this episode see Christensen, *Kayanides*, 110.

27. The references to Ḥimyar and Qaḥṭān denote South Arabian associations. Qaḥṭān was the fictitious ancestor of all the South Arabian tribes. See *EI*², s.v. Ḳaḥṭān.

They agreed therefore that Kayqāwus was to be handed over to Rustam, and that warfare was to be abandoned. Rustam and Kayqāwus then departed for Babylon. Kayqāwus granted Rustam freedom from slavery to the king, endowed him with the fiefs of Sijistān and Zābulistān,[28] gave him a gold-woven *qalansuwah*,[29] crowned him, and ordered that he sit on a silver throne with legs of gold. That land remained in the hands of Rustam down to the death of Kayqāwus and for a long time thereafter. He reigned for 150 years.

Persian scholars assert that the first to mourn by wearing black was Shādūs[30] b. Jūdharz who mourned for Siyāwakhsh. He did this on the day Kayqāwus learned of his son's death—the victim of a treacherous assassination by Frāsiyāt. Wearing black, Shādūs came to Kayqāwus and announced to him that he did so because it was a day of darkness and blackness.

Ibn al-Kalbī's report that the ruler of the Yaman captured Qabūs is verified by a poem of al-Ḥasan b. Hāni':[31]

> Qabūs spent the hot season in our chains
> for seven years, enough for one to compute them.

---

28. The highlands of the Kandahar country in Afghanistan. See LeStrange, *Lands*, 334.

29. A headgear with a high conic shape, often worn in Islamic times by highly placed persons such as caliphs, wazīrs and qāḍīs. See Dozy, *Vêtements*, 365–371.

30. For Shādūs, see Justi, *Iran Nb*, 294, s.v. Šēdōs, who assumes that the name contains an *imālah*, i.e., a change of the first vowel from *-a-* to *-ē-*.

31. That is the famous poet of the 'Abbāsid period, Abū Nuwās, who died ca. 200 (815). See *EI*², s.v. Abū Nuwās.

Kaykhusraw

After Kayqāwus, his grandson Kaykhusraw, the son of Siyāwakhsh b. Kayqāwus b. Kayabīwah b. Kayqubādh became king. When Bayy b. Jūdharz brought him and his mother Wisfāfarīd (she is often referred to as Wasfafrah), the daughter of Frāsiyāt,
[605] from the land of the Turks to Kayqāwus, the latter made him king. When Kaykhusraw followed his grandfather Kayqāwus as ruler and was crowned, he delivered an eloquent speech to his subjects in which he announced that he would seek to avenge the blood of his father Siyāwakhsh upon Frāsiyāt the Turk. Then he wrote to Jūdharz, the general, who was in Iṣbahān and the regions of Khurāsān, ordering him to appear before him. When Jūdharz arrived, the king informed him of his decision to avenge the murder of his father. He instructed him to review the army, select thirty thousand men, attach them to Ṭūs b. Nūdharān, and to send the latter with them to the land of the Turks. Jūdharz carried out the order and joined Ṭūs. Among those who came with him were Burzāfrah[32] b. Kayqāwus, the paternal uncle of Kaykhusraw, Bayy b. Jūdharz, and a large number of his brothers. Kaykhusraw instructed Ṭūs to pursue

---

32. Burzāfrah (or Burz-farrah) occurs in some traditions as Fariburz. See Justi, *Iran Nb*, 73, s.v. Burzafrah; Bal'amī, *Ta'rīkh*, 603 n.1. For the alternative reading Burzafarrah see the name Barzapharnes in Justi, *Iran Nb*, 65; Christensen, *Kayanides*, 115 n.3.

Frāsiyāt and his warlords but not through the Turkish territory where Furūdh[33] b. Siyāwakhsh lived; he was a brother of Kaykhusraw—born to a mother called Burzāfarīd,[34] a woman Siyāwakhsh had married in a Turkish town on his way to Frāsiyāt. Later Siyāwakhsh left her while she was with child. She gave birth to Furūdh, and he grew up in this town. They say that Ṭūs committed a fatal error: namely, when he was near [606] the city in which Furūdh dwelled somehow hostilities broke out between them. In the course of these hostilities Furūdh perished. When the news reached Kaykhusraw, he wrote a harsh note to his uncle Burzāfrah telling him that Ṭūs b. Nūdharān had fought his (that is Kaykhusraw's) brother Furūdh. Ṭūs was to be delivered in chains and shackles, and Burzāfrah was to take over the command of the army. When the message reached Burzāfrah, he gathered the military commanders, read them the order to put Ṭūs in chains, and dispatched him with trustworthy messengers to Kaykhusraw. Burzāfrah took over the army command and crossed the river known as Kāsrūd.[35] When Frāsiyāt learned of this, he sent some of his brothers and warlords against Burzāfrah. They met at Wāshin[36] in the land of the Turks. Among them were Fīrān b. Wīsaghān and his brothers, Tarāsf[37] b. Jūdharz, Frāsiyāt's brother-in-law, and Hamāsf[38] b. Fashinjān. They fought a furious engagement. As Burzāfrah perceived the seriousness of the situation and the great number of dead, he lost courage, and retreated with the banner to the mountains. The Jūdharz clan became confused, [607] and in that massacre seventy of them were slaughtered in one battle. Many were killed on both sides. Burzāfrah and his reti-

33. Possibly to be read Farūdh. See Justi, *Iran Nb*, 99; Christensen, *Kayanides*, 115, where the name is read Frōd.

34. See Justi, *Iran Nb*, 73.

35. The name, which should probably be read Kāsa(g)-rōd, is identified by Markwart, *Wehrot*, 5, with present-day Kashaf-rūd. See also Justi, *Der Bundehesh*, 205, s.v. Kasp; Spiegel, *Eranische Alterthumskunde*, I, 627ff.

36. Wāshin may be the place often referred to in the Arabic geographical works as Wāshjird or Wēshjird. A discussion of its location is in Markwart, *Wehrot*, 54ff.

37. For Tarāsf, or better Tarāsp, see Justi, *Iran Nb*, 322.

38. Hamāsf, or better Hamāsp, is possibly a corruption of Hamazasp, a well-attested Iranian name. See Justi, *Iran Nb*, 124 ff.

nue left for Kaykhusraw. So disturbed and stricken were they that they wished they were dead. They were also in terror of chastisement. When they came before Kaykhusraw, he began to upbraid Burzāfrah violently and said, "You were deceived because you disobeyed my order; contravening a royal command brings misfortune and causes regret." So grievous were Kaykhusraw's words that Burzāfrah was pained and could neither eat nor sleep.

A few days after their arrival, Kaykhusraw sent for Jūdharz. When he entered, Kaykhusraw displayed compassion. Then Jūdharz complained of Burzāfrah, stating that it was Burzāfrah who had caused the flight with the banner and the desertion of his (Jūdharz's) sons. Kaykhusraw then said, "Your loyal service to our ancestors has been continuous; our troops and treasuries are at your disposal in the pursuit of revenge." He ordered Jūdharz to prepare and ready himself to march against Frāsiyāt in order to slay him and lay his country desolate.

When Jūdharz heard what Kaykhusraw said, he rose at once, kissed his hand and said, "O victorious King, we are your sub-
[608] jects and slaves. Should a calamity or accident occur, may it be upon the slaves, not upon the king, and may my slain sons be a sacrifice for you. We shall wreak vengeance upon Frāsiyāt, avenging ourselves upon the kingdom of the Turks. May the king not be troubled by what occurred and let him not abandon his pleasure, for warfare is subject to turns of fortune." He assured the king that he was in full control and left content.

The next day Kaykhusraw summoned the commanders of his armies and the notables of the realm, and when they arrived he told them of his decision to fight the Turks. He wrote to the governors (*ʿummāl*) of the provinces informing them thereof and ordering them to present themselves at an appointed time in the steppe called Shāh Ustūn[39] in the Balkh region. The military chieftains arrived at the place, as did Kaykhusraw with his generals (*isbahbadh*) and their men. Among them was his paternal uncle Burzāfrah with his clan, and Jūdharz with his remaining sons. When everything was

---

39. Balʿami, *Tārīkh,* 605, gives Shāh-Sīr.

ready for war, the *marzbāns*[40] were assembled, Kaykhusraw personally reviewed the army so that he might know their numbers and positions. Then he called Jūdharz b. Jashwādghān[41] and Mīlād[42] b. Jurjīn[43] and Aghaṣ[44] b. Bihdhān.[45] Aghaṣ was the son of a lady-in-waiting under Siyāwakhsh; she was called Shūmāhān.[46] [609]

The king told them that he wanted the troops to enter the territory of the Turks from four directions to surround them on land and on water, and that Jūdharz had been put in charge of most of the troops. The assault was launched from Khurāsān by those (troops) under his uncle Burzāfrah and Bayy b. Jūdharz, and a great number of commanders were attached to Jūdharz. The king handed over to him on that day the great banner which they called *dirafsh-e-Kābyān.*[47] They say that the banner had never before been handed by any king to any general, but princes used to carry it when entrusted with grave missions. He ordered Mīlādh to enter from a spot adjacent to China, and assigned to him a large number of troops, apart from those assigned to Jūdharz. The king ordered Aghaṣ to enter from the side of the Khazars[48] with a force equal to that given Mīlādh. To Shūmāhān he assigned her brothers and nephews and fully thirty thousand men, and ordered her to enter on a road between the paths of Jūdharz and Milādh. They say that Kaykhusraw drew Shūmāhān into the campaign be-

---

40. The term *marzbān* designated some kind of highly placed official in the Sasanian period, and is here used in a loose sense for the mythological period. See Kolesnikov, *Palestinskij Sbornik,* 27 (1981), 49–56; Ph. Gignoux, *JSAI,* 4 (1984), 1–29.

41. See Justi, *Iran Nb,* 114, s.v. Gēšwād; Nöldeke, *Das iranische Nationalepos,* 8.

42. Mīlād is a form of the Iranian name Mihrdād. See Markwart, *ZDMG* (1895), 633 ff. This and some of the adjoining names indicate the Parthian provenance of certain elements in these heroic stories. See Markwart, op. cit., 641ff.; Nöldeke, *Nationalepos,* 7.

43. Jurjīn is the same name as Armenian Wrkēn. See Markwart, *ZDMG,* 49 (1895), 634 n. 3; Justi, *Iran Nb,* 355, s.v. Warkaina.

44. For this name see Justi, *Iran Nb,* 7, s.v. Aghus.

45. Perhaps a corruption of Iranian Wēh-dādān (or else of Wēh-dēn). See Justi, *Iran Nb,* 360, s.v. Wehadān.

46. The name is not clear. See Justi, *Iran Nb,* 314.

47. The actual meaning of the term is "the banner of the Kavians." See Christensen, *Sassanides,* 212.

48. That is from the Caucasus and, later, Central Asia. See *EI*², s.v. Khazar.

cause of her connection with Siyāwakhsh, whose blood she had vowed to avenge. All these marched ahead. Jūdharz entered the land of the Turks from the direction of Khurāsān, clashing first with Fīrān b. Wīsghān. A fierce battle ensued, in
[610] which Bīzan[49] b. Bayy slew Khumān[50] b. Wīsghān in single combat; also, Jūdharz killed Fīrān, and then went for Frāsiyāt. The three armies pressed upon him, each from the direction where it had entered, and the great mass followed Kaykhusraw himself. Following in the direction of Jūdharz, the king made his entry (into the land of the Turks) and reached the army of Jūdharz. He led an onslaught upon the Turks, slew Fīrān, the leading general of Frāsiyāt and heir to the throne, as well as many of his brothers, such as Khumān, Ostahan,[51] Julbād,[52] Siyāmaq,[53] Bahrām,[54] Farashkhādh[55] and Farakhlād.[56] He
[611] also slew some sons of his, such as Rūyīn[57] b. Fīrān, who was a dignitary (*muqaddam*) of Frāsiyāt, and several brothers of Frāsiyāt, among them Zandarāy,[58] Andirmān,[59] Isfakhram[60]

---

49. The name Bīzan is a reflection of Iranian Wēw-zana, meaning "of the family of Wēw." See Markwart, *ZDMG*, 69 (1895), 642. If this interpretation is correct, Bīzan means the same thing as "son of Bayy" which follows in the text.

50. The older form of the name Khumān is probably Hōmān, derived from the name of the *haoma* plant, sacred to the ancient Iranians. See Justi, *Iran Nb*, 132.

51. The name of this person occurs as Nastihan in the *Shāhnāmah*. In the Pahlavi account this person's name could be read Khwastirikht, but this reading is uncertain. See Justi, *Iran Nb*, 52, s.v. Ausahr; 182, s.v. Xwast-irixt; 226, s.v. Nastihen.

52. In the *Shāhnāmah* the form attested is Gulbād. See Justi, *Iran Nb*, 119, s.v. Gulbād.

53. See Justi, *Iran Nb*, 299.

54. In the *Shāhnāmah* the name of this person is Bārmān. See Justi, *Iran Nb*, 64, s.v. Bārmān.

55. In the *Shāhnāmah* his name is Faršīdward; the Middle Persian form may have been Frasaward. The Avestan name which may be identified here is Frašhāmvareta. See Justi, *Iran Nb*, 104.

56. Possibly Farrukhlād. The form in the *Shāhnāmah* is Lahhāk. See Justi, *Iran Nb*, 96, s.v. Farruxlād; 183, s.v. Lāwahāk.

57. The name Rūyīn means "brazen". See Justi, *Iran Nb*, 267.

58. Zandarāy may correspond to the name Zangulah in the *Shāhnāmah*. See Justi, *Iran Nb*, 379, s.v. Zandalan.

59. The name Andirmān corresponds to Avestan Vandaremainiš. In the *Shāhnāmah* it is spelled Andarīmān. See Justi, *Iran Nb*, 347, s.v. Wandaremainiš; Christensen, *Kayanides*, 25; Darmesteter, *Études Iraniennes*, II, 228f.

60. The older Iranian form of Isfakhram is Spahram. See Justi, *Iran Nb*, 307.

and Akhust.[61] He took prisoner Barwā[62] b. Fashinjān, the assassin of Siyāwakhsh. He found that Jūdharz had counted the dead and the captives, and the booty in animals and valuables; the count was thirty thousand captives, over five hundred sixty thousand slain, and animals, silver and valuables which were [612]
beyond reckoning.

The commander ordered each chieftain who was with him to place his Turkish prisoner or victim near his banner, so that Kaykhusraw might see them upon his arrival. When Kaykhusraw reached the troops and the battleground, the men lined up, and Jūdharz and the other generals received him. Upon entering the camp, he began to pass by the banners, and the first corpse he saw was that of Fīrān next to the banner of Jūdharz. When he saw it, he stopped, then said, "O hard-sheltered mountain of slopes impregnable, did I not warn you of this war, and of setting yourself in our path? All to protect Frāsiyāt in this pursuit. Did I not exert great effort for your sake? Did I not seek to offer my kingship to you? But you made a fatal choice. Was I not truthful, the protector of brethren, the keeper of secrets? Did I not warn you of Frāsiyāt's cunning, of how little he valued loyalty? But you did not do what I commanded you to do; you proceeded with your dream until lions surrounded you to keep you from fighting us and the sons of our kingdom. What good was Frāsiyāt to you? You departed from this world, and brought to an end the line of Wīsghān. Woe to your reason and understanding; woe to your generosity and truthfulness. We are truly grieved today by what has happened to you."

Kaykhusraw continued to lament Fīrān until he arrived at the banner of Bayy b. Jūdharz. When he stopped there, he found Barwā b. Fashinjān alive, a prisoner in the hands of Bayy. Upon learning that it was Barwā who had mutilated Siyāwakhsh after murdering him, Kaykhusraw came close to him, bowed his head and prostrated himself in gratitude to God. He then said, "Praise to God who enabled me to seize you, O Barwā. You are

61. The form of this name in the *Shāhnāmah* is Axwāst. See Justi, *Iran Nb*, 13.

62. Possibly the same name as attested under the form Parwā in the Sasanian period. See Justi, *Iran Nb*, 244. For Fashinjān, see above, n. 15.

[613] the man who slew Siyāwakhsh and mutilated him; you are the one who took away his finery. You, of all the Turks, undertook his destruction; you planted by your deed this tree of hostility, stirred up between us this war, kindled in both parties a burning fire. Through your hands his shape was changed and his strength sapped. O Turk, did you not stand in awe of his beauty? Why did you not leave the rising light upon his face? Where are your courage and strength today? Where is your brother the magician who failed to help you? I shall not slay you for having slain him, but for volunteering for the evil deed that you should not have committed. I shall kill him who, in wickedness and crime, slew Siyāwakhsh." Then he ordered that Barwā's limbs be cut off while Barwā was still alive, and only after that should he be slain; which was carried out by Bayy.

Kaykhusraw continued from banner to banner, from general to general (*isbahbadh*). As he reached each one, he would say something like the aforementioned remarks. Then he arrived at his campsite. When he settled down there, he summoned his uncle Burzāfrah, and when the man entered, the king seated him at his right, and expressed his satisfaction that Burzāfrah had slain Julbādh b. Wīsaghān in single combat. He richly rewarded Burzāfrah, making him ruler of the regions of Kirmān[63] and Mukrān.[64] Then he summoned Jūdharz, and when the latter entered, the king said to him, "O faithful general, kind and mature, this mighty victory is indeed due first to our God, without any stratagem or power on our part; then to your devotion to our interest and to your readiness to sacrifice yourself and your sons. This we have on record. We grant you the title of *buzurjframadhār*,[65] which is the wazīr's office, and we assign to you Iṣbahān[66] and Jurjān[67] and their mountains.

63. On the province of Kirmān in Islamic times see LeStrange, *Lands*, 299ff., and EI^2.

64. On the province of Mukrān (Makrān) in Islamic times see LeStrange, *Lands*, 329ff., and EI^2.

65. On the title *buzurjframādhār*, which literally means "the great commander," see Christensen, *Sassanides*, 518ff., and Nöldeke, *Geschichte*, 9 n.2.

66. On this town see EI^2, s.v. Isfahān; LeStrange, *Lands*, 202ff.

67. On the Islamic province of Jurjān, which is equivalent to the modern

Take good care of their people." Jūdharz gave thanks, and left [614]
content and happy.

The king then summoned the outstanding generals who had been with Jūdharz and distinguished themselves, those who were responsible for the slaying of the Turkish *tarkhāns*,[68] the progeny of Fashinjān and Wīsghān. These generals included Jurjin[69] b. Mīlādhān, Bayy, Shādūs, Lakhām,[70] Jadmīr[71] b. Jūdharz, Bīzan b. Bayy, Burāzah b. Bīfaghān,[72] Farūdhah b. Fāmdān,[73] Zandah b. Shāburīghān,[74] Bistām b. Kazdahman,[75]
and Fartah b. Tafāraghān.[76] They entered one by one. Some [615]

---

province Astarābādh, see *EI*², s.v. Gurgān, and Astarābādh; LeStrange, *Lands*, 376ff.

68. *ṭarkhān* is a title used in Islamic times for a Turkish nobleman or prince. Its use in this context is of course an anachronism, like most of the titles of office and many of the geographical names.

69. For this name see above, n. 43.

70. In the *Shāhnāmah* Lakhām is Ruhhām. See Justi, *Iran Nb*, 257, s.v. Rahām.

71. Jadmīr is possibly the same person who is named in the *Shāhnāmah*, Katmārah (see the note to the Leiden edition in this place).

72. Burāzah b. Bīfaghān is the person called in the *Shāhnāmah* Gurāzah *sar tukhma-i* Gīwagān (see note to the Leiden edition on these words). See Justi, *Iran Nb*, 349, s.v. Warāzaka. The patronymic of this person is a reflection of the name Gēwag, related to the name Wēw already encountered here (see above, n. 16).

73. Both the personal name and the patronymic are uncertain as to their reading as well as their meaning. The latter may be read perhaps Qāmdān and be regarded as a corruption of Kām-dēn, a name which may mean a person "whose religion is [according to] desire," i.e., the desire of God. See Justi, *Iran Nb*, 99, s.v. Ferūdeh.

74. The reading of the first name is doubtful. In the *Shāhnāmah* the form is Zanga, and the father's name is given as Shāwarān. The confusion has been attributed to the ambiguities of the Pahlavi script, where *d* and *g* have the same shape. This implies that the Islamic recensions used by Ṭabarī and Firdawsī were based on a reading of the stories written in Pahlavi script. If the correct reading is with *d*, the first name means "living", and gives a fairly late form of the word, *zinda*. The father's name, Shāburīghān, is apparently related to the widely attested name Shā(h)pu(h)r, which means "king's son, prince." See the note to the Leiden edition, and Justi, *Iran Nb*, 385, s.v. Zengeh, and 386, s.v. Zindeh.

75. In the *Shāhnāmah* the name occurs as Gustaham son of Gazhdaham. The older form of the first name was Wistaxma. See Justi, *Iran Nb*, 371, s.v. Wistaxma, and 114, s.v. Gezdehem.

76. In the *Shāhnāmah* the first name is Parta, probably to be derived from the word for battle, Old Iranian *parta-*. The patronymic is uncertain. It has the form Tawānah in the *Shāhnāmah*, while in the Ṭabarī manuscripts it has the

were appointed to rule the celebrated lands, some were assigned to court duties. Soon he received messages from Mīlādh, Aghaṣ and Shūmahān indicating that they had attacked the land of the Turks, and had put Frāsiyāt's armies to flight one after the other. He wrote them that they should persevere in warfare, and meet him at an appointed place within the land of the Turks. They say that when the four armies surrounded Frāsiyāt, and he learned of the havoc that death and capture had wrought in his ranks and of the destruction of his land, he was in dire straits; of all his sons only Shīdah,[77] who was a sorcerer, remained with him. Frāsiyāt sent him well prepared and equipped to Kaykhusraw. When Shīdah reached Kaykhusraw, the latter was informed that Shīdah had been sent by his father, Frāsiyāt, to make an attempt on his life. Kaykhusraw therefore gathered his generals, and cautioned them to be on guard against Shīdah's design. It is said that Kaykhusraw was apprehensive of Shīdah that day. He feared him, and believed himself helpless against him; it is also said that the battle between them continued for four days, and that one of Kaykhusraw's retinue, Jurd b. Jarhamān[78] by name, aligned Kaykhusraw's men in the best battle order. Many were slain from the opposing armies; the men of the world (*khunyarth*)[79] fought fiercely and defiantly. Shīdah, certain that he could not overcome
[616] them, fled, pursued by Kaykhusraw and his men. Jurd overtook Shīdah and struck him on the head with a mace from which he fell dead. Kaykhusraw stood over the dead body, eyeing it in its abominable ugliness. The army of the Turks became Kaykhusraw's booty. The news reached Frāsiyāt, who then advanced with all his *tarkhān*s. When Frāsiyāt and Kaykhusraw met, a ferocious battle erupted, the like of which, it may be said, has

form Fāraghān. See the annotation in the Leiden edition and Justi, *Iran Nb*, 244, s.v. Parteh.

77. For this Iranian name, which means "resplendent", see Justi, *Iran Nb*, 293f., s.v. Šēdah.

78. The reading is uncertain. See Justi, *Iran Nb*, 121, s.v. Gurd.

79. This word, usually spelled *xnyrθ*, is the Arabic transcription of the Iranian term Xvanirath, which denotes the central clime, or region, of the world, where human habitation is concentrated. The phrase here is likely to mean simply "the men of the world." The phrasing in Arabic seems in this case to be taken from a composition which bears the marks of style of heroic poetry. For the concept of Khvanirath, see Christensen, *Sassanides*, 164.

never before been fought upon the earth. The men of the guard and the Turks mingled, and the battle continued until all the eye could see was a stream of blood. Jūdharz and his sons, Jurjīn, Jurd, and Bistām were taken prisoner. Frāsiyāt noticed they were defending Kaykhusraw like ferocious lions, whereupon he fled. It is reported that the number of the slain that day reached a hundred thousand. Kaykhusraw and his men persisted in the pursuit of Frāsiyāt. The latter, stripped of arms, fled from country to country until he came to Ādharbayjān,[80] where he hid in a body of water known as Bi'r Khāsif.[81] Then he was apprehended. When Kaykhusraw arrived, he made sure to have Frāsiyāt put in irons. After three days', he summoned Frāsiyāt, and asked him what his excuse was in the matter of Siyāwakhsh. But Frāsiyāt had neither excuse, nor argument. Whereupon Kaykhusraw gave the order that he be put to death. Bayy b. Jūdharz arose and slew Frāsiyāt as Frāsiyāt had slain Siyāwakhsh. His blood was brought to Kaykhusraw who dipped his hand into it, and said, "This is in blood vengeance for Siyāwakhsh, and because you wronged him and outraged him." Victorious, successful and content, he left Ādharbayjān. [617]

It is reported that some of the sons of Kayabiwah,[82] the great-grandfather of Kaykhusraw, and their sons, were with Kaykhusraw in the battle against the Turks. Among them were Kay Arash[83] b. Kayabiwah, who was in charge of Khūzistān[84] and the adjacent land of Babylonia, and Kay Bih Arash,[85] who was in charge of Kirmān and its environs. Also with him was Kay Ojī b. Kay Manūsh[86] b. Kay Fāshīn[87] b. Kayabiwah. This

---

80. For this area in northwestern Iran see EI^2 and *Enc. Iran.*, s.v.

81. Not identified. Khasav-yurt, a river in the Khazar country, is unsuitable in this context.

82. See above, n. 2.

83. The ancient form of the name was Arsham, which means "man, a male animal." See Justi, *Iran Nb*, 29ff., s.v. Aršam.

84. See LeStrange, *Lands*, 232ff., and EI^2, s.v.

85. This name seems to be a reflection of the Old Iranian name Vanghu-Aršya, attested in the Avesta. See Justi, *Iran Nb*, 347, s.v. Wanhu-Aršya. Justi does not quote the form occurring here.

86. On the varieties of the spellings of Kay-Ojī (Kayūjī), see Justi, *Iran Nb*, 231ff. For Kay-Manūsh, see op. cit. 191.

87. The ancient form of the name is Pisina, attested in Yašt 13:132. See Justi, *Iran Nb*, 252f.

Kay Ojī was the father of King Kay Luhrāsf.[88] It is said that a brother of Frāsiyāt, Kay Sharāsf[89] by name, went to the land of the Turks after his brother was put to death by Kaykhusraw, and seized power there. He had a son called Kharzāsf,[90] who reigned after him and who was an arrogant tyrant. He was the nephew of Frāsiyāt, the king of the Turks who had fought Manūshihr.[91] Jūdharz was the son of Jashwādaghān[92] b. Ba-
[618] sakhrah[93] b. Farruyīn[94] b. Jabar[95] b. Raswūd[96] b. Ūrath[97] b. Tāj[98] b. Rabasang[99] b. Aras[100] b. Wēdīnaj[101] b. Raghar[102] b. Nawadjah[103] b. Mashwagh[104] b. Nawdhar[105] b. Manūshihr.

---

88. This name is a late rendering of the ancient Iranian name Arvat-Aspa. See the material collected by Justi, *Iran Nb*, 41f., s.v. Aurwadaspa, and 183 for his remarks on the form Luhrāsp.

89. Kay-Sharāsf is probably to be read Shawāsf, according to some of the variants listed in the Leiden edition. This name is a reflection of Ancient Iranian Syavaspa, which means "a possessor of black horses." See Justi, *Iran Nb*, 300, s.v. Syāwāspa.

90. This is possibly a corruption of the name Arjasp, Old Iranian Arjataspa. See Justi, *Iran Nb*, 21f.

91. The name occurs in an earlier part of Ṭabarī's account, 430 and 432. See Justi, *IranNb*, 191–193.

92. See above, n.41.

93. The reading is uncertain. See Justi, *Iran Nb*, 67, s.v. Besaxrah.

94. The reading is uncertain. See Justi, *Iran Nb*, 96, Farruxīn.

95. The reading is uncertain. See Justi, *Iran Nb*, 106.

96. See Justi, *Iran Nb*, 340f. He prefers the variant reading Wasūd, which he connects to the well-attested late Persian name Wahsūd, which means "of good benefit."

97. Of the several variants, the reading Urath, for Old Iranian Huraθya, is probably to be preferred. See Justi, *Iran Nb*, 133, s.v. Hurath.

98. The reading is problematic. See Justi, *Iran Nb*, 323, s.v. Tāz.

99. On this doubtful name see Justi, *Iran Nb*, 27, s.v. Arpas.

100. This name occurs as Harasf above, in Ṭabarī I, 530. On the other forms of this name, see Justi, *Iran Nb*, 126, s.v. Harasp.

101. Possibly a reflection of the Avestan name Vahudaēnā, which means "an adherent of the Good Religion" (or alternatively, "one whose inner religion is good"). See Justi, *Iran Nb*, 347, s.v. Wanghudaēnā.

102 Raghar occurs earlier in Ṭabarī, I, 530 as Aranj. The reading is extremely doubtful. See Justi, *Iran Nb*, 257, s.v. Raghar.

103. Nawadjah is possibly a corruption of Nawadgāw, a name which apparently means "possessor of ninety cows." See Justi, *Iran Nb*, 227, s.v. Nawadgāw.

104. See Justi, *Iran Nb*, 200, s.v. Maswak.

105. The Old Iranian form of this name is Nautara, which means "junior". See Justi, *Iran Nb*, 226 f., s.v. Nautara; Nöldeke, *Das iranische Nationalepos*, 8 and n. 8. See also above, n. 19.

After Kaykhusraw avenged himself and felt secure in his realm, he renounced his kingship and became an ascetic. He announced to the notables of his people and to the nation at large that he was going to relinquish power. They were overcome with anxiety, and their estrangement from him grew. They appealed to him, beseeched and implored him, and sought to persuade him to continue to direct their kingdom. But their effort was in vain. When they despaired, they all said, "If you persist in your intention, name a man to whom you would entrust the realm. Luhrāsb was present. Kaykhusraw pointed to him and announced that he was his choice and heir. Luhrāsb accepted the legacy, and the people flocked to him. Kaykhusraw disappeared. Some say that Kaykhusraw absented himself for acts of devotion, and it is not known where or how he died. Some tell other stories. Luhrāsb assumed power and conducted the realm as he saw fit. [619]

The children of Kaykhusraw were Jāmās,[106] Asabahar, Ramī and Ramīn.[107] He reigned for sixty years.

---

106. The Old Iranian form of this name is Jāmāspa. See Justi, *IranNb*, 109.
107. See Justi, *Iran Nb*, 258, for the last two names.

The Kingdom of the Children of Israel After Solomon, the Son of David[108]

Returning to the story of the Children of Israel, after Solomon, the son of David, all the Israelites were ruled by his son Rehoboam. It is said that his reign lasted seventeen years, but it is reported the kingdom of the Israelites split after Rehoboam. Abijah b. Rehoboam ruled over the tribes of Judah and Benjamin but not over the other tribes; the rest of the tribes made Jeroboam their king—he was the son of Nabat, a servant of Solomon. This occurred because of the sacrifice offered by Solomon's wife at his home—she had offered locusts to an idol,[109] whereupon God threatened (Solomon) that part of the kingdom would be taken away from his son. Rehoboam is reported to have reigned three more years before he died.

Then Asa b. Abijah reigned over the two tribes that his father had ruled over, that is, Judah and Benjamin, for forty-one years up to his death.[110]

---

108. See I Kings 15:1–8. Rehoboam ruled 928–911 B.C., Abijah 911–908 B.C. For biblical chronology, see *New Westminster Dictionary of the Bible,* 168–175.

109. A scarab serving as a cult object?

110. Asa ruled 908–867 B.C. See I Kings 15:9–24; 16:8–29; II Chronicles 14–16.

The Story of Asa b. Abijah and Zerah the Indian[111]

According to Muḥammed b. Sahl b. ʿAskar Ismāʿīl b. ʿAbd al-Karīm—ʿAbd al-Ṣamad b. Maʿqil—Wahb b. Munabbih:[112] A king of the Israelites called Asa b. Abijah was a righteous man, [620] and he was lame. (And at that time there) was an Indian king called Zerah—a corrupt tyrant—calling upon men to worship himself. (Now) Abijah[113] had been an idolworshiper. He had worshiped two idols, not God, and he called upon men to worship those two idols, thus misleading most of the Israelites. He continued to worship the idols until his death.[114] Following

---

111. See II Chronicles 14:8–15. In biblical lore Zerah is an Ethiopian. Note the expression "from India to Ethiopia," a Hebrew expression derived from Esther 1:1 about far-away places. See also Ginzberg, *Legends, II, 125; IV, 184.* Here the Ethiopian has become an Indian. The Arabic text has Zarj for Zerah.

112. Wahb b. Munabbih is the major authority in Islamic literature for biblical lore. His data are based primarily on biblical information, partly on post-biblical legends (*aggadah*) and partly on Islamic elaborations, sometimes with references to the Qur'ān. His nephews Ismāʿīl b. ʿAbd al-Karīm and ʿAbd al-Ṣamad b. Maʿqil served as transmitters of his material. See R.G. Khoury, *Wahb b. Munabbih*, Wiesbaden, 1972.

113. The text reads *abiya*; perhaps read *abiyyan*. See next note.

114. Earlier Abijah is portrayed as a righteous man. Moreover, this reference to him as an idol-worshiper appears in a story concerning his son Asa and Zerah the Indian. This may derive from a confusion of Abiyya (= Abijah) with *abiyyan* (scornful), a quality of Zerah. It was Abijah's son Asa who was involved with Zerah.

that, his son Asa took over. When he became king over the Israelites, Asa sent a herald proclaiming:

> There, unbelief is dead and so are the unbelievers; faith and the believers are alive. The idols and their worship are overturned, obedience to God and acts of faith reappear. As of today, no unbeliever shall raise his head among the Israelites in unbelief in my land and reign, or else I shall slay him. For the flood came upon the world and its population, God made cities sink into the ground, brimstone and fire rained from heaven, only because obedience to God was abandoned and disobedience was displayed. Therefore, it behooves us not to suffer any disobedience to God, nor spare any effort in obedience to God, until we have cleansed the earth from its impurity, and purged it from its pollution. We shall fight whoever opposes us therein by warfare and expulsion from our land.

When his people heard these words, they became resentful and clamorous. They went to the mother of King Asa, complaining of her son's action against them and their deities, and of his appeal to abandon their religion and embrace the worship of the Lord. She undertook to speak to him and deflect him to the worship of his father's idols. As the king was sitting with the nobles of his people, their leaders and chieftains, the
[621] king's mother entered. The king rose, and, giving her her due and honoring her, he offered her his seat. She refused and said, "You are not my son unless you respond to my appeal, obey me in doing what I command you to do. If you obey me, you will do right and be happy; should you disobey me, you will forfeit your good fortune and wrong yourself. It has reached me, my son, that you have started your people on a stupendous affair; you have called upon them to violate their religion, reject their deities, and to turn away from their ancestors' religion. You set a new path for them, launching heresy among them. You claim you sought thereby to enhance your dignity and position in order to strengthen your rule. But your step is a misstep and a disgrace. You provoke everybody to oppose you, and you set out single-handedly to fight them. You seek to enslave the free, and to turn the weak into strong support. Thereby you make

the opinion of the learned appear foolish, you contradict the sages, and follow the fools. I swear, my son, it is only your great fickleness, youth, and lack of learning that urge you to act this way. If you reject my words, and do not recognize that I am in the right, you are not of your father's progeny, and kingship is not for a man of your ilk. O my Son, what is it that you propose to your people? Have you been granted revelation in writing, like Moses when he went to Pharaoh whom he [622]
drowned, and thus saved his people from evil?[115] Or have you perchance been granted strength like David, who killed the lion for his people, who followed the wolf and split its jawbone, and who slew, unaided, Goliath the giant?[116] Or have you been granted more of royalty and wisdom than Solomon the son of David—that head of sages whose wisdom has become proverbial even for generations to come?[117] O my Son, anything fortunate that comes to you makes me most happy; anything else makes me most distressed about your distress."

As the king heard her, his wrath and annoyance grew. He said to her, "O Mother, it does not behoove me to eat at one table with my friend and enemy; nor does it behoove me to worship any deity but my Lord. Now then, either you follow me, and you will be on the right path, or you desist, and you will be misguided. You must worship God and renounce any other deity. Whosoever rejects this, is but an enemy of God. I lead to God's triumph for I am His servitor."

She said to him, "I shall not relinquish my idols nor the religion of my ancestors and people. I shall not abandon them for your tenet nor shall I worship the Lord you invoke." The king replied, "O Mother, this speech of yours severs the relations between us."

Then, upon the king's command they took her away and banished her. He further ordered the head of his guard and court to put her to death should she so much as question his position. When the tribes around him heard this, they felt out-

115. Exodus 14:21–31.

116. I Samuel 17.

117. Solomon's wisdom was a subject given considerable attention in the Islamic legends that were told about him. Note in particular his contact with Bilqīs, the Queen of Sheba.

[623] maneuvered and overawed, and they submitted to him. They said, "If this is how he treats his mother, how would he treat us if we should oppose his order, and not respond to his religion?" They tried all manner of evasion, but God sustained him, and crushed their cunning. Discontented and unwilling to give up their religion, they conspired to escape from his country and settle elsewhere.

They set out for Zerah, the king of India, seeking to incite him against Asa and his followers. When they came before Zerah, they prostrated themselves. He said to them, "Who are you?" They said, "We are your slaves." Said he, "Which slaves of mine are you?" They said, "We are from your country, Palestine (*al-Shā'm*). We are admirers of your reign. A youthful king, tender of age and foolish, appeared among us, changed our religion and declared our view foolish and our fathers unbelievers. He disregarded our resentment; therefore, we came to you to advise you of this. You will be worthier to rule our land of which we are the leaders. It is a land of much wealth, a weak population, and easy living; (a land of) much beauty, with the treasures and assets of the thirty kings defeated by Joshua the son of Nun, the successor (*Khalīfah*)[118] of Moses who led his people through the sea.[119] We and our land are yours, our country is your country. Nobody in it will oppose you. The people stretch out their hands to you, pleading peacefully for their lives and possessions."

Zerah said to them, "By my life, I shall not respond to your appeal, nor shall I respond to a call to combat a people who are perhaps more compliant than you, until I have sent to them trusted agents from among my people. If what you tell me is
[624] true, it will accrue to your advantage, and I shall make you rulers over the land; if, however, it proves to be false, I shall punish you for having lied to me." The men said, "You have spoken justly, and your verdict is fair; we are pleased with it." Zerah gave orders for their maintenance, and they were given

118. Note the use of *khalīfah*, which used in the same way denotes caliph, that is, the successor to Muḥammad the Prophet.

119. Joshua defeated thirty-one kings in his conquest of Canaan. See Joshua 12, especially the last verse.

pay. He selected from among his people trusted agents to be sent as spies. He threatened them with severe chastisement for false reports but promised to reward them if they reported truthfully. Zerah said to them, "I am dispatching you because of your loyalty, your religious strictness, and your good reputation, in order to inspect one of my lands. Report to me about its people, its ruler, the numbers of its armies, the quantity of its waters, the paths and roads, the points of entrance and departure, and its weaknesses and strengths. Report this so that I might, as it were, see it with my own eyes and know it as if I were there in person. Take along from the treasuries some sapphires and pearls and raiment that might appeal to the people, and induce them to purchase the goods from you."

He opened his treasures to equip them for travel on land and by sea. He described the people whom they might encounter and who would show them how to proceed. They set out as merchants, and reaching the coast they boarded a ship and arrived at the coast of Jerusalem (Iliya).[120] Then they went on until they entered Jerusalem. Depositing their baggage there, they displayed their wares and goods, inviting the people to buy from them, but the people were not eager for the goods and trade was slack. They began to sell much at low prices, lest they be expelled from the city before they could learn of its affairs and obtain the data that their king had instructed them to [625]
seek.

Now King Asa had warned the women of the Children of Israel that an unmarried woman should not appear in the garb of a married woman, lest she be put to death or exiled to some island in the seas. Woman is the strongest snare used by the devil to confuse the pious. Unmarried women were to go out only (if they were) veiled and in shabby clothes, and thus unrecognizable.

As these spies were selling their goods, accepting one dirham for what was worth a hundred, the women of the Children of Israel began buying covertly. They bought at night and in secret, so that none of the pious men would notice them. The

120. After Aelia Capitolina, the name given the city by the Romans after the Barkochba revolt in A.D. 135.

spies sold all their goods and obtained in turn what they were looking for. They accumulated data about the city, its fortresses, and the water supply. But they had concealed their main wares, their best pearls, corals and sapphires, as a gift for the king. From people they encountered in the city they began to inquire about the king who had bought nothing from them. They said, "How is it that the king has bought nothing from us? If he is rich, we have wondrous goods to supply him with, whatever he wants, the like of which has never entered his treasuries; if he is poor, what prevents him from visiting us, so that we might give him whatever he desires without any payment?" The men from the city who visited them said, "His
[626] wealth, treasures, and various possessions are immeasurable. He took over the treasures which Moses had carried out of Egypt, and the jewels the Israelites had brought.[121] He also took over what Joshua the son of Nun, the successor to Moses, had accumulated, and the great wealth and inestimable vessels that Solomon, the head of the sages and kings, had assembled."

The spies inquired, "How is he at warfare? What is his strength? What about his troops? Suppose, some king attacked and invaded his realm, how would he fight him? What is the king's equipment, the number of his troops? How many cavalry and horses are at his disposal? Or is it that his great treasures inspire people with awe for him?" The people replied, "King Asa's equipment and resources are poor but he has a friend who, if called upon to help move mountains, would do so. As long as the friend is with him, nothing can overcome him." Then the spies asked, "Who is Asa's friend? How numerous are his troops? How can he be confronted? How does he fight? How many soldiers and chariots does he have? Where is his base and home?" At this, the people answered, "His abode is above heaven, he is upright on his throne, his troops are innumerable, and all creation is at his service. Should he command the sea, it would deluge the land; should he command the rivers, they would dry up. He is not visible and his base is not known. Such is Asa's friend and helper."

The spies began to record everything they had been told

121. The allusion is to Exodus 12:36.

about Asa. Some of these spies came before Asa and said, "O King! We have a gift we should like to offer you from among the curiosities of our land, or you might wish to purchase it from us, and we would sell it cheaply." He said to them, "Bring it so that I might look at it." When they brought it to him, he said, "Will this remain forever with the owners, and they with it?" They answered, "No, this will wane, and so will its owners," whereupon he replied, "I have no need of it; what I am seeking is something whose splendor remains with the owners, unabated, and whose owners will remain with it." [627]

He returned their gift, and they left him. They traveled from Jerusalem (Bayt al-Maqdis)[122] toward their king, Zerah the Indian. Upon arriving, they unrolled the report before him and informed him of what they had learned about King Asa and his friend. Zerah adjured them by his power, and by the sun and the moon which they worshiped and prayed to, not to conceal from him what they had seen among the Israelites. They gave a truthful account. When they had completed their report of Asa and his friend, Zerah said to them, "The Israelites, suspecting that you were spies inquiring about their weakness, mentioned Asa's friend. They lied. They wanted to terrify you. Asa's friend cannot muster an army larger than mine, nor better equipped, nor one with stouter hearts or more valor in battle than mine. If he came against me with thousands,[123] my forces would easily surpass his."

Zerah then urged every province under his rule to send a fully equipped army. He sought the support of Gog and Magog,[124] and the Turks and Persians, and the rest of the subject [628]
nations. He wrote:

---

122. Bayt al-Maqdis is the Arabic equivalent of Hebrew *bet hammiqdash*, that is, "the sanctuary, the temple," and more generally "the holy city." Jerusalem is more commonly called al-Quds in Arabic, based on the Hebrew *ʿīr haqqodesh*, "the holy city."

123. The text reads *alf*, "thousand"; perhaps read *alf alf*, "million".

124. Gog and Magog represent the names of obscure and distant peoples of great might. See Genesis 10:2; Ezekiel 28:2; 39:6. Tradition connected them with eschatological events. Note Qurʾān 18:92ff.; 21:96 which mentions Yājūj and Mājūj, connecting them with the wall that Alexander erected against invaders. See *SEI*, s.v. Yādjūdj wa-Mādjūdj.

> From Zerah, the mighty Indian, King of the lands, to whomever my messages reach, I have a land whose crop is drawing close, whose fruit is ripe, and I should like you to send me workers upon whom I shall bestow whatever they reap. This land is distant from me, and its people seized some fringes of my land and subdued my subjects who came under their rule. I leave their fate in the hands of those who rise along with me to fight them; if your strength fails, I shall be your strength; and my treasuries are inexhaustible.

They rallied to him from every direction, supporting him with cavalry, men, and equipment. When they assembled, he supplied them from his stores with arms and implements, and ordered a count of their number and a review. Their number reached 1,100,000, apart from his own countrymen. He ordered a hundred ships. Mules were hitched, four in a set, carrying a couch and tent, in each tent a slave girl. In each ship were ten servants and five of his elephants. Each of the armies had a hundred thousand men. The retinue which rode with him consisted of a hundred commanders. In each army, he placed experts whom he addressed and spurred on to battle. As he observed them and rode with them, his prestige rose greatly in the hearts of those present.

Then he said, "Where is the friend of Asa? Can he protect Asa from me? Who can defeat me? If Asa and his friend but looked at me and my army, they would not dare fight me. For
[629] against each of his soldiers, I have one thousand. For sure, Asa will enter my country as a prisoner, and I shall lead his captive people amidst my troops."

Zerah began to disparage Asa and talk about him abusively. Asa now learned of Zerah's activities and preparations for war. He prayed to God saying:

> Oh God, you have created in your power heaven and earth and all those in them, all under Your control. You are of tender patience and mighty wrath. I ask of You not to remember our sins toward You, nor chastise us for disobeying You, but to remember us in your mercy which you did apply to creatures. See our weakness and the

strength of our enemy; see how few we are and how numerous is our enemy; see the straights and trouble we are in, and the joy and satisfaction of our enemy. Drown Zerah and his hosts in the sea with the might with which you plunged Pharaoh and his hosts into the sea while saving Moses and his people. I ask You to surprise Zerah and his men with a sudden chastisement.

Asa had a dream in which God announced to him:

Know that I have heard your word; your supplication has reached My Throne. If I drowned Zerah the Indian and his people, the Children of Israel would not know of it, nor would anybody else. But I shall display to you and to those who follow you My power against Zerah and his people. I shall save you from this trouble and grant you their booty, and I shall place their troops in your hands, so that your [630]
enemies may learn that the protégé of 'the friend of Asa' is invincible; his army will not be put to flight nor will the friend's devotee be frustrated. I shall bide My time until he completes his scheme, then I shall lead him to you as a slave, and his troops will be chattels for you and your people.

Zerah and those with him set forth, then camped on the coast of Tarshish.[125] Within a day the rivers dried up; the meadows turned barren; the people were harassed by the birds and could not escape the beasts. They proceeded, and when they were two days' journey from Jerusalem, Zerah dispatched some of his troops to the city. The countryside, mountains and plains were replete with the enemy. The people of Palestine were filled with terror, and feared destruction.

King Asa heard about the enemy; he sent a vanguard of his people toward them, and ordered the vanguard to inform him about the number and array of the troops. The men sent by Asa set out and saw the troops from the top of a hill. Then they returned to Asa, informing him that human eyes had not seen

---

125. Tarshish is a biblical coastland outside of Palestine. In this text Palestine is called al-Sha'm, which is the term for Syria, as the area from Iraq to Egypt.

nor had human ears heard anything like it; what with their elephants and horses and horsemen, "We would not have believed that there are such numbers of men and equipment. Our minds did not suffice to count them. We would not know how to fight them, and we lost hope." The city's people heard about it, rent their garments, covered their heads with dust, lamented in the alleys and marketplaces, and began to bid each other farewell.
[631] They then came to the king and said, "We are all going out to those people; we shall stretch out our hands to them, and perchance they will pity us and permit us to remain in our country."

King Asa said to them, "God forbid (that we) surrender to the unbelievers, abandon the House of God and His scripture to the wicked!" They said, "Then find us a ruse; ask your friend and Lord, Whose help you used to promise us, and in the belief in Whom you used to call us to rally. If He rids us of this calamity, well and good. Otherwise, we shall submit to our enemy; perhaps this will save us from massacre."

Asa replied, "My Lord is invincible and can be moved only by supplication, chastity, and humbleness." The people then said, "Then turn to Him. Maybe He will respond to you and have pity on our weakness. A friend will not abandon his friend in such a position."

Asa went into the prayer chamber, took the crown off his head, changed his robes for sackcloth, and sprawled in the dust. With a heavy heart he stretched out his hand calling upon the Lord. In supplication and profusion of tears, he said:

> Oh God, Lord of the seven heavens, Lord of the mighty throne, the God of Abraham, Ishmael, Isaac, and Jacob and his sons. You are concealed from Your creation when it pleases You. Your abode is unknown, and the depth of Your might is inscrutable. You are the waking one who sleeps not; the ever-alert whom days and nights will not weary. I ask of You what Your friend Abraham asked of You when, to rescue him, the fire was extinguished.[126]

---

126. Qur'ān 4:12: "And God took Ibrāhīm [Abraham] for a friend [*khalīl*]." Hebron, where the patriarchs are reportedly buried, is called in Arabic al-Khalīl. Abraham was saved from the fire into which his heathen compatriots

You brought the righteous to join him in the fire. I pray to You with the prayer that Your confidant Moses offered, when You saved the Children of Israel from evil and thereby liberated them from slavery, leading them across the sea to land, while drowning Pharaoh and those who [632] followed him. I implore You as did David whom You raised and granted strength after weakness, giving him victory over Goliath, the giant whom You put to flight. It is a request like that of Solomon Your prophet, whom You endowed with wisdom, and to whom You granted high rank, and sovereignty over all living beings. You revive the dead and destroy the world, remaining alone in eternity, indestructible. Oh, my God, I beseech You, have pity on me. Respond to my prayer. For I am wretched, lame, one of Your weakest worshipers, with the least notion of what to do. Yet a great trouble and grave danger has befallen us, and only You are able to remove it. We have no strength or power but in You. Please, then, have pity on our weakness. For You pity whomever pleases You, however it pleases You.

Outside, the learned among the Israelites began to pray to God:

Oh God, respond today to Your servitor for he takes refuge in You alone; do not abandon him to Your enemy. Remember his love for You, how he separated himself from his mother and all people, except those obedient to You.

While Asa was in his prayer chamber prostrated, God made him fall asleep, and then, they say, a divine messenger came to him saying:

Oh Asa, a friend will not abandon his friend. God says, "I extend my love to you; my aid to you is forthcoming. It is I who shall rid you of your enemy; for he who trusts in Me shall not be humiliated, nor will he who takes courage in Me prove weak. You remembered Me amidst prosperity,

---

had thrown him. See Qur'ān 37:97ff; 21:68–70; 29–24. Also *EI*², s.v. al-Khalīl; Ginzberg, *Legends*, I, 176, 202ff., 206, 216ff. See also Speyer, *Erzählungen*, 142–144.

and I shall keep you safe amidst adversity. You prayed to Me in trust; I shall keep you safe while you are afraid." Al-
[633] mighty God says, "I swear that even if heaven and earth with everything in them should turn against you, I shall secure for thee a way of escape. It is I who shall send some of My tormentors [*zabāniyatī*][127] to slay My foes. I am with you, and none shall come near you and those with you."

Asa, his face aglow, and thanking God, left his prayer chamber. He told the people what he had heard. The believers gave credence to his words but the hypocrites considered these words lies, and said to one another, "Asa walked in lame, and lame did he walk out. Had he told us the truth and had God responded to him, his leg would be sound; but he is beguiling us and wants us to indulge in hope until war starts and he can destroy us."

As the king was telling them of God's act for their sake, the messengers arrive from Zerah. They entered Jerusalem with messages from Zerah to Asa that were replete with abuse against Asa and his people, and with the denial of God. Zerah wrote in them, "Call on your friend, with talk of whom you have misled your people. Let him challenge me with his troops, and let him appear to me; though I know that neither he nor anybody else can prevail over me, for I am King Zerah the Indian."

When Asa read the messages delivered to him, tears welled up in his eyes. He entered the prayer-chamber, and spread those messages before God, and said:

O God, nothing is more desirable to me than to stand before Thee, but I fear lest this light which Thou hast shown in these, my days, should peter out. These messages have arrived, and Thou knowest their contents. If I were their
[634] butt, that would be a slight matter; but Thy slave Zerah turns against Thee, insults Thee, speaks vaingloriously and falsely, and Thou art witness thereto.

127. These are mentioned in Qur'ān 96:18.

Then, they say God revealed to Asa:

> There is no change in My words, no variation in My promise, no alteration in My command. Therefore go out of thy prayer-chamber, order thy troops to rally, and lead them and those who follow thee until you reach an elevated piece of ground.

Asa came out and related what he had been told, and twelve chieftains, each with his unit, set out. As they were departing they took leave of their families, intimating that they would not return alive. They stood on a hill opposite Zerah, and from there they saw Zerah and his people. When Zerah saw them, he shook his head jeeringly and said, "For fellows like these I came from my country and spent my money?" He then summoned those who had described Asa and his people to him, and exclaimed, "You have deceived me. You asserted that your people are numerous." He then ordered that they and the spies whom he had sent to obtain information all be put to death.

Meanwhile Asa was imploring God, taking refuge in Him. Zerah said, "I do not know what to do with these people, nor how few of them there are against us. I consider them too few for warfare, and I think I shall not fight them."

Zerah sent a message to Asa, "Where is your friend whom you were threatening us with and who, you claimed, would save you from my blows? Will you surrender, so that I can carry out my judgment upon you? Or do you seek to fight me?" Asa's reply was, "O wretch, you neither know nor grasp what [635]
you are saying. Do you wish to wrestle with your Lord, to outnumber Him? He is the strongest, greatest, most powerful and forceful, and His creatures are too humble and weak to actually see Him. He is with me here and no one who is with God shall be defeated. Exert yourself to the utmost, oh wretch, until you have learned what is to befall you."

When Zerah's men lined up, and took their positions, Zerah commanded his archers to shoot. But God sent His angels from every heaven, they say—and God knows best—to help and aid Asa and his people. Asa had them retain their positions. When the enemy shot their arrows the unbelievers kept the sunlight from the earth, as if a cloud were rising. The angels diverted it from Asa and his people. Then the angels struck the people of Zerah with the cloud of arrows, and each man was hit by his own arrow, with the result that the archers were all slain. During that time, Asa and his people were praying to God and loudly extolling Him, and they say the angels became visible. When the wretch Zerah saw them, he was seized with terror and bewilderment, and exclaimed, "Great is Asa's cunning, superb his sorcery. Such are the Israelites, unsurpassed, unmatched in cunning. They learned it from the Egyptians; that is how they crossed the sea."

The Indian called out among his people, "Unsheath your swords, attack them, crush them." They pulled out their swords, attacked the angels, and the angels slew them and none of the humans remained except Zerah with his women and slaves. At the sight of this, Zerah took to flight with his
[636] retinue, exclaiming, "Asa is victorious overtly, and his friend has destroyed me covertly. I was looking at Asa and those who were standing with him and not fighting, while the battle was taking its toll of my people."

When Asa saw that Zerah was fleeing, he exclaimed, "Oh God, Zerah is fleeing, and if You do not separate us, he will again rally his people against us." But God revealed to Asa, "You have not slain them; I have slain them. Now remain in your place. If I were to leave it to the two of you, they would slay you all. Rather, let Zerah squirm in My palm. None will help save him from Me; he has no escape. I grant as a gift to you and your people his encampments, with their silver, valuables, and animals. This is the reward for your adherence to Me, and I seek no reward for aiding you."

Zerah reached the sea intent on flight. One hundred thousand people were with him. They prepared their ships and boarded them, but at sea God sent winds upon them from every direction of land and sea, and the waves were stormy. The ships struck one another and were smashed while Zerah and his men drowned. The waves were so stormy that the people of the surrounding towns were in terror; the earth trembled. Asa sent men to find out what had happened. But God revealed to him, they say—and God knows best—"Come down, you and your people, and the people of your towns to pick up the booty that God has bestowed upon you by His power. Be grateful for it. I allow every man to take from these camps [637] whatever he chooses." They rushed down praising and hallowing God. They say and God knows best that for three months they carried that booty to their towns.

After Asa, his son Jehoshafat reigned for twenty-five years, until his death. After that reigned Athaliah—she is also known as Ghazaliah—the daughter of Omri, and mother of Ahaziah. She had slain the sons of the kings of the Children of Israel; only Joash, the son of Ahaziah, was hidden from her. Joash and his men slew her. Her reign lasted seven years. Then Joash b. Ahaziah reigned until his men killed him, the man who had slain his grandmother. His reign lasted forty years. Then Amaziah b. Joash reigned for twenty-nine years until he was slain by his men. After that Uzziah (also called Ghuzziah) b. Amaziah reigned for fifty-two years until his death. Then Jotham b. Uzziah reigned for sixteen years until he died. Then Ahaz b. Jotham b. Uzziah reigned for sixteen years until his death. After that Hezekiah b. Ahaz reigned until his death. They say he was a friend of Isaiah, and that Isaiah had announced to him the end of his lifetime. But he implored the Lord, and God added to Hezekiah's lifetime, granting him a respite, and instructed Isaiah to inform him thereof. But Muhammad b. Ishaq maintained that the friend of Isaiah to whom this story refers was called Zedekiah.[128]

---

128. The chronology of these reigns is as follows: Asa in Judea, 913–873 B. C. or 910–869 B. C.; Uzziah, 783–742 B.C. or 767–739 B.C.; Hezekiah, 715–687 B.C.; Zedekiah, who ruled from 598–587 B.C., is misplaced here. Isaiah's activity falls into the period between Uzziah and Hezekiah. Hezekiah's illness, imminent death, and the grant of fifteen years of life beyond this moment is announced by Isaiah. See II Kings 20:1–11; Isaiah 38.

[638]

The Story of Isaiah's Friend; the Kings of the Children of Israel and Sennacherib

According to Ibn Ḥumayd—Salamah b. al-Faḍl—Ibn Isḥāq: In the divine scripture revealed to Moses, in the account of the Israelites and of what they were going to do after him, it is said,[129] "And We decreed for the Children of Israel in the Book, 'You shall do corruption in the earth twice, and you shall ascend exceedingly high' . . . and We have made Gehenna a prison for the unbelievers." So there were the Israelites with their history and sins, and God was letting them go unpunished, out of compassion for them, favoring them. Then God brought (punishment) upon them for their sin, as He had warned them in the Mosaic text. The first of these incidents concerned one of their kings called Zedekiah. When he ascended the throne, God had sent a prophet to instruct and direct him, thus making the prophet an intermediary between the king and God. God thus spoke to Zedekiah about the Israelites, not by books revealed, but rather by commanding them to follow the Torah and its stipulations, and by deterring them from disobedience, as well as by calling upon them to return to

129. Qur'ān 17:4–8.

obedience. When this king began to reign, God sent to him Isaiah the son of Amoz. That was before the time of Jesus, Zechariah, and John the Baptist.[130] It was Isaiah who announced the advent of Jesus and Muḥammad. The king reigned over the Children of Israel and Jerusalem for some time. But as his reign was coming to a close, grave events took place while Isaiah was with the king. God sent against them Sennacherib, king of [639] Babylon, with six hundred thousand men,[131] and he advanced until he reached the environs of Jerusalem.

The Israelite king was suffering from a rash on his leg. The prophet Isaiah came to him and said, "O King of the Children of Israel, Sennacherib, king of Babylon, has arrived with six hundred thousand of his forces. The people are terrified and fleeing before them." This depressed the king, who said, "O Prophet of God, do you have a divine revelation for us about what has happened. How will God treat us and Sennacherib and his forces?" The prophet then replied, "No revelation has come to me about you." Just then God revealed to the prophet Isaiah, "Go to the king of the Children of Israel, and command him to prepare his testament and to appoint whomever he desires from among the members of his house to succeed him." The prophet Isaiah then came to the king of the Children of Israel, Zedekiah, and said to him, "The Lord has revealed to me that I should command you to prepare your testament and to appoint whomever you desire of your family as your successor, for you shall die."

As Isaiah said this to Zedekiah, the king turned to the sanctuary and prayed. He praised God and called upon him, weeping and imploring amidst tears, his heart sincere and full of reliance upon God, with endurance and a clear conscience, "Oh God, Lord supreme, God supreme most holy, compassionate, merciful and gracious, whom no slumber or sleep affects! Remember my acts and deeds, and my good rule over the Children of Israel. All that was from You, and You know it better

---

130. The prophet Zechariah is confused here with the New Testament figure who is the father of John the Baptist (Yaḥyā b. Zakariyyā). See Luke 1:5, 11–13, 59ff.

131. Sennacherib of Assyria invaded Judah in 701 B.C. See II Kings 18:13, 19–36; Isaiah 36–37.

[640] than I myself, for both my conscience and my manifest behavior are open to You." God responded to him for he was a pious worshiper. God inspired Isaiah to inform King Zedekiah that his prayer had been heard, and that God was merciful, "God saw your tears. He has postponed your death by fifteen years and shall deliver you from your enemy, King Sennacherib of Babylon and his hosts."

Upon hearing this the king was relieved of pain, suffering and grief. He prostrated himself and said, "O my God and God of my fathers, You have I worshiped, praised, honored and glorified. You grant kingship to whomever You desire, and withdraw it whenever it pleases You. You exalt or humble whomever it pleases You. You know the concealed and the manifest. You are the first and the last, Master of the innermost and of the manifest. You have mercy, and answer the prayer of those in straits. You responded to my prayer, and pitied me when I implored You."

As he raised his head, God instructed Isaiah, "Tell King Zedekiah to command one of his servitors to bring him a piece of the fig and let the king apply it to his rash, and he will be healed. By morning, he will have recovered." The king did accordingly, and was healed. He then said to Isaiah the prophet, "Ask the Lord to give us a sign of what He is going to do to our enemy." God said to the prophet Isaiah, "Tell him, I shall dispose of your enemy and save you from them. They will all be dead by morning except for Sennacherib and five of his scribes."

When they awoke in the morning, a herald came to the king, and announced at the gate of the city, "O King of the Children of Israel, God has disposed of your enemy. Come forth, for Sennacherib and his host have perished." When the king went forth to look for Sennacherib, he was not found among the dead. The king then dispatched men to search for him, and he
[641] was found in a cave with five of his scribes, one of whom was Nebuchadnezzar. They were paraded in public places, and then were brought before the king of the Israelites, who, upon seeing them, prostrated himself from sunrise till afternoon. Then he said to Sennacherib, "What do you think of the act of our Lord concerning you? Has He not slain your host with His power

while both we and you were unaware?" Sennacherib replied, "I had heard, even before I left my country, of your Lord and His aid to you as well as His mercy upon you. But I did not obey the right counsel. It is only my foolishness that plunged me into this misery. Had I listened or been reasonable, I would not have attacked you. But misery struck me and my men." The king of the Children of Israel exclaimed, "Praise God, the mighty Lord whom it pleased to save us from you. Our Lord left you and those with you alive, not in order to honor you but to confront you with increased misery in this world, and chastisement in the world to come; also to have you tell those whom you left at home what you have seen of the act of our Lord, and to warn those who will come after you. Were it not for that, He would not have preserved you. Your blood and that of those with you is worth less before God than the blood of a tick, should I happen to kill one."

Then the king of the Children of Israel ordered the chief of his guard to parade them before the populace, and for seventy days he paraded them in Jerusalem, while feeding them two loaves of barley bread per man daily. Sennacherib said to the king, "Death is better than what you are doing to us. But do what you were ordered to do." The king gave orders to place them in the death-chamber, but God revealed to Isaiah, "Tell the king to send Sennacherib and his men away, in order to [642]
warn their people; let the king honor them and transport them until they have reached their country. The prophet Isaiah informed the king thereof. So Sennacherib and those with him departed for Babylon. When they arrived, he assembled the people and informed them of what God had wrought with his troops. His sorcerers and soothsayers told him, "O King of Babylon, we used to tell you about their Lord and their prophet, and the divine revelations to their prophet, but you did not listen to us. They are an invincible people, because of their Lord." The story of Sennacherib frightened them. But God spared them, and it turned into a warning and an admonition. Sennacherib lived seven years thereafter.

Some scholars from among the People of the Book assert that this king of the Israelites attacked by Sennacherib was lame as a result of sciatica, and that Sennacherib coveted his realm because Zedekiah was chronically ill and weak, and that another king of Babylon had set out against him, one Lifar by name. Nebuchadnezzar, the son of his uncle, was his scribe.[132] God sent upon him a wind that destroyed his army while he and his scribe escaped, and Lifar was slain by his own son; but Nebuchadnezzar in his fury about his master's death slew the son, the parricide. Sennacherib later set out against Zedekiah. Sennacherib dwelled then in Nineveh with the current king of Ādharbayjān—he was called Salmān the Left-handed. Sennacherib and Salmān clashed and fought until their armies annihilated one another, so that whatever they possessed became the booty of the Children of Israel.

[643] Some say, that the one who attacked Hezekiah, the friend of Isaiah, was Sennacherib, the king of Mosul, and that when he surrounded Jerusalem with his armies, God sent an angel to kill 185,000 of Sennacherib's men in one night.

Hezekiah's reign lasted twenty-nine years. It is said that he was succeeded by Manasseh, son of Hezekiah, who ruled for fifty-five years. Amon, his son, succeeded him for twelve years but was slain by his courtiers. After him, his son Josiah ruled for thirty-one years. He was slain by the pharaoh of Egypt, the mutilated cripple.[133] Josiah's son Jehoahaz succeeded him. Raided by the mutilated pharaoh who captured him, he was carried off to Egypt. The pharaoh made Jehoahaz's son, Jehoiakim, king over his father's domain and imposed upon him, so they assert, a tribute to be paid to the pharaoh for twelve years. They further assert that Jehoiakim exacted the money from the Israelites to pay the pharaoh.

Jehoiachin, the son of Jehoiakim, ruled after him. After a reign of three months he was attacked by Nebuchadnezzar,

---

132. For the legends connected with the story of Sennacherib see Ginzberg, *Legends*, VI, 267–270, 300–301; VI, 362–365. Here Sennacherib and Nebuchadnezzar are related and take part in the invasion of Judah, thus connecting the invasion of 701 B.C. and the fall of Jerusalem over a century later.

133. For the Pharaoh Necho, see II Kings 23:29; also Ginzberg, *Legends*, IV, 160; X, 297 n.71. The name of the pharaoh is construed as a derivative of the root *NKY* which means "to injure" or "to cripple" in both Hebrew and Arabic. The ancient Syriac Bible and the *Targum* make use of this etymology.

who captured him and carried him off to Babylon. His uncle Mattaniah was made king in his stead and was named Zedekiah. He rebelled but Nebuchadnezzar defeated him, bound him in fetters, and carried him to Babylon after slaying Zedekiah's son before his eyes. He then tore out Zedekiah's eyes, and destroyed the city and the temple. Nebuchadnezzar led the [644]
Israelites into captivity in Babylon where they remained until Cyrus, the son of Jamasb, the son of Asb, returned them to Jerusalem because of the relationship that existed between them. For his mother was Esther, the daughter of the Jew Abihail. The reign of Zedekiah, including the three months of Jehoiachin's reign, lasted, it is said, eleven years and three months. After that the kingdom of Jerusalem and Palestine became the possession of Ushtasb b. Lahrasib, and Nebuchadnezzar was his governor over all that land.

According to Ibn Ḥumayd Muḥammad b. Isḥāq—Salamān:[134] When Zedekiah, the aforementioned king of the Jews, passed away, the affairs of the Jews became confused. There was rivalry for the kingship. They killed one another to attain it, and though their prophet Isaiah was among them, they did not turn to him nor did they listen to him. We heard that because they acted in this way, God said to Isaiah, "Rise among thy people, let me send a revelation through you." When he rose, God inspired him. The prophet admonished them and filled them with fear about the vicissitudes of fate; he enumerated God's favors and fate's vicissitudes. As Isaiah finished his speech, they turned upon him to kill him, but the prophet fled from them. A tree that he passed split open, and he entered it. But Satan caught him and seized a fringe of his gar- [645]
ment, which he showed to the pursuers. They set a saw across the middle of the tree and sawed through it, and Isaiah was sawn in half.[135]

134. The Ibn Ḥumayd tradition may go back to the lost Qur'ān commentary of Ibn Jubayr (d. 95 A.H./713/4). See *GAS*, I, 28ff.

135. On the martyrdom of Isaiah, see Ginzberg, *Legends*, IV, 279; VI, 371, 374ff. It may be noted that the legend concerning Isaiah's death is similar to that told of the Iranian Yima (Jamshēd). For a discussion of this similarity see Christensen, *Premier homme*, II, 73ff.

Muḥammad b. Sahl al-Bukhārī also told me the story of Isaiah and his people, the Children of Israel, and of his death at their hands. He said: We were told by Ismāʿīl b. ʿAbd al-Karīm —Ṣamad b. Maʿqil—Wahb b. Munabbih.

The Account of Luhrāsb and His Son Bishtāsb; the Expedition of Nebuchadnezzar Against the Israelites and How He Destroyed Jerusalem[136]

After Kaykhusraw, the Persians were ruled by Luhrāsb, son of Kayūjī b. Kaymanūsh b. Kayfāshīn, who was selected by Kaykhusraw. When the crown was set upon his head, he said, "We prize piety above all." He sat on a gold throne, adorned with all kinds of jewels. By his order the city of Balkh was built for him in Khurāsān, and he named it "The Beautiful." He introduced government agencies, strengthened his reign with a select guard, cultivated the land, levied taxes to support the troops, and sent Nebuchadnezzar, whose Persian name was Bukhtrashah,[137] so it was said, against the Israelites.

---

136. In this conception the legendary kings of Persia succeeded one another as supreme rulers throughout the ancient Near East. Nebuchadnezzar is, therefore, merely a governor serving them. His geographical domain is limited to west of the Tigris. See Ezra 7:21; Nehemiah 2:9. The name Nebuchadnezzar itself, as it is given in the Arabic sources, has a Persianized form. It is consistently written Bukht-Naṣ(ṣ)ar, where the first part is identical to the Persian word meaning "saved".

137. The text reads Bukhtrashah, perhaps read Bukhtrasha. It is not clear

I was told on the authority of Hishām b. Muḥammad: Luhrāsb, the nephew of Qabūs,[138] became king and built the city of Balkh. Since at that time the power of the Turks was growing, he dwelt in Balkh fighting the Turks. Nebuchadnezzar was
[646] his contemporary and was the commander (*isbahbadh*) over the area between al-Ahwāz and Western Asia (Arḍ al-Rūm) to the west of the Tigris. He personally concluded the peace with the people of Damascus, and he sent one of his officers to Jerusalem. The latter concluded a peace treaty with the king of the Israelites, a man of David's progeny. The officer took hostages and departed. But by the time he reached Tiberias, the Israelites attacked their king and slew him, saying, "You gave hostages to the Babylonians and humiliated us." They then prepared to fight. Nebuchadnezzar's officer reported to him what had happened, and he was instructed to stay on until Nebuchadnezzar's arrival and to behead the hostages he was holding. Nebuchadnezzar then set out for Jerusalem, took the city by force of arms, slew the fighting men, and took the children captive.

We received word that he found the prohet Jeremiah in the Israelite prison. God had sent him as a prophet to warn the Children of Israel of what Nebuchadnezzar was to bring upon them, and to tell them that unless they repented and gave up their evil deeds, God would visit upon them the power that would slay their fighting men and capture their children. Nebuchadenzzar said to Jeremiah, "What is it you want?" Jeremiah then told him that God had sent him to warn the Israelites of what was to befall them, but they did not believe it and imprisoned him. Nebuchadnezzar said, "Wretched people, they defied their Lord's messenger." He released Jeremiah and treated him well. The residue of the unfortunate Israelites gathered around the prophet and said, "We were wrong and wicked, but we are repenting before God the evil we have per-

---

what the second element was deemed to denote in either Bukht-Naṣ(ṣ)ar (the Arabic-Persian form of Nebuchadnezzar) or Bukht-Rasah (if the reading of the latter name is correct).

138. This form of the name is a corruption of Kay-Us. See Justi, *Iran Nb*, 334, s.v. Usan, and above, n. 1.

petrated. Pray to God to accept our repentance." He prayed, and the Lord revealed to him that they were not sincere saying, "If they are [sincere] let them stay with you in this city." Jeremiah told them of the divine command, but they said, "How shall we stay on in a town that was destroyed and whose people have aroused divine wrath?" They refused to remain there.[139] Nebuchadnezzar then wrote to the king of Egypt, "Some of my slaves have run away from me to you; send them to me, or else I shall attack you and send my cavalry to conquer your land." The king of Egypt wrote back, "They are not your slaves, but free men and the sons of free men." So Nebuchadnezzar attacked him, slew him, took the Egyptians captive, and proceeded through North Africa (Maghrib) until he reached its very farthest point. He then returned (home) with many captives from Palestine and Transjordan, among them Daniel and other prophets. [647]

That was the time when the Israelites dispersed. Some of them settled in the Hijāz, at Yathrib and in the Wādī al-Qurā, and elsewhere.[140] According to a report reaching us, God then inspired Jeremiah thus, "I am restoring Jerusalem. Therefore, proceed to settle there." So he set out, and arriving there he found it in ruins. He said to himself, "God be praised, He commanded me to settle in this city and announced to me that He would restore it. But when will He rebuild it, and when will He revive it? After its death?" He then put his head down and fell asleep. His donkey and provision-basket were with him. He remained asleep seventy years, so that Nebuchadnezzar was gone, as was the great king above him, that is, Luhrāsb. His reign lasted 120 years, and he was succeeded by his son Bishtāsb.[141] Word reached the latter about Palestine, that it was in

139. See Jeremiah 39:11–14; 40:2–10; 42, 43.

140. The settlement of the Jews in Arabia is connected here with the destruction of the Judean kindgom and the Babylonian captivity in 586 B.C. See Y. Hirschberg, *Israel in Arabia* (Hebrew), and C.C. Torrey, *The Jewish foundations of Islam*; J. Montgomery, *Arabia and the Bible*; D.S. Margoliouth, *The Relations between Arabs and Israelites.* The Wādī al-Qurā contained a chain of settlements between Syria and North Arabia. See Yāqūt, *Muʿjam*, IV, 877.

141. Bishtāsb or Gushtāsp is a late form of Old Iranian Vishtāspa. See Justi, *Iran Nb*, 372f. The theory that this early figure of a king, who was said to be

ruins and that wild beasts had become numerous there, and that no humans remained there. He announced in Babylonia among the Israelites that whosoever wished to return to Palestine could do so, and he made a man of the progeny of David king over them. He ordered him to rebuild Jerusalem and to re-
[648] construct its temple (*masjid*); consequently, the Israelites returned and rebuilt it. Then God opened Jeremiah's eyes, and the prophet looked at the city as it was being rebuilt. He had slept until he was a hundred years old, but when God revived him he thought he had been asleep for only an hour. He remembered the city in ruin and desolation. When he saw it now, he exclaimed, "I know that God is powerful over everything."[142]

The Children of Israel settled in Jerusalem and their government was returned to them. They multiplied there until the Romans were victorious over them in the period of the regional princes (*mulūk al-ṭawā'if*).[143] After that they no longer had a commonwealth (*jamā'ah*).

It was in the time of Bishtāsb that Zoroaster (Zarādasht), whom the Zoroastrians consider their prophet, appeared. Some scholars from among the People of the Book in Palestine assert that Zoroaster was a servant of one of the prophet Jeremiah's disciples, and that he was close to the latter and favored by him.[144] But he betrayed his master and slandered him. The

---

the patron of the prophet Zoroaster, was identical with the Achaemenian king of the same name (the father of Darius I), has been propounded by E. Herzfeld in *Zoroaster and his world*, but criticized by other scholars. See especially W.B. Henning, *Zoroaster, Politician or Witch-doctor?*

142. The prototypes for this story are the rabbinic legends of Ḥoni the Circle-maker and Jeremiah's disciple Baruch ben Neriah. See Ginzberg, *Legends*, VI, 409ff.; also Speyer, *Erzählungen*, 425. The story may echo Jeremiah 29:1–7 or 40:7–10. The apocalyptic theme concerning sleeper and donkey is found in Qur'ān 2:261 and is also used by 'Abbāsid propagandists who cite the Qur'ānic verse.

143. That is, the period between Alexander the Great and the Sasanian dynasty. The term *mulūk al-ṭawā'if* may also be rendered as princelings, petty kings, petty dynasties, and so forth. More specifically, it refers here to the Diadochs.

144. Note that Jeremiah had a secretary, one Baruch ben Neriah. For the rabbinic legends concerning him, see Ginzberg, *Legends*, IV, 322, 324; VI, 411ff. The identification of Zoroaster with Baruch ben Neriah is made in several Syriac and Arabic sources. See Jackson, *Zoroaster*, 165f.; Bidez and Cumont, *Les*

master invoked wrath, and the man thus became a leper. He reached Ādharbayjān where he started the Zoroastrian faith. Later he went to Bishtāsb, who was then at Balkh. When Zoroaster came to Bishtāsb and offered him the new faith, the king admired it, forced the people to embrace it, and perpetrated a great massacre among his subjects in this connection. They followed his religion. Bishtāsb reigned for 112 years.

But another scholar well versed in antiquity said that Kay Luhrāsb was commended by the people of his realm. He was repressive towards the rulers around Iran (Irānshahr), strict with his associates, high-minded, and absorbed in construction, irrigation and cultivation. The kings of Rome, North Africa, and India, and other rulers, used to pay him a set annual tribute and impost, and they addressed him with reverence, recognizing [649]
him with awe as King of Kings.

It is said that Nebuchadnezzar brought him treasures and valuables from Jerusalem. When Luhrāsb felt he was becoming weak, he made his son Bishtāsb king. He thus retired from rule while entrusting it to his son. Luhrāsb is said to have reigned 120 years. It was asserted that this Nebuchadnezzar who attacked the Israelites was called Bukhtrashah, and that he was a Persian of the progeny of Jūdharz. It is also asserted that he lived a long life of over three hundred years, and that he was in the service of King Luhrāsb, the father of Bishtāsb. It was Luhrāsb who sent him to Palestine and Jerusalem in order to exile the Jews from there. He went there and later withdrew. After serving Luhrāsb, he served his son Bishtāsb and, later, Bahman[145] who lived in the city of Balkh, called "The Beautiful."

It is also asserted that it was Bahman who ordered Bukhtrashah to go to Jerusalem to exile the Jews from there. The rea-

mages hellénisés, I, 49f.; 41ff., where other Jewish identifications of Zoroaster are discussed. See also H.S. Nyberg, *JCOI*,39 (1958), 45ff. and J. Neusner, *JBR*, 32 (1964), 359–360. See also the Hebrew medieval stories connected with the name of Ben Sira (Sirach), discussed in E. Yasif, *Sippure Ben Sira*.

145. The ancient form of this name is Vohu Manah, "of good mind," which also serves as a name for one of the Amesha Spenta, the group of abstract divine figures around Ahura Mazda. On this mythical king see Justi, *Iran Nb*, 374, s.v. Wohu-Manah.

son therefore was that the ruler of Jerusalem attacked the messengers Bahman had sent to him, and slew some of them. When Bahman learned of this he called Bukhtrashah. He made him king of Babylon and ordered him to proceed there, and then to go to Palestine and Jerusalem, specifically against the Jews, to slay their fighters and seize their young ones. Bahman gave him a free hand to select from among the nobles and officers whomever he wished, and Bukhtrashah selected from the royal house Darius[146] the son of Mahrī, of the progeny of
[650] Madai b. Japhet b. Noah.[147] Darius was Bukhtrashah's nephew. He also selected Cyrus Kaykawān,[148] one of the sons of Elam b. Shem who was in charge of the treasury of Bahman, and Ahasuerus b. Cyrus b. Jāmāsb,[149] who was nicknamed the sage, as well as Bahrām b. Cyrus b. Bishtāsb.[150] Bahman assigned to him these four of his kin and retinue, and also some dignitaries of the *asāwirah* and their leaders. There were three hundred of them and fifty thousand soldiers of the army. Bahman permitted him to exact whatever he needed to maintain them.

Buktrashah now marched with them southward until they reached Babylon. He stayed there for a year to prepare for the campaign. A vast number of people came to him. Among them was a man of the progeny of Sennacherib, the king who had raided King Hezekiah b. Ahaz in Palestine and Jerusalem. The latter was of the progeny of Solomon and David, and the friend of Isaiah. The man's name was Nebuchadnezzar b. Nebuzaradan b. Sennacherib (ruler of Mosul and its environs) b. Darius b. ʿAbīrī b. Tīrī b. Rūbā b. Rāyā b. Solomon (Salāmūn) b. David b. Ṭāmī b. Hāmil b. Harmān b. Fūdī b. Hamūl b. Daramī b.

---

146. The Old Persian form of this name is, in the nominative, Dārayavahuš (although the *-h-* is not expressed in the Old Persian script). The late Persian tradition preserves this name as Dārāb, Dārā. See Justi, *Iran Nb*, 78–80.

147. Genesis 10:2.

148. There is some confusion about this person, which Justi, *Iran Nb*, 167, s.v. Kuru, No. 2, tries to correct by emending the name to read Kay-Arish son of Kay Kawād.

149. See Justi, *Iran Nb*, 167, s.v. Kuru, No. 1.

150. The name Bahrām is a development of Old Iranian Verethraghna. On this person see Justi, *Iran Nb*, 361, s.v. Werethraghna, No. 3.

Qamā' il b. Sāmā b. Raghmā b. Nimrod b. Kush b. Ham b. Noah. [651]

This man came to Bukhtrashah because of the tribute that Hezekiah and the Israelites had brought to his ancestor Sennacherib when the latter waged war on them. Thus he ingratiated himself with Bukhtrashah, who sent him out with a large force. Then Bukhtrashah followed him. When the soldiers massed at Jerusalem, Bukhtrashah proved victorious over the Israelites because God wanted to punish them. As a result, he took them prisoner, destroyed the Temple, and retired to Babylon with Jehoiachin b. Jehoiakim, a descendent of Solomon. Jehoiachin was king of Israel at the time. Bukhtrashah returned after appointing Mattaniyā, uncle of Jehoiachin, to be king, renaming him Zedekiah. When Nebuchadnezzar arrived in Babylon, Zedekiah rebelled. Nebuchadnezzar attacked him again, and defeated him; he destroyed his city and the temple. After slaying Zedekiah's sons and putting out his eyes, Nebuchadnezzar carried Zedekiah in chains to Babylon. The Children of Israel remained in Babylon until they returned to Jerusalem. According to our source, Nebuchadnezzar, the one named Bukhtrashah, lived forty years after the conquests of Jerusalem. He was succeeded by his son, Merodakh, who ruled the area for twenty-three years. Then the latter died and was succeeded by a son called Belshazzar b. Merodakh, who ruled [652]
for a year.

When Belshazzar became king, he became confused in his rule. Bahman dismissed him, and in his stead he appointed Darius the Mede[151] over Babylon and the adjoining regions of Syria and the other districts. Darius was related to Mādhī b. Japheth b. Noah. Darius then slew Belshazzar, and reigned over Babylon and the region of Syria for three years. Then Bahman dismissed him and appointed instead Cyrus the Elamite,[152] of the progeny of Elam b. Shem b. Noah, who had gone to Gomer with Madai when Gomer went eastward. When power was in-

151. This mythical figure is mentioned in Daniel 9:1 and in Josephus, *Ant.* 10.11:2,4,7. See Justi, *Iran Nb*, 78, s.v. Dārayawa(h)u, No. 2.

152. The same person was called Cyrus Kay-Kawān. See above, n. 148.

vested in Cyrus, Bahman wrote to him instructing him to be kind to the Israelites, to permit them to settle wherever they wished, to return to their country, and to appoint whomever they chose to lead them. They chose the prophet Daniel, and he took charge of their affairs. Cyrus ruled Babylon and the adjacent territory for three years. These years—from the time of the victory of Nebuchadnezzar to the end of his power and that of his son, and the reign of Cyrus the Elamite, counting from the destruction of Jerusalem—are referred to as the period of Nebuchadnezzar, a period of seventy years.[153]

After that, Babylon and its environs were ruled on behalf of Bahman by one of his relatives called Ahasuerus b. Cyrus b. Jāmāsb. Nicknamed the sage, he was one of the four dignitaries selected by Bukhtrashah when he set out for Palestine on behalf of Bahman. Ahasuerus had come to Bahman well recommended by Nebuchadnezzar, and it was at that time that Bahman appointed him to rule Babylon and its environs. He was
[653] appointed, so it is asserted, because a man who had administered the region of India (Sind and Hind) for Bahman, Karardashīr b. Dashkāl,[154] rebelled with six hundred thousand followers. Bahman therefore appointed Ahasuerus over the region and ordered him to go to Karardashīr, which he did. He waged war on the rebel, slaying him and most of his supporters. Bahman continued adding to the administrative duties of Ahasuerus, giving him various parts of the realm to rule over. The latter stayed at Susa, gathered nobles around him and wined and dined them; he ruled the region from Babylon to India, and Ethiopia and the coast. On a single day he gave each of one hundred twenty military commanders a banner and a thousand choice soldiers, each of whom equalled one hundred warriors.

Ahasuerus became entrenched in Babylon but spent much time at Susa, and he married a woman from among the Israelite captives. She was called Esther, the daughter of Abihail. She

153. Jeremiah 29:10. Note, however, that Jerusalem fell in 587 B.C. and the return began in 539 B.C., the beginning of Cyrus's reign.

154. See Justi, *Iran Nb*, 156, s.v. Kara, No. 3.

had been raised by an uncle of hers, Mordechai, who was her milch-brother, as Mordechai's mother milk-fed Esther. The reason he married her was that he had killed one of his wives, a noble, beautiful, bright woman, named Vashti. He had ordered Vashti to appear before the people in order that they might see her majesty and beauty, but she refused. Ahasuerus slew her but then became anxious about it. It was suggested to him that he review the women of the world, which he did. He became attracted to Esther by a divine design for the sake of the Israelites. The Christians assert that she bore him a son on his way to Babylon, and that he named it Cyrus. They also assert that the rule of Ahasuerus lasted fourteen years, that Mordechai taught him the Torah, and that Cyrus embraced the faith of the Israelites and learned from the prophet Daniel and his compan- [654]
ions, Hananiah, Mishael and Azariah. They asked the king to permit them to proceed to Jerusalem but he refused, saying, "Even if a thousand of your prophets were with me, no one would leave me as long as I live." He appointed Daniel as judge and transferred to him all his power, ordering him to remove from the treasuries and return to Jerusalem whatever Nebuchadnezzar had taken from there. The king started the reconstruction of Jerusalem. It was built and completed in the days of Cyrus b. Ahasuerus.[155]

The reign of Cyrus was within that of Bahman and Khumānī[156] and lasted some twenty-two years. Bahman died after thirteen years of the rule of Cyrus, and Cyrus died four years after Khumānī assumed power. The total reign of Cyrus b. Ahasuerus lasted twenty-two years. This is what those versed in biography and history report about Nebuchadnezzar and his relations with the Children of Israel. Old (Muslim) authorities among the learned gave different reports about the matter.

Thus I was told by al-Qāsim b. al-Ḥasan—Ḥajjāj—Ibn Jurayj Yaʿlā b. Muslim—Saʿīd b. Jubayr: An Israelite was reading un-

155. Cyrus b. Ahasuerus is Cyrus the Great. See Justi, *IranNb*, 167, s.v. Kuru, No. 3.

156. Another form of the name attested is Humā, Humāy, both daughter and wife of Bahman. See Justi, *IranNb*, 132, s.v. Huma, No. 2.

til he reached the passage, "We sent against you servants of Ours, men of great might."[157] He wept bitterly, closed the scripture, and said, "Such is the time God intended." Then he
[655] said, "O Lord, show me this man by whose hand You will accomplish the destruction of the Children of Israel." He was shown in his dream a wretch in Babylon, Nebuchadnezzar by name. The Israelite was a rich man, and he set out with money and servants. He was asked, "Where are you going?" and replied, "I want to trade." He settled in a house in Babylon and took it on lease. Alone there, he began to invite the beggars and was kind to them. Giving something to everyone who came, he would ask, "Are there not any other poor men?" They said, "Yes, a wretch in such and such neighborhood, a sick man, Nebuchadnezzar by name." He said to his servants, "Come." He walked until he reached that man, whereupon he asked, "What is your name?" "Nebuchadnezzar," he replied; whereupon he said to his servants, "Carry him." They carried him to the house, where the Israelite nursed him until the man recovered, and gave him clothes and adequate support. Then the Israelite announced he was going to leave, and Nebuchadnezzar wept. "Why are you crying?" the Israelite asked. The other man replied, "I am crying because you treated me in this manner, and I find nothing with which to reciprocate." At this, the Israelite said, "Oh yes, I want a slight matter from you: Should you become king, you should obey me."[158] The other man began following him saying, "You are mocking me"—he was prepared to do as requested but he felt that he was being mocked. The Israelite wept, and said, "I know that what prevents you from granting my request is that God wishes to carry out what He decreed and wrote in His scripture."

[656] Fate struck its blow. Ṣayḥūn—the Persian king in Babylon—said, "What if we sent a vanguard to Palestine?" (His advisors) said, "Not a bad [idea]." He then asked, "Whom would you

157. Qur'ān 17:5.

158. *in malakta aṭa'tanī*, "If you become king, you would accede to my wish." In Ṭabarī's commentary on the Qur'ān 15:5–7, vol. XV, 29 (ed. 1954), Ibn Jubayr is quoted for this story. It is evident that there is a confusion of *aṭa'tanī*, "you would obey me," and *a'ṭaytanī*, "you would give or grant me."

consider [sending]?" They said, "Such and such." So he sent a man with an army of a hundred thousand, and Nebuchadnezzar went along in his kitchen, in order to eat his fill. When he arrived in Palestine, the head of the vanguard found that God's country abounded in horses and sturdy men, which made him wary; but he did not investigate (the situation). Nebuchadnezzar began to take part in the councils of the native population, and he would say, "What prevents you from attacking Babylon? If you raided it, you would have access to its wealth." They replied, "We are not good at fighting and do not fight." So he abandoned the councils of the native population. Then the vanguard returned, and its commander informed their king of what he had seen. Nebuchadnezzar began talking to the king's cavalry, "If the king called me, I would inform him otherwise." This was reported to the king who called him in, whereupon Nebuchadnezzar informed him, "When that commander of the vanguard saw that country so rich in horses and sturdy men, he became wary and made no inquiry; but I left no gathering there unattended, and I told them such and such, and they told me such and such"—that is the version of Sa'īd b. Jubayr. The chief of the vanguard then said to Nebuchadnezzar, "You have disgraced me; I'll pay you a hundred thousand (coins) if you withdraw what you said." He replied, "If you gave me Babylon's treasury, I would not withdraw it." [657]

The wheel of fate turned. The king said, "Suppose we send a cavalry detachment to Palestine; and if they find the going easy, let them proceed, and if not, let them wrest from it as much as they can." (His advisors) said, "Not a bad [idea]." Then he asked, "Whom would you consider [sending]?" They said, "Such and such." Said he, "[I would] rather [send] the man who informed me." He called in Nebuchadnezzar, and then dispatched him with four thousand horsemen. They departed, spied out the entire land and captured what they could, but without destroying or killing.

It so happened that Ṣayḥūn died and was being buried. Some said, "Appoint a successor." Others said, "Don't rush! Let your men, your choice cavalry arrive, lest they be resentful." So they tarried until Nebuchadnezzar came with the captives and the spoils, which he proceeded to distribute among the people. Then they said, "We see nobody more worthy of kingship than he." So they made him king.

Other (Muslim) scholars say that Nebuchadnezzar went out against the Israelites because of a conflict that arose when they killed John, the son of Zechariah.[159]

---

159. Yaḥyā b. Zakariyyā', that is, John the Baptist.

The Reason Why Nebuchadnezzar Destroyed Jerusalem

According to Mūsā b. Hārūn—ʿAmr b. Ḥammād—Asbāṭ—al-Suddī, and the chain of authority we mentioned above: Ṣayḥā'īn dispatched Nebuchadnezzar to wage war on the Israelites when their king slew John the son of Zechariah and word reached Ṣayḥā'īn about his death.

According to Ibn Ḥumayd—Salamah—Ibn Isḥāq: According to what I learned, Almighty God appointed over the Israelites, after Isaiah, a man called Josiah b. Amoz. Then God sent them [658]
al-Khaḍir[160] as a prophet—his name, as Wahb b. Munabbih asserted on the authority of Israelites, was Jeremiah b. Hilkiah, of the tribe of Aaron.[161]

As for Wahb b. Munabbih, what he related about al-Khaḍir, I heard from Muḥammad b. Sahl b. ʿAskar al-Bukhārī—Ismāʿīl b. ʿAbd al-Karīm—ʿAbd al-Ṣamad b. Maʿqil who said: I heard Wahb b. Munabbih relate. . . .

According to Ibn Ḥumayd—Salamah—Ibn Isḥāq—an unquestionable authority: Wahb b. Munabbih al-Yamanī used to tell as follows: Almighty God told Jeremiah when he sent him

160. Also rendered al-Khiḍr. For this prophet, who is a hero of Arabic folklore, see *EI*², s.v. al-Khaḍir.

161. Jeremiah 2:8. Here al-Khaḍir is identified with Jeremiah.

to be a prophet among the Israelites, "Before I created you, I selected you, and before I shaped you in the womb of your mother, I consecrated you, and before I removed you from your mother's womb I purified you, and before you could walk I made you a prophet, and before you reached manhood I tested you, and I elected you for an important task." For Almighty God sent Jeremiah to that king of the Israelites, to instruct and direct him, to bring him the divine message in whatever arose between him and Almighty God.

Then the affairs of the Israelites became grave. They were guilty of acts of disobedience, violated prohibitions, and forgot what God had done for them, and that He had saved them from their enemy Sennacherib and his hosts. Then Almighty God revealed to Jeremiah, "Go to thy people, the Children of Israel, and tell them that which I shall command you; remind them of My favors to them, make known to them their misfortunes."
[659] Jeremiah said, "I am weak, unless You strengthen me. I fail, unless You grant me attainment. I err, unless You instruct me. I am forsaken, unless You help me. I am humble, unless You honor me."

Almighty God replied,

> Do you not know that everything issues from My will, and that all hearts and tongues are in My hands? I turn them at My will, and they obey Me. I am the incomparable God. By My word arose heaven and earth and whatever is in them. I address the seas, and they hearken to My word. I command them, and they comply with My order. I set limits to them in the plain, and there is no violation of My boundary. In mountain-like waves they come but when they reach the limit I have set, in fear and cognizance of My decree, they are enveloped in humbleness of obedience to Me. I am with you, and no evil will come to you while I am with you. I send you to a great host of My creatures, to convey to them My messages. Thereby will you merit the reward of those of them who will hearken to you; it will not be less than their rewards. And, should you fail therein, you will merit the burden of him whom you have left, and in his blindness, no less. Go to your people and

tell them, "God remembers the good of your ancestors. This urged Him to call upon you, O sons, to repent." Ask them, how their fathers found the effect of obedience to Me, and how they found the consequence of disobedience toward Me. Do they know anyone before them who obeyed Me but was wretched in obedience to Me, or was disobedient toward Me, yet prospered in that disobedience? Beasts remembering their goodly domiciles, return to them; but these people graze in the meadows of perdition. Their rabbis and monks took My worshipers as servants, and the people worship them, not Me, and they [the rabbis and monks] judge them not in accordance with My scripture. They made the people ignore Me, forget Me. Their princes and leaders disregard My favor, believe they are safe from My cunning, spurn My scripture, forget My covenant, alter My procedure, and My creatures believe in them with the loyalty due only to Me. The people obey [660]
the leaders in disobeying Me, and follow them in heresy against My religion and in insolence, heedlessness and deception toward Me and My messengers. By My majesty, exaltedness, and power! Is it seemly that I create creatures to serve as divinities? Their readers and legists practice devotion in sanctuaries, and display religiosity in erecting them for a deity other than Myself, as they seek worldly advantage in religion. They study there not for knowledge, and learn not for deed. The sons of prophets are outnumbered, overpowered, deluded, "plunge along with the plungers."[162] They desire that I help them as I did their fathers, and honor them as I honored their fathers.

Without truth, thought and consideration they assert that none is worthier thereof than they. They do not remember how their fathers assisted Me, and how they exerted themselves for Me, when heretics wrought alternations. Nor do they remember how their ancestors sacrificed their very lives, how they suffered but believed, until My order prevailed and My religion was victorious. I have been patient with these people—perhaps they will

162. Qur'ān 74:76.

> respond. I gave them time, I forgave them—perhaps they will repent. I gave them long life—perhaps they will reflect. I forgave throughout, I gave them rain, and made the earth grow plants for them, granted them health and victory over the enemy. But they merely became more wicked, more removed from Me. How long will they struggle with Me? [How long] will they deceive Me? I swear by My Majesty, that I shall foreordain for them a hardship
> [661] that will confuse the forebearing; the sensible man's sense will go astray, and so will the wise man's wisdom. Then shall I give mastery over them to a harsh and violent tyrant, whom I shall clad in awe, and from whose heart I shall remove mercy, compassion and leniency; who will be followed by a host like the blackness of the dark of [the] night, with soldiers like flocks of clouds, and chariots like the raging sea. The flutter of his banners is like the flight of eagles, the attack by his horsemen like the eagles' scream.

Later, Almighty God revealed to Jeremiah, "I shall destroy the Children of Israel at the hand of Japheth." Japheth refers to the people of Babylon who are the progeny of Japheth, the son of Noah. When Jeremiah heard the divine revelation, he cried out and wept, rent his clothes and poured dust on his head,[163] and said, "Cursed be the day wherein I was born,[164] the day I learned the law; my worst day is the one when I was born. I was left to be the last of the prophets only for what is evil unto me. If He wished me well He would not make me the last of the prophets of the Children of Israel. Through me, wretchedness and destruction shall strike."

When God heard al-Khaḍir imploring, crying, and exclaiming, He called unto him, "O Jeremiah, does my revelation grieve you?" He then replied, "Yes, O Lord, destroy me before I see calamity overwhelm the Children of Israel." But Almighty God said, "By My majesty and glory, I shall not destroy Jerusalem and the Children of Israel until the decree comes from

---

163. These were traditional signs of mourning among the Jews. See Jeremiah 20:14.

164. Jeremiah 20:14–18.

you." Jeremiah rejoiced at hearing what his Lord had said. His soul became uplifted and he replied, "No, by Him who sent the truth through Moses and His prophets, never shall I urge my Lord to destroy the Children of Israel." Then he came to the king of the Children of Israel and announced to him what God had revealed. The king rejoiced at hearing the good news and became jubilant. He said, "Should the Lord chastise us, it [662]
would be for the many sins we have perpetrated, but it is within His power to forgive us."

For three years after this revelation they increased their refractory behavior and persevered in their evil ways; all this at the time when their destruction was approaching. They were not thinking of the world to come. Revelation was withheld from them as worldly matters continued to distract them. Their king said to them, "O Children of Israel, desist from these doings before divine force steps in, before God sends against you a people who will have no pity on you; the Lord is close to the repentent." But they refused to desist from any of their behavior.

God moved Nebuchadnezzar b. Nabuzeradan b. Sennacherib b. Darius (Dāryās) b. Nimrod (the one who disputed with Abraham concerning his Lord) b. Peleg b. Eber to proceed to Jerusalem and to accomplish there what his grandfather Sennacherib had intended to do.[165] He set out for Jerusalem with an army of six hundred thousand men. When he departed, the news reached the king of the Israelites, "Nebuchadnezzar and his army have set out to fight you." Then the king sent for Jeremiah. When the prophet arrived, the king said, "O Jeremiah, what about the revelation that God would not destroy the people of Jerusalem except by your urging?" Jeremiah said to the king, "The Lord does not revoke a promise, and I put my trust in Him." When the time approached, and the end of their realm was at hand, and God decided that they should be destroyed, He dispatched an angel to whom He said, "Go to Jere- [663]
miah and ask him for his opinion." And (God) instructed him what to ask of Jeremiah. Disguised as an Israelite, the angel

165. For Nimrod, see Genesis 10:8ff.; for Peleg, 10:25. See also Qur'ān 2:260 concerning a dispute with God.

came to Jeremiah. The prophet said to him, "Who are you?" The angel replied, "An Israelite, asking you about a concern of mine." The prophet consented, and the angel said to him, "O Prophet, I came to ask you about my kith and kin whom I have treated kindly in accordance with divine command. I have treated them with kindness throughout, and have not failed to honor them. But the more I honor them, the more they rage against me. Give me your opinion of them, O Prophet." Jeremiah said to him, "Improve relations between yourself and God, treat the relatives in accordance with divine command, and may you be happy." The angel then departed. A few days later he reappeared in the same guise. Jeremiah asked, "Who are you?" "I am the man who came to you to consult you about my kith and kin," he replied. The prophet asked, "Has there been no improvement yet in their attitude? Are you still dissatisfied?" He responded, "O Prophet, by God, I know no manner of honoring relatives which I have not attempted or improved upon." To this Jeremiah then said, "Go back to your people, be good to them, and ask God, who encourages the virtuous, to better your relations, so that all of you will please God and be spared His wrath."

The angel left, and was absent for several days. Nebuchadnezzar and his troops descended upon Jerusalem. They were more numerous than locusts. The Israelites were in terror, and
[664] the king of the Israelites was distressed. Summoning Jeremiah, he said, "O Prophet, what of the divine promise?" "I trust the Lord," replied the prophet. Then the angel approached Jeremiah as he was sitting on the wall of Jerusalem, smiling and rejoicing at the promised divine help. He sat down in front of the prophet who asked him, "Who are you?" "I am the one who came to you twice about my relatives," he replied. "Is it not time for them to rouse themselves?" asked Jeremiah. "O Prophet, I have borne with patience all that I suffered from them to this day, although I knew their purpose was to anger me. But when I came to them today, I saw them in an act that will displease God," he said. "What act?" asked Jeremiah. He answered, "O Prophet, a grave act to anger God. Had they continued their previous behavior, my anger would not have become vehement, I would have suffered and hoped; but today I

became furious for the sake of God and of you. So I came to tell you about them, and I ask you, by God who sent you to announce the truth, would you not invoke God to destroy them?" Jeremiah then exclaimed, "O King of heaven and earth, if they are right and just, leave them be, but if they anger and displease You, destroy them." No sooner did the word pass Jeremiah's lips than God sent from heaven a thunderbolt upon Jerusalem. The sacrificial alter caught fire, and the seven city gates collapsed. When Jeremiah saw that, he shouted, rent his garment, poured dust on his head, and exclaimed, "O King of heaven, Most Merciful, where is your promise to me?" Then it [665]
was announced (from heaven), "O Jeremiah, what befalls them, comes by your decision announced to Our messenger."

The prophet realized that it was his decision—which he had uttered thrice to the Lord's messenger. He lost his mind and mingled with wild beasts. Nebuchadnezzar with his troops entered Jerusalem, conquered Palestine, slew the Israelites until he annihilated them, and destroyed the temple. He then ordered each of his troops to fill his shield with dust, and to throw it upon the temple. They did so, filling the site. He then left for Babylon, taking the captive Israelites. He ordered all those from Jerusalem to assemble. All young and old Israelites assembled, and he selected from among them a hundred thousand youths. When the booty of his army was sorted and he was about to distribute it among the soldiers, the chieftains (*mulūk*) present said, "O King, take all our booty, and distribute among us (instead) these youths elected by you from among the Israelites." He complied, and each of them was given four youths. Among these were Daniel, Hananiah, Azariah and Mishael. There were also seven thousand of the progeny of David, eleven thousand of the tribe of Joseph and his brother Benjamin, the sons of Jacob, and eight thousand of the tribe of Asher. Included as well were fourteen thousand of the tribes of Zebulun and Naphtali, four thousand of the tribes of Reuben and Levi, four thousand of the tribe of Judah, and what [666]
remained of the Children of Israel.

Nebuchadnezzar divided them into three groups: one-third he left in Palestine, one-third he took into captivity, one-third he slew. He brought the Temple vessels to Babylon, also the seventy thousand youths. This was the first blow God brought down upon the Israelites for their evildoing and iniquity. When Nebuchadnezzar started out on his way back to Babylon with the Israelite captives, Jeremiah came on his donkey, carrying a vessel of grape juice and a basket of figs. When he reached Jerusalem and saw how it lay in ruins, he began doubting. How would God revive this city after its death? God then caused him to lie dead for a hundred years, with donkey vessel and basket just as they were when he died. God made him invisible. Then God raised him up, saying,[166] "How long have you tarried?" He said, "I have tarried a day, or part of a day." Said He, "No, you have tarried a hundred years. Look at your food and drink—it has not spoiled; and look at your donkey. We shall make you a sign for the people. Look at the bones [of your donkey]—We shall set them up and then clothe them with flesh."

Then Jeremiah looked at his donkey and saw how the veins and nerves were being joined, though the animal had died at the same time as he. Then he saw how God clothed it all with flesh, until it stood up and became animate and brayed. The prophet then looked at his juice and figs, and behold, they were as when he had put them down, unchanged. Confronted with
[667] such divine might, he exclaimed, "I know that God is powerful over everything." Thereupon God gave long life to Jeremiah, and he is seen in the desert areas.

Nebuchadnezzar ruled as long as it pleased God. Then he saw a dream that perturbed him, for he saw a thing that struck him and made him forget what he saw.[167] He summoned Daniel, Hananiah, Azariah and Mishael, who were of the seed of prophets, and said, "Explain to me a dream I saw; something struck me and made me forget the dream, yet it amazed me." They said to him, "Tell us about it that we might let you know its interpretation." He said, "I do not remember. If you do not interpret it for me, I shall cut off your shoulders." They left him and prayed to God, imploring His help, and asked Him to let them know the dream. He granted their request. Then they

166. Qur'ān 2:261. See also n. 142.
167. Daniel 2.

came to the king and told him, "You saw a statue." "Right you are," he said. They continued, "Its feet and legs were of clay, its knees and thighs of copper, its belly of silver, the chest of gold, head and neck of iron." "Right indeed!" he said. They continued, "As you were looking at it, it surprised you, but God sent a rock from heaven, and it smashed the statue. It is the rock that made you forget the dream." The king responded, "That is right. But what does it mean?" They said, "It means that you saw the reigns of kings; some were weaker, others better, some stronger. The first reign was of clay, it was the weakest and meekest. Above it was copper—it is the better and the stronger one. Above copper was silver, which excels copper and is finer [668]
than it, and above silver was gold which is better and nobler than silver. Next was iron, your realm, the strongest of the kingdoms, and more powerful than any before it. The rock you saw, sent by God from heaven to smash it, points to a prophet God will send from heaven to smash it all, and power will revert unto Him."

The people of Babylon said to Nebuchadnezzar, "Have you seen these Israelite youths whom you gave to us upon our request? By God, we have become estranged from our women since the youths came to stay with us. We saw our women attracted to them, turning toward them. Get them out of our midst, or slay them." The king replied, "As you wish. Whoever prefers to slay those in his possession, let him do so." They removed them but as the youths were led to be slain, they implored God, "O Lord, we are the victims of other people's sins." God had mercy upon them, and promised to revive them after they had been slain. They were slain, except for those Nebuchadnezzar kept alive, among them Daniel, Hananiah, Azariah and Mishael.

When Almighty God wanted Nebuchadnezzar to perish, the latter hastened to address the Israelites in his power, "Do you see this house which I destroyed, and these people I have slain? Who are they, and what house is it?" They said, "It is the house of God, a temple of His, and the people were His people. They were of the seed of the prophets. But they were wicked, and transgressed, showing their disobedience; because of their sins you were made ruler over them. Their Lord is the God of

[669] heaven and earth, and Lord of all human beings. He both grants and deprives them of honor. He makes them powerful, but if their deeds call for it, He destroys them and imposes alien rule over them."

The king then said, "Tell me, what could make me rise to high heaven? Perhaps I shall rise to heaven, slay those who are there, and take it over as my realm. For I am through with the earth and its people." They answered, "You cannot do that; no creature can." And Nebuchadnezzar said, "You must do this or I shall slay you to the last [man]!" They cried to God, imploring Him. To show the king how weak and negligible he was, God sent upon him a gnat that entered his nostril, penetrated his brain, and bit into the very center of the brain, until the king was unable to sit or rest without pain in his head at the center of the brain. When he felt death was close, he said to his retinue, "After I die, split my head open, and find out what it was that killed me." When he died, they split his head open, and found the gnat biting at the very center of this brain, so that God might show men His might and dominion.[168]

God saved the Israelites who were under the king's rule. Taking pity on them, he returned them to Palestine and Jerusalem, and to the sacred Temple. They multiplied, and were more prosperous than ever before. They say—and God knows best—that God revived those who were slain, and that they joined the others. When they returned to Palestine, they had no divine scripture, for the Torah had been seized and burned, and it perished. Ezra, one of the captives in Babylon who re-
[670] turned to Palestine, spent day and night grieving over it, in solitude. While he was in waterless valleys and in the wilderness, grieving over the Torah and weeping, lo and behold, a man approached him as he sat, and (the man) said, "O Ezra, what grieves you?" Ezra said, "I grieve over God's scripture and covenant which was among us, but our transgressions and the Lord's wrath against us came to such a pass that He made our enemy prevail. They slew our men, destroyed our country and

168. The story of the gnat is found also in the rabbinic legends concerning Titus, the Roman emperor who destroyed the Second Temple. See Ginzberg, *Legends*, V. 60, n. 191.

burned our divine book, without which our worldly existence and our life to come has no meaning. What shall I weep over if not this." The man said, "Would you like it to be returned to you?" Ezra asked, "Is that possible?" "Yes," the man replied. "Go back, fast, cleanse yourself, and cleanse your garments. Then be at this place tomorrow."

Ezra went back, cleansed himself and his garments, and went to the appointed place. He sat there, and the man came carrying a vessel filled with water—he was an angel sent by God—and gave Ezra to drink from that vessel. The Torah then presented itself in Ezra's consciousness. Ezra returned to the Children of Israel and set down the Torah for them, so that they might know what it permits and what it prohibits, its patterns, precepts and statutes. They loved it as they had never loved anything before. The Torah was established among them, and with it their cause fared well. Ezra stayed among them to carry out the divine truth. Then he died. In the course of time, the Israelites considered Ezra to be the son of God. God again sent them a prophet, as He did in the past, to direct and teach them, and to command them to follow the Torah.[169]

Others relate, on the authority of Wahb B. Munabbih, different stories about Nebuchadnezzar and the Israelites, and (about) his expedition against them. We omitted them, for the sake of brevity. [671]

---

169. Qur'ān 9:30 concerning alleged Jewish claims that Ezra was the son of God.

The Story of Nebuchadnezzar's Raid Against the Arabs

According to Hishām b. Muḥammad: It is mentioned—and God knows best—that the settlement of the Arabs in Iraq, their establishment there, and their taking of al-Ḥīrah and al-Anbār as their domicile, began when God inspired Berechiah b. Hananiah[170] b. Zerubabel b. Shealtiel (Hishām said that al-Sharqī said Shealtiel is the first who made the dish *ṭifshīl*),[171] of the tribe of Judah, saying, "Go to Nebuchadnezzar and command him to raid the Arabs whose houses have no locks, nor gates.[172] Let him conquer their land with soldiers, slay their fighting men, and despoil their wealth. Tell him that they do not believe in Me, that they have taken other deities, and that they deny My prophets and messengers."

---

170. The name Hanahiah is uncertain in the text. The editor suggests it follows I Chronicles 3:19.

171. *Ṭifshīl* (the form *ṭafayshal* is also attested) is a dish of grains; see de Goeje, *Glossarium*, p. CCCXLI; Dozy, *Supplément*, II, 48. Persian knows a dish called *tafshīla* (variant forms: *tafshīra, tafshara*, etc.), consisting of meat, eggs, carrots and honey, but other ingredients are also mentioned; see *Burhān-i Qāṭi'*, 502. The word seems to be of Aramaic origin, See JAram. *tabshila*, a kind of broth; see Jastrow, *Dictionary*, 1646.

172. Jeremiah 49:31 regarding Kedar and Hasor. The Hebrew expression "inhabitants of the tents of Kedar" had become synonymous with the Arabs of the desert.

Berechiah proceeded from Najrān,[173] until he reached Nebuchadnezzar at Babylon—his name was Nebuchad Nazr but the Arabs arabicized it.[174] The prophet announced the revelation, and told him as he was charged. That was at the time of Maʿadd b. ʿAdnān.[175]

Nebuchadnezzar pounced upon the Arab merchants who were in his land. They used to come to buy and sell, securing grain, figs, clothes, and so forth. He assembled those whom he succeeded in seizing and built an enclosure around them on a sand hill. The king fortified it, concentrated them therein, and appointed guards and watchmen over them. Thereupon he announced the expedition against the Arabs. While the expedition was in preparation, the news spread to the neighboring [672]
Arabs. Groups (*ṭawāʾif*) of them came out to him suing for peace and guarantees of safety. Nebuchadnezzar consulted Berechiah about them, and the latter said, "Their coming out of their land to meet you before you start to march upon them is a sign of repentence over their practices; accept it and treat them kindly." So Nebuchadnezzar settled them in the Sawād,[176] on the bank of the Euphrates, where they later developed the site of their military encampment into the city of al-Anbār.[177] He left the people of al-Ḥīrah[178] undisturbed, and the Arabs settled there during the lifetime of Nebuchadnezzar. When he died, they joined the people of al-Anbār, and that fenced-off area (al-Ḥīrah) remained a ruin.

---

173. Najran, which is situated in the Yaman, was a Christian center in pre-Islamic times.

174. On the form of the name in Arabic, Bukht-Naṣar, see above, n. 136.

175. ʿAdnān was the legendary ancestor of the northern Arabs. See *EI*^{2}, s.v. ʿAdnān.

176. The fertile black land of southern Iraq. See LeStrange, *Lands*, 24.

177. On Anbār see LeStrange, *Lands*, 65f.; *EI*^{2}, s.v. al-Anbār. See also F.C. Andreas in *Pauly's Realencyclopädie der classischen Altertumswissenschaft*, ed. G. Wissowa, Stuttgart, 1893-., I, 1790–1795, s.v. Ambara. Anbār is identified by some scholars with the important Jewish center of learning Pumbedita of the talmudic period. Detailed information in Oppenheimer, *Babylonia Judaica*, 362ff.

178. Ḥīrah is located southwest of present-day Najaf in Iraq, and was the capital of the Lakhmid dynasty in the pre-Islamic period. See LeStrange, *Lands*, 75f.; *EI*^{2}, s.v. al-Ḥīra; *CHI* 3(1), 597ff. The most detailed treatment of the history of Ḥīrah is in Rothstein, *Dynastie der Laḫmiden*, 12ff.

Apart from Hisham, another scholar versed in antiquity mentioned that when Maʿadd b. ʿAdnān was born, the Israelites began slaying their prophets. The last of those slain was John b. Zechariah (the Baptist). This does not include those slain by the men of al-Rass and the people of Ḥaḍūr.[179] When they had the audacity to attack God's prophets, He decreed the destruction of that generation, to whose prophets Maʿadd b. ʿAdnān belonged. So God set Nebuchadnezzar upon the Israelites. After the destruction of the Temple and the towns, and the dispersion of the Israelites and their captivity in Babylon, the king was urged in a dream—or some prophet was instructed to command him to do it—to enter Arabia, wipe out man and beast, and obliterate it completely, leaving no sign of life there. Nebuchadnezzar concentrated cavalry and infantry
[673] between Aylah and al-Ubullah.[180] They entered Arabia and massacred every living being they had come upon and seized. God had revealed to Jeremiah and Berechiah, "God has warned your people but they did not desist, so after having had a kingdom they became slaves, and after an affluent life, they became beggars. Similarly I warned the people of ʿArabah but they were obstinate. I imposed Nebuchadnezzar's rule over them to take revenge upon them. Now rush to Maʿadd b. ʿAdnān of whose progeny will be Muḥammad, whom I shall bring forth at the end of time to seal prophethood and lift humility."

Setting out, the two rushed through the land as the earth folded under them miraculously.[181] They preceded Nebuchadnezzar and met ʿAdnān who received them, whereupon they rushed him to Maʿadd who was then twelve years old. Berechiah carried him on al-Burāq[182] and sat behind him. At

---

179. For these evildoers, see Qur'ān 25:40 and 50:12. Ḥaḍūr is also mentioned in Bayḍāwī's commentary of Qur'ān 21:14. See also Yāqūt, *Muʿjam*, II, 289; III, 73; index, 100.

180. Aylah is in northwest Arabia at the gulf of Akabah. See *EI*^{2}, s.v. al-Ayla. For Ubullah, which is in Iraq, see LeStrange, *Lands*, 47. What is implied here is that Nebuchadnezzar ranged his forces east-west all along the border with Arabia.

181. "The earth folded under them" is analogous to the Hebrew *qefiṣath hadderekh*.

182. That is, the wondrous beast of Muhammad's celestial journey to reach a distant sanctuary, interpreted as Jerusalem. See *EI*^{2}, s.v. al-Burāḳ.

once they reached Ḥarrān. The earth miraculously folded up and rushed Jeremiah to Ḥarrān.[183] Thus ʿAdnān and Nebuchadnezzar met in battle. Nebuchadnezzar put ʿAdnān to flight, and he proceeded through Arabia down to Ḥāḍūr in pursuit of ʿAdnān. Most of the Arabs of the ʿArabah area gathered at Ḥāḍūr, and the two forces established defensive trenches. . . . Nebuchadnezzar set an ambush, some assert the very first ambush ever. A heavenly voice called out, "Woe to the slayers of the prophets." Swords struck them from behind and in front. They repented their sins and called out in distress. ʿAdnān was prevented from reaching Nebuchadnezzar, and the latter from reaching ʿAdnān. Of those who were not at Ḥāḍūr and had escaped before the defeat split into two groups, one force betook [674] itself to Raysūt[184] under ʿAkk, the other set out for Wabar and a group of settled Arabs.

It is to them that the Qur'ānic passage refers: "How many a city that was evildoing We have shattered [of miscreants; yet when the chastisement descended upon the cities and engulfed them at the last blow, they were about to flee but failed to do so]. Then when they perceived Our might [to take revenge of them], behold, they ran headlong out of it [fleeing; swords struck them in front and from behind]. Run not! [Do not flee!] Return to the luxury that you exulted in, [to the pleasant life for which you were not grateful], and to your dwelling places; haply you shall be questioned."[185]

When they understood what was striking them, they admitted their sins, exclaiming, "'Alas for us! We have been evildoers.' So they ceased not to cry, until We made them stubble, silent and still [dead and slain by the sword]."

Nebuchadnezzar returned to Babylon with captives from the land of the Arabs (ʿArabah),[186] and placed them at al-Anbār; as a result it was called al-Anbār of the Arabs. Later the Aramaic speakers mingled with them. When Nebuchadnezzar returned, ʿAdnān died, and Arabia remained in ruins during Nebuchad-

183. For Ḥarrān which is in northern Syria, see *EI*^{2}, s.v. Ḥarrān.
184. The text reads Raysūb; read Raysūt, as in Yāqūt, *Muʿjam*, III, 633.
185. Qur'ān 21:11–15.
186. For ʿArabah see Yāqūt, *Muʿjam*, III, 633.

nezzar's lifetime. After Nebuchadnezzar's death, Maʿadd b. ʿAdnān marched with the prophets, that is, the prophets of the Israelites, until he came to Mecca. He restored its landmarks and performed the pilgrimage, as did the prophets with him.
[675] He then marched on until he came to Raysūt. Maʿadd questioned its people, inquiring about the remnant of the clan of al-Ḥārith b. Muḍāḍ al-Jurhumī—he was the one who had fought Daws al-ʿAtq. Most of the Jurhum had been wiped out by Daws; however, he was told that Jūsham b. Julhumah was alive. Maʿadd married his daughter Muʿānah, and she bore him Nizār b. Maʿadd.

Returning to the Story of Bishtāsb, His Reign and Its Events, Initiated by Him as well as Others, Such as His Governors; Also the Deeds of Nebuchadnezzar

Arab and Persian scholars well-versed in the lore of the ancient peoples say that Bishtāsb, son of Kay Luhrāsb said on this coronation day, "We are directing our thought, activity and knowledge toward everything through which righteousness is secured."

It is said that he built in Fārs the city of Fasā.[187] And in India and elsewhere he built sanctuaries for fire-worship, appointing priests to serve there. It is also said that he set up seven dignitaries,[188] each of them as a king in a region given to him; and it is said that Zoroaster the son of Isfīmān[189] ap- [676]

187. On Fasā see LeStrange, *Lands*, 290 and EI^2, s.v.

188. The motif of the seven highly placed dignitaries in the Persian court who are closest to the person of the king was fairly widespread in antiquity. It occurs, for example, in Esther 1:14. The story of the seven conspirators in the court of the pseudo-Smerdis, one of whom was the future Darius I (Herodotus III:71ff.) may go back to a similar idea. See further Nöldeke, *Geschichte*, 437.

189. Zaradusht-i Spitamān is a Middle Iranian form of the name of the founder of the religion of ancient Iran, called in English, following the Greek

peared after thirty years of Bishtāsb's reign. He claimed prophethood and counseled the king to embrace the new faith; the latter at first refrained from doing so, but later gave credence to his claim and accepted his tenets and the scripture which Zoroaster claimed was divinely revealed. It was written on twelve thousand cow skins, that is, carved on skins and painted in gold.[190] Bishtasb sent it to a place called Diz Nibisht in Iṣṭakhr[191] to which he assigned priests. He prohibited teaching it to the rank and file.[192] In those days Bishtāsb kept his peace with Kharzāsf b. Kay Sawāsf,[193] brother of Frāsiyāt, king of the Turks, observing a kind of truce. A condition of that truce was that Bishtāsb should have at the gate of Kharzāsf a royal mount, reserved, as befits royalty.[194] Zoroaster instructed Bishtāsb to break with the Turkish king. Accepting the suggestion, Bishtāsb sent for the horse and the man in charge, and took them over. The news was broken to Kharzāsf who was angered by it—he was a powerful sorcerer. He decided to fight Bishtāsb, and wrote him an insulting and roughly worded message, informing him that a major incident has occurred. He also reproved him for embracing Zoroaster's

---

tradition, Zoroaster. The name Zaradusht and some of the legends connected with his person occur quite frequently in Arabic sources. For a survey of the Arabic material see H.S. Nyberg, "Sasanid Mazdaism according to Moslem sources," *JCOI*, 39 (1958), 1–63. For a modern scholarly theory of Zoroaster's life and religious conceptions see M. Boyce, *History of Zoroastrianism*, especially I, 181ff. The traditional materials are collected and analyzed in Jackson, *Zoroaster*.

190. For the legend that the Avesta was written on twelve thousand cow skins, see Nyberg, op. cit., 15ff.

191. Iṣṭakhr is ancient Persepolis, where an important Achaemenid palace and center of government existed. The meaning of the term *diz (i) nibisht* is "the fortress of the writings." An attempt, not entirely convincing, to distinguish two separate traditions in ancient Iran, one connected with Iṣṭakhr and the other with Shīz, in ancient Media, was made by S. Wikander, *Feuerpriester*, esp. 132ff.

192. For the tradition about the secrecy in which the Avesta was to be kept see Shaked, *Proceedings of the Israel Academy*, 3 (1969), 175–221, esp. 187f.

193. On this person, the Sasanian form of whose name was probably Arjasp (the older form was Arejat-aspa) son of Syāwasp, see Justi, *IranNb*, 21f., s.v. Arejadaspa, and 300, s.v. Syāwaspa. See also Nöldeke, *Persische Studien*, II, 6.

194. We have evidence for the notion that such a custom existed in the Sasanian court. See S. Shaked, *JSAI*, 7 (1986), 75-91, esp. 79.

faith, and ordered him to extradite Zoroaster or else, he swore, he would attack and shed the blood of Bishtāsb and his house. When the messenger brought the letter to Bishtāsb, the latter assembled his kith and kin and the great men of his realm, among them Jāmāsb,[195] their scholar and reckoner, and Zarīn b. Luhrāsb.[196] Then Bishtāsb wrote the king of the Turks an insulting letter in reply to his message; it declared war and an- [677] nounced that he would not desist even if his rival did. Both were on the move, each with an innumerable fighting force. With Bishtāsb was Zarīn,[197] his brother, Nastur b. Zarīn,[198] Isfandiyār[199] and Bushūtan,[200] the two sons of Bishtāsb, and the men of Luhrāsb. With Kharzāsf were his brothers Jawharmaz[201] and Andirmān[202] his family, and Bidarafsh the sorcerer.[203] In the battles that ensued Zarīn was killed, which grieved Bishtāsb. Zarīn's son Isfandiyār lamented his father in fine music. He slew Bidarafsh in single combat. Fate turned against the Turks, and they lost men heavily. Kharzāsf fled, and Bishtāsb returned to Balkh. Some years later a certain Jurazm[204] slandered Isfandiyār and turned Bishtāsb against him. The king sent Isfandiyār on one campaign after another; then he ordered him to be chained and had him sent to a castle which served as a prison for women.

Bishtāsb went to Kirmān and Sijistān, then to the mountain

---

195. Jāmāsp(a) was a famous sage of Iranian antiquity. See Justi, *Iran Nb*, 109, s.v. Jāmāsp, No. 2.

196. The reading of the name is uncertain. See Justi, *Iran Nb*, 378, s.v. Zaẹnigà, and 41, s.v. Aurwadaspa.

197. A corruption of Zarēr. See Nöldeke, *Persische Studien*, II, 2; Justi, *Iran Nb*, 382, s.v. Zairiwari; Jackson, *Zoroaster*, 105.

198. The correct form of the name is probably Bastwar b. Zarēr. See Nöldeke, *Persische Studien*, II, 3; Justi, *Iran Nb*, 65, s.v. Bastawairi; Jackson, *Zoroaster*, 105.

199. See Justi, *Iran Nb*, 308, s.v. Spentōdāta, No. 1. The correct form of the name, as given by Justi, means "adhering to the holy (or bounteous) law."

200. That is, Peshōtan. See Justi, *Iran Nb*, 251, s.v. Peschotanu.

201. See Justi, *Iran Nb*, 112, s.v. Gauhormizd.

202. For Andirmān see above, n. 59.

203. More details about this person in Justi, *Iran Nb*, 368, s.v. Widrafš.

204. The text reads Jurazm; the name should be read Kurazm, one of the sons of Vishtāspa. The Avestan form of the name is Kavarazem. See Darmesteter, *Études Iraniennes*, II, Paris, 1883, 230f.; Justi, *IranNb*, 159, s.v. Kawarazem; Jackson, *Zoroaster*, 117.

[678] Ṭamīdhar[205] to study his religion and perform acts of devotion. He left his father Luhrāsb in the city of Balkh, an old man and invalid; his treasures, his wealth and his women he left with his wife Khaṭūs.[206] Spies carried the news to Kharzāsf; upon receiving it, he rallied innumerable troops and marched from his land toward Balkh, in the hope of taking advantage of Bishtāsb and conditions in his realm. As he reached the border of the kingdom of Fārs, he sent ahead Jawhurmuz, his brother, who was to succeed him as king, with a large fighting force. He sent him with an order to speed towards the center of the kingdom, smite the people, and attack villages and towns. Jawhurmuz acted accordingly and spilled blood, committing untold infamies. Kharzāsf followed suit; he burned the archives, slew Luhrāsb and the priests, destroyed the fire-worship sanctuaries, seized the wealth and treasures, and captured two daughters of Bishtāsb, one called Khumānī[207] and the other Bādhāfrah.[208] Among the things seized was the great banner called *dirafsh-e-kābyān*.[209] He pursued Bishtāsb, who kept fleeing until he finally took up a fortified position in that region, near Fārs, in the mountain known as Ṭamīdar. Bishtāsb was hard-hit by adversity. It is said that when the situation became desperate, he sent Jāmāsb to Isfandiyār to set him free from his detention and rush him to the king. When Isfandiyār was brought in, the king apologized and promised to crown him and treat him as Luhrāsb had treated him (that is, Bishtāsb). He put him in charge of the army and of fighting Kharzāsf.

When Isfandiyār heard his words, he forgave the king. He

205. There are a number of variants listed for this name in the manuscripts of Ṭabarī, among them Tindhar and Tahmandar, but none seems to be connected to a known locality. The name may possibly be reconstituted as Tahm(ān)-diz, "the Fortress of the Brave."

206. The name of Vishtāspa's wife as attested in the Iranian sources is Hutaosa. See Justi, *Iran Nb*, 139, s.v. Hutaosa; Jackson, *Zoroaster*, 70. She was, like her husband, of the Naotarya family (some sources present her as his sister, in accordance with the Iranian custom of incestuous marriages).

207. He is known as Huma or Huma'i in the Zoroastrian and late Iranian traditions. See Justi, *Iran Nb*, 131; Jackson, *Zoroaster*, 72.

208. The name, according to Firdawsi, is Weh-āfrīd, which means "created well." See Justi, *IranNb*, 348, s.v. Waṅuhi-āfriti; Jackson, *Zoroaster*, 72.

209. See above, n. 47.

rose[210] and immediately took charge of the army review and selection and of all the urgent matters. He spent the night occupied with the mobilization. At dawn he ordered the trumpets sounded; the soldiers assembled, and he led them against the Turks' position. When the Turks saw his army, they rushed out to face it. Among them were Jawhurmuz and Andirmān. Fighting flared up between the opposing forces. Isfandiyār, spear in hand, struck like lightning amidst the people, eager to pounce upon the enemy. Soon enough he made a mighty breach in their position. The rumor now spread among the Turks that Isfandiyār had been released from prison, and they took flight in panic. Isfandiyār pressed forward, regained the great banner, and carried it unfurled. When he came before Bishtāsb, the latter was delighted by his victory and ordered him to pursue the enemy. One of his directives was to slay Kharzāsf, if possible, in retribution for Luhrāsb's death, and to slay Jawhumuz and Andirmān as revenge for the death of the princes. Moreover, he was to destroy the Turks' fortress and put the torch to their cities. He was to slay their inhabitants in order to avenge the followers of the faith whom they had killed; and he was to save the captives. Bishtāsb sent along with him the generals and chieftains needed.

They say that Isfandiyār entered the land of the Turks from a direction never before attempted, and that in controlling the army, killing wild beasts, and striking the ʿAnqā',[211] he performed unparalleled feats. He forced his way into the Turkish [680]
city named Dizru'īn[212] which in Arabic means "the one of brass." He killed the king, his brothers and fighters, seized the king's wealth, captured his women, saved his two captive sisters, and reported the victory to his father. After Isfandiyār, the greatest share in that battle fell to his brother Fashūtan, to Ādarnūsh,[213] and to Mahrīn, the son of his daughter.[214]

---

210. An account of the war led by Isfandiyār, based on the various sources, is in Jackson, *Zoroaster*, 116f.

211. For this fabulous bird see EI^2, s.v. al-ʿAnḳā'.

212. Diz-rūyīn, or, as the name is given in the *Shāhnāmah*, Rūyīn-diz, means "the brazen fortress."

213. Ādarnūsh occurs under the form Nūsh-Ādar in the *Shāhnāmah*. See

It is said that they reached the city only after crossing mighty rivers—the Kāsrūd, the Mihrūd,[215] and another of their mighty rivers. It is also said that Isfandiyār entered a city called Wahishtkank[216] which belonged to Frāsiyāt, and that he subjugated the land (of the Turks), reaching its farthest limits, up to Tibet and the Ṣūl Gate.[217] After that he divided up the land and, upon the conclusion of peace, entrusted each region to a Turkish dignitary, and he set the tribute due annually from each of them to Bishtāsb. Thereupon he retired to Balkh. Furthermore, it is said that Bishtāsb envied his son Isfandiyār for the valor he displayed, and therefore he sent him to Rustam in Sijistān.

[681] According to Hishām b. Muḥammad al-Kalbī: Bishtāsb declared that his son Isfandiyār would succeed to the throne. He sent Isfandiyār to wage war against the Turks, and the crown prince returned victorious to his father. The latter said, "This man Rustam is in the very midst of our land; he is disobedient because he claims that Qabūs has released him from submission to the empire. Therefore go to him and bring him to me." Isfandiyār rode out to Rustam and fought him, but Rustam killed Isfandiyār.[218]

Bishtāsb died after a reign of 112 years.

An author mentions that an Israelite by the name of Samī, who was a prophet, was sent to Bishtāsb. He set out to meet him at Balkh, and entering the city he met Zoroaster, the Magian teacher, and the learned Jāmāsb b. Qaḥad. Samī spoke in Hebrew; Zoroaster knew that tongue and recorded in Persian

---

Justi, *Iran Nb*, 17, s.v. Anōš (under Anōšādar); Jackson, *Zoroaster*, 113. The name means "immortal fire" or "possessor of immortal fire."

214. Mahrīn (Mahrēn or rather Mihrēn) is unknown from parallel sources. The translation given here, "son of his daughter" is doubtful.

215. For Kāsrūd see above, n. 35. The river Mihrūd is probably the same as Mihrā(n) Rūd, occurring in the Bundahishn. See Markwart, *Wehrot*, 97ff., 113.

216. This toponym should be read Wahisht-kang. The form given in the *Shāhnāmah* is Kang-i bihisht. See Nöldeke, *Nationalepos*, 168; Markwart, *Wehrot*, 165.

217. Ṣūl is a city near Derbend in the Caucasus. See Yāqūt, *Muʿjam*, s.v.

218. On this episode as it is told in the *Shāhnāmah* see Nöldeke, *Nationalepos*, 166; Jackson, *Zoroaster*, 121.

what Samī was saying in Hebrew. Jāmāsb joined them, and that is why Jāmāsb was called "the Learned."[219]

A Persian authority asserts that Jāmāsb was the son of Qaḥad b. Hū[220] b. Hakāw[221] b. Nadhkaw b. Fars b. Raj b. Khurasraw b. Manūshihr the King; and that Zoroaster was the son of [682]
Yūsīsf[222] b. Fardwāst b. Urudaḥd b. Mabjadsaf b. Jakhshanash b. Fatarasf b. Alhadī b. Hardān b. Saqmān b. Bidasht b. Adrā b. Raj b. Khurasraw b. Manūshihr. [683]

It is said that Bishtāsb and his father Luhrāsb embraced the religion of the Sabians,[223] until Samī and Zoroaster came to Bishtāsb with their tenets. This occurred after thirty years of his reign had elapsed. This authority said that Bishtāsb's reign lasted 150 years; he was one of those who considered Bishtāsb one of the seven noble men whom they call Bihkanid.[224] Bishtāsb lived in Dihistān of Jurjān and was a contemporary of Falhawī who dwelled at Māh Nihāwand, of Sūrīn Falhawī who dwelled in Sijistān, and of Isfandiyār Falhawī who dwelled at al-Rayy.[225]

Others say Bishtāsb ruled for 120 years.

---

219. This story, like the tradition about Zoroaster being identical with Baruch, Jeremiah's secretary, combines Iranian and Jewish traditions. The prophet Samī is unknown from other sources.

220. Hū is probably a form of Hvogva, Hvova, one of the prominent people of the early Zoroastrian period. See Justi, *Iran Nb*, 140, s.v. Hwogwa. His son's name is unclear; it could be read Fhd, etc.

221. Hakāw is possibly Jakāw. The following names are not clear.

222. Yūsīsf is quite likely to be a corruption of Bushtāsf, a variant form of Wishtāsp.

223. The Sabians are mentioned in Qur'ān 2:59; 5:73; 22:17. The pre-Islamic group mentioned in these passages were perhaps the Mandaeans of Iraq. In Islamic times down to the eleventh century the term applied to a group centered in Ḥarrān whose religion consisted of an amalgam of ancient pagan elements, especially star worship, with philosophical interpretations. See *EI*^{1}, s.v. Ṣaba'iyya; Tardieu, *JA*, 274 [1986], 1-44.

224. The reading of the word is uncertain. For the idea of the seven noble men in the Persian court see above, n. 188.

225. For these locations see LeStrange, *Lands*, 379ff.; 196ff.; 334ff.; 214ff.

The Account of the Kings of the Yaman in the Days of Qābūs, And After Him, to the Age of Bahman b. Isfandiyār.

Abū Jaʿfar says: As reported previously, some assert that Qābūs lived in the age of Solomon the son of David. We have also mentioned the kings of the Yaman in the age of Solomon, and the story of Bilqīs, the daughter of Īlsharah.[226]

According to Hishām b. Muḥammad al-Kalbī: After Bilqīs, kingship over the Yaman went to Yāsir b. ʿAmr b. Yaʿfūr who
[684] was called Yāsir Anʿam. He was named Yāsir Anʿam (the Gracious) because of the gifts he bestowed upon them, which strengthened their realm and their loyalty.

The people of the Yaman assert that he conducted raids westward until he reached a dried out river bed (*wādī*) called Wādī al-Raml which had never been reached by anybody before him. Once there, he found no passage beyond it, so abundant was the sand (*raml*). However, while staying there, the sand opened up. He then ordered a man of his house, ʿAmr by name,

226. That is, the Queen of Sheba who visited Solomon. See I Kings 10; Qur'ān 27:20–45. The story of their meeting receives wide prominence in the Arabic *Isrā'iliyyāt* literature. See EI^2, s.v. Bilḳīs. Abū Jaʿfar-Ṭabarī, the author.

to cross with his companions. They crossed but did not return. Seeing that, he ordered a copper statue to be cast and set on a rock at the edge of the valley, and on its chest it carried an inscription in South-Arabian, "This is the statue of Yāsir Anʿam of Ḥimyar. There is no passage beyond it. Let no person attempt it lest he perish."

After him ruled a king (*tubbaʿ*), that is, Tibān Asʿad, the father of Karib b. Malkī Karib Tubbaʿ b. Zayd b. ʿAmr b. Tubbaʿ, that is, Dhū al-Adhʿār, the son of Abrahah Tubbaʿ Dhī al-Manār b. al-Rāʾish b. Qays b. Ṣayfī b. Sabaʾ. He was called al-Rāʾid.[227]

This king lived in the days of Bishtāsb and Ardashīr Bahman [685] b. Isfandiyār b. Bishtāsb. He emerged from the Yaman on the road taken by al-Rāʾish (and travelled) until he reached two mountains of the Ṭayyiʾ. He then marched toward al-Anbār, but when he reached al-Ḥīrah—this was at night—he became confused (*taḥayyara*) and stopped, and that place was named al-Ḥīrah.[228] He left some men there of the tribes of the Azd,[229] Lakhm Judhām, ʿĀmilah, and Quḍāʿah. They built it up and remained there. Later they were joined by people from the tribes of the Ṭayyiʾ, Kalb, Sakkūn, Balḥārith b. Kaʿb and Iyad. The king advanced to al-Anbār, then to Mosul, and then to Ādharbayjan, where he encountered the Turks. He put them to flight, slaying their fighting men and capturing the children. Following this, he returned to the Yaman where he spent many years; the kings held him in awe and respect, and they brought him gifts.

A messenger of the king of India came to him with gifts and presents of silk, musk, aloe and other precious products of India. He saw things the like of which he had not seen before, and said, "My, is all that I see found in your country?" The messen-

---

227. *Tubbaʿ* was the title of the kings of the Yaman. Most of the following accounts have their origins in the Alexander Romance. See Friedländer, *Chadirlegende*; Nagel, *Alexander der Grosse in der frühislamischen Volksliteratur*.

228. The pun indicates that the name of al-Ḥīrah is derived from the root *ḥ-y-r*, "to get confused."

229. On the Azd and many of the other Arab tribes mentioned in these pages see the relevant entries in *EI*.

ger replied, "Bless you, some of what you see is available in our country; most of it is from China." The messenger then described China to the king: its vastness, fertility, and the extent of its borders. The king swore to conquer it. He set out at the head of the Ḥimyar along the coast, until he reached al-Rakā'ik[230] and the wearers of black headgear. He sent one of his men—a man called Thābit—with a large force to China. However, Thābit was wounded; so the king (himself) proceeded until he entered China. He killed its defenders and
[686] plundered what he found there. They assert that his expedition to China, his stay there, and the return took seven years, and that he left in Tibet twelve thousand horsemen from Ḥimyar. They are the people of Tibet, and assert nowadays that they are Arabs. They are Arabs in constitution and pigmentation.

According to ʿAbdallāh b. Aḥmad al-Marwazī—his father —Sulaymān—ʿAbdallāh—Isḥāq b. Yaḥyā—Mūsā b. Talḥah: A king (*tubbaʿ*) set out with a few Arabs until they lost their way outside (what is now) Kūfah. It became one of the stations where some infirm men remained. It was called Ḥīrah because they had lost their way (*taḥayyur*). The king proceeded on his way but later returned to them. In the meantime, they had built up the place as a permanent settlement. The king left for the Yaman but they stayed on, and among them were people from all the Arab tribes such as Banū Liḥyān, Hudhayl, Tamīm, Juʿfī, Ṭayyi', and Kalb.[231]

230. Al-Rakā'ik is not a known place name. It may be regarded as a plural form of the adjective which means "shallow-minded".

231. On these tribes see the appropriate entries in *EI*.

The Account Concerning Ardashīr Bahman and His Daughter Khumānī

Bishtāsb was succeeded by his grandson Ardashir Bahman. They say that on his coronation day he said, "We uphold loyalty and we compensate our subjects generously." He was called Ardashīr the Mighty,[232] and was nicknamed thus, so it is said, because he took whatever was within reach in the surrounding kingdoms, and thus ruled all the climes. It is said [687]
that he built a city in the Sawād and named it Ābād Ardashīr. This is the village known (today) as Humaniyyah on the Upper Zāb.[233] In the Tigris region he built a city and named it Bahman Ardashīr, which is (today) Ubullah.[234] He set out for Sijistān to avenge his father, slew Rustam and Rustam's father

232. The term used in Arabic, *al-ṭawīl al-bāʿ*, may be translated "powerful", as done here. The original Persian term *darāz-dast*, which literally means, like the Arabic expression, "of long hands, longimanus," signifies "oppressive, rapacious." See Balʿamī, *Tārīkh*, 683.

233. The place name Abād-Ardashīr, which means "the inhabited place of Ardashīr," in not preserved. The text has *Humayniya*, to be read *Humayniyya*, also known as Humaniyyah, possibly from the Iranian divine name Wahuman. See LeStrange, *Lands*, 37; O. Blau, *ZDMG*, 27 (1873), 295–363, esp. 325; T. Nöldeke, *ZDMG*, 28 (1874), 93–102, esp. 94 n. 1.

234. On al-Ubullah, ancient Apologos, see LeStrange, *Lands*, 46f.; Oppenheimer, *Babylonia Judaica*, 253f.

Dastān, his brother Azwārah,[235] and his son Faramurz.[236] Ardashīr levied huge taxes to maintain the army and to sustain the clergy, the fire sanctuaries and so forth. He was the father of Darius (Dārā) the Great and Sāsān,[237] the progenitor of the other Persian kings, that is, Ardashīr son of Bābak, and his sons. Khumānī,[238] the daughter of Bahman, was the mother of Darius.

Hishām b. Muḥammad relates: After Bishtāsb, there ruled Ardashīr Bahman b. Isfandiyār b. Bishtāsb. He was, as they mention, humble, and well liked. His messages were issued, "From Ardashīr, worshiper of God, servitor of God who guides your affairs." It is said that with a million soldiers he waged war on the invading Romans. A source other than Hishām reports: Bahman died before the birth of Darius. Khumānī was made queen, out of gratitude to her father Bahman, and the kings of the earth continued to pay tribute to Bahman. He is said to have been the most distinguished and successful Persian king; his writings and messages excelled those of Ardashīr and his age.

[688] Bahman's mother was Astūryā, that is Esther, the daughter of Jair[239] b. Shimei b. Kish b. Misha b. King Saul (Ṭālūt) b. Kish b. Abiel b. Zeror b. Beçorath b. Aphiah b. Jesse b. Benjamin b. Jacob b. Isaac b. Abraham, God's friend. The mother of Bahman's son was the slave Rahab bint Pinchas, of the children of Rehoboam b. Solomon b. David. Bahman appointed Rahab's brother Zerubabel b. Shealtiel king over the Israelites, transferred to him the office of the exilarch, and returned him to Palestine, upon Rahab's request.[240] Bahman died and left (the following) offspring: two sons, Darius the Great and Sāsān, and daughters Khumānī, who ruled after him, and Franik[241]

---

235. The name Azwārah occurs as Zuwārah or Zawārah in the *Shāhnāmah*. See Justi, *Iran Nb*, 337, s.v. Uzwārak.

236. Faramurz occurs in the *Shāhnāmah* with a long vowel in the second syllable. See Justi, *Iran Nb*, 90.

237. These persons occur further on in the book.

238. On Khumānī see Justi, *Iran Nb*, 132, s.v. Huma, No. 2.

239. In Jewish sources Mordechai is listed as the son of Jair. See Esther 2:5; I Samuel 9:1. See also Ginzberg, *Legends*, VII, 320.

240. Ezra 2:2; 3:2,8.

241. Text reads Farīk; Franik seems to be the reading to be preferred here (the

and Bahman Dukht.[242] "Bahman" translated into Arabic means "the well-intentioned.[243] He ruled for 112 years. As for Hishām b. al-Kalbī, he says that Bahman's reign lasted eighty years.

Khumānī, Bahman's daughter, succeeded to the throne. As some authorities mentioned, they made her queen out of love for her father Bahman, out of gratitude for his benevolence, and because of her excellent mind and beauty, and her vigor and valor. She was nicknamed Shahrāzād.[244] [689]

One authority said that Khumānī reigned after her father Bahman. When she was pregnant with Darius the Elder, she asked Bahman to crown the yet unborn child and grant him preference to the throne. He complied, and made the unborn child crown prince. Sāsān,[245] Bahman's other son, was at the time an adult, and had no doubt as to his future kingship. But when Sāsān saw what his father had done in this respect, he traveled to Iṣṭakhr, became an ascetic, and abandoned his earlier life-style. He practiced piety, acquired some sheep, and he himself tended his animals. The people considered his behavior disgraceful, and were shocked by it. They said, "Sāsān has become a shepherd." This is why people connected him to shepherding.[246] Sāsān's mother was the daughter of Sheal-

---

third consonant is uncertain in the manuscripts). See Justi, *Iran Nb*, 106, s.v. Freni, No. 8.

242. Bahman-dukht simply means "the daughter of Bahman" and does not look like a genuine personal name. See Justi, *Iran Nb*, 375, s.v. Wohu-Mananh (Ableitungen und Zusammensetzungen No. 2).

243. Bahman is a late development of the form Vohu Manah, which means "possessor of a good mind." It is the name of one of the Amahraspands, the divine beings forming the retinue of Ohrmazd. A man who possesses this quality and in whom Bahman dwells is, among other things, peaceful and generous, and he helps the poor (see Shaked, *Wisdom*, 29, para. 78).

244. The proper form of this name, as can be seen from the variants and the parallel versions, is Chihrāzād, which means approximately "one whose countenance is noble." The name is derived from an epithet of the goddess Anahita. See Justi, *Iran Nb*, 163, s.v. Čihrāzād.

245. Sāsān is the reputed ancestor of the Sasanian dynasty, that ruled Iran from about A.D. 224 to the Arab conquest. The story of Sāsān as given here and in other sources makes him a direct descendant of the Achaemenids. This is done at the cost of ignoring the centuries which separate Darius (522–486 B.C.) from Ardashīr, the founder of the Sasanian dynasty. On the name Sāsān see Frye, *History*, 284f.; *CHI* 3(1), 116f.

246. The romance of Ardashīr, describing the origins of the dynasty of the

tiel(?) b. Jochanan b. Oshia b. Amon b. Manasseh b. Hezekiah b. Ahaz b. Jotham b. Uzziah b. Joram b. Jehoshaphat b. Abijah b. Rehoboam b. Solomon b. David.

They say that Bahman died before his son Darius was born to Khumānī; she gave birth to Darius a few months after she ascended to the throne. She refused to expose the matter. She therefore put the child in a coffer and floated it on the Kurr River of Iṣṭakhr, adding a precious jewel.

[690] Another source says: It was the Balkh River, and the coffer reached a miller of Iṣṭakhr who had lost a young child. When the man found the coffer, he brought it to his wife, and she rejoiced in the child because he was beautiful and because the thing that was found along with him was precious. They nursed him. Later, when the boy grew up, the incident became known, and Khumānī admitted her wrongdoing in exposing him to danger. When he matured, he was tested and was found extremely well endowed with princely character. She then transferred the crown to him, and he took charge of the realm.

Khumānī left, settled in Fārs, built the city of Iṣṭakhr, and sent army after army against Rome. She was victorious, subduing enemies, while preventing them from seizing any of her territory. The subjects enjoyed prosperity and comfort during her reign. When Khumānī raided Roman territory, many prisoners were taken and brought to her country. She ordered the builders among them to build for her within the area of Iṣṭakhr, tall, wondrous Roman-type structures. One of these is in Iṣṭakhr; another is on the through route to Darābjird, a *farsakh* (six km) from this city; the third, four *farsakh*s (twenty-four km) away on the road to Khurāsān.[247] She sought to please Almighty God, and was granted aid and victory. She eased the burden of taxation on her subjects. Her reign lasted thirty years.

Sasanians, makes him grow up as a shepherd, his royal descent being at first unrecognized.

247. For Dārābjird see LeStrange, *Lands*, 288f., 294, 296.

The History of the Israelites and the Synchronization of Their Chronological Data with Those of the Persian Kings [691]

We have previously mentioned that some of the Israelite captives who were brought by Nebuchadnezzar to Babylonia went to Jerusalem, and that this happened in the days of Cyrus b. Ahasuerus and during Cyrus's reign in Babylonia on behalf of Bahman b. Isfandiyār during Bahman's lifetime. It continued for years after Bahman's death in the reign of his daughter Khumānī. We also mentioned that Khumānī lived twenty-six years after the death of Cyrus b. Ahasuerus. In all, her reign was thirty years. The period during which Jerusalem lay in ruins, from the destruction by Nebuchadnezzar to its rebuilding, was seventy years, according to the Jews, the Christians, and scholars of history. All of the period falls partly in the days of Bahman b. Isfandiyār b. Bishtāsb b. Luhrāsb, and partly in the days of Khumānī, as explained previously in the present work.

Some have asserted that Cyrus (Kīrash) was actually Bishtāsb. But others deny this, saying: Kay Arash[248] was, rather,

248. The name of Cyrus was not preserved in the Iranian historical and legendary sources available to Ṭabarī and his contemporaries. It occurs in the biblical account of the rebuilding of Jerusalem after the Babylonian exile. Ṭabarī, or one of the authorities on which he relies, tries to harmonize the Jewish and Iranian accounts by identifying Cyrus either with Bishtāsb (Wishtāspa), a his-

the uncle of Bishtāsb's grandfather; or, Kay Arash was the brother of Kayqāwus b. Kayabiwah b. Kayqubādh the Great, and King Bishtāsb was the son of Kayluhrāsb b. Kayujī b. Kaymanūsh b. Kayqāwus b. Kayabiwah b. Kayqubādh the Great. Kay Arash never reigned; he was merely appointed to rule Khuzistān and the contiguous Babylonian territory on behalf of
[692] Kayqāwus and on behalf of Kaykhusraw b. Siyāwakhsh b. Kayqāwus, and, after that, on behalf of Luhrāsb. He (Cyrus) had a long life and was a man of great consequence. When Jerusalem was rebuilt and its people, the Israelites, returned there, Ezra was among them. I have already described what happened to him and to the Israelites. The ruler over them was an appointee of the Persians, either a Persian or an Israelite. This was the case until their region came under the rule of the Greeks and the Romans following the victory of Alexander, and the assassination of Darius, the son of Darius (the Elder). All occurred, it is said, within a period of eighty-eight years.

---

torical ancestor of Darius, or with Kay Arash, whose name sounds similar enough to Koresh (the Hebrew form of the name Cyrus).

The Account of Darius [Dārā] the Elder and His Son Darius the Younger. How He Perished and the Account of Alexander [Dhū-l-Qarnayn][249]

Darius b. Bahman b. Isfandiyār b. Bishtāsb became king. He was nicknamed Jihrāzād,[250] meaning, noble-natured. They say that he dwelt in Babylon, that he sternly administered his realm, and that he subdued the kings around him and they paid him tribute. He built in Fārs a city which he called Darābjird. He cut the tails of the riding beasts (that carried) the royal mail[251] and arranged the animals in proper order. He was amazed by his son Darius. Because of his love for him, he named him after himself and designated him as successor to the throne. He had a wazīr, Rastīn[252] by name, a man of fine mind. But intrigue and enmity arose between Rastīn and a youth called Bīrī[253] who was raised with the younger Darius. [693]

---

249. See n. 227 above.

250. This is the same name as Shahrāzād, discussed above, n. 244.

251. On the postal system in the Parthian period, see *CHI* 3(1), 564.

252. The name is unpointed, but is probably to be read as Rashnīn. See Justi, *Iran Nb*, 259, s.v. Rašnīn.

253. Perhaps, as surmised by Justi, *Iran Nb*, 252, s.v. Pīrī, this is to be read Pīrī.

Rastīn slandered him to the king, and it is said that the king gave Bīrī a drink from which he died. The prince bore a grudge against the wazīr and the group of military commanders who had supported the wazīr against Bīrī. Darius reigned for twelve years.

He was succeeded by his son, Darius b. Darius b. Bahman. His mother was Māhiyāhind[254] the daughter of Hazārmard[255] b. Bihradmah. At his coronation Darius said, "We shall neither force anyone into the abyss of destruction, nor hold back one who tumbles into it." It is said that he built the city of Dārā (Darius) in the Jazīrah. He employed Bīrī's brother and made him wazīr, because of his sympathy for him and his brother. But the wazīr instigated the king against his aides and induced him to kill a number of them. This angered the notables and the public, and they loathed the king who was a heedless, excitable, malicious, and violent young man.

According to Hishām b. Muḥammad: After Darius b. Ardashīr, his son Darius ruled for fourteen years. He mistreated his subjects and slew their leaders, and Alexander attacked him at that time. The people of his realm were fed up with him and
[694] detested him, and they wished to be rid of him. Many of their leaders and dignitaries joined Alexander. By exposing Darius's weak points, they strengthened the invader. In the Jazīrah, the contenders met and battled for a year. Then some of the intimates of Darius pounced upon him, slew him, and brought his head to Alexander. He ordered that they be put to death, saying, "This is the reward for him who dares an attempt on his king's life." Alexander married Darius's daughter, Rūshanak. He invaded India and the lands to the east, after which he withdrew, intending to go to Alexandria. But he died in the region of the Sawād, and his remains were taken to Alexandria in a gold casket—his reign had lasted fourteen years. Greek rule

254. The correct reading of the name is probably Māh-(A)nāhīd, combining two divine names into a compound personal name, "Moon-Anāhitā (= Venus)." See Justi, *Iran Nb*, 187, s.v. Māh-nāhīd (where a different explanation of the name is given).

255. Hazārmard may mean "equal to a thousand men." See Justi, *Iran Nb*, 128. The father's name should be read Bih-dād-māh, the first part signifying "follower of the Good Law." Māh (Mah) may mean either "moon" or "greater".

had become centralized, whereas before Alexander it was dispersed; (on the other hand) Persian rule was dispersed, whereas before Alexander it had been centralized.

According to a source other than Hishām: When Darius's son Darius became king, he ordered a vast city to be built in the Jazīrah, and he named it Dāranawā—it is called Dārā[256] today. He also reports that Darius built and equipped it with everything necessary, and that Philip, the father of Alexander the Greek, reigned over a Greek land known as Macedonia and other lands that he had occupied. He concluded a peace treaty with Darius, under which he paid an annual tribute to the latter. Philip died, and his son Alexander succeeded him, but he did not send the tribute that his father used to send. This brought the wrath of Darius upon him; Darius wrote to him upbraiding him for the misdeed of stopping the payment of the [695] tribute his father used to pay, and so forth, and (saying) that it was youth and ignorance that led him to withhold what his father used to send in tribute. Darius sent to Alexander a polo mallet (*sawlajān*), a ball, and a load of sesame. In a written message he stated that Alexander was a boy, and that he should play with the polo mallet and ball, but not function or parade as a king. Should he not confine himself to this order, and should he assume kingship and rebel, then he, Darius, would send an emissary to fetch him in shackles; and (he stated) that the soldiers of Darius were as numerous as the grains of sesame (he) sent to Alexander.

In reply, Alexander wrote to Darius that he understood the message. (He said) that he had looked at the polo mallet and the ball sent to him, and saw therein a good omen (that is, he would) throw the thrower of the ball to the mallet, and drag him with the ball. He likened the earth to the ball, and declared that he would drag the realm of Darius to his own kingdom and country, (and this) into his domain. In the same light, he viewed the sesame sent to him; although abundant, it was neither bitter nor pungent. Along with his letter, he sent Darius a sack of mustard and told him that what he was sending was small in size but that in pungency, bitterness and [696]

256. On Dārā see LeStrange, *Lands*, 96.

strength, it equalled the gift of sesame, and that his army fully answered this description.

When Alexander's message reached Darius, the latter assembled his army and prepared to fight Alexander, who in turn made preparations and set out toward the land of Darius. The news thereof reached Darius who advanced to meet him. The two forces met and engaged in the fiercest of battles; and fate turned against the army of Darius. Two men of his guard—it is said they were of Hamadhān—stabbed him from behind and dragged him from his saddle. They expected thus to gain Alexander's favor and good grace, but Alexander had announced that Darius should be captured but not slain. When Alexander was informed of the fate of Darius, he went to meet him, and saw that he was about to die. Alexander dismounted, sat by the head of Darius, and told him that it had never occurred to him to slay him, and that what happened was not of his initiative. He said to Darius, "Ask me for whatever you wish, and I shall help you." Whereupon Darius said to him, "I have two requests. First, take revenge upon the two who assaulted me," and he named them and their province; "second, marry my daughter Rūshanak." Alexander granted both requests. By his order, the two men who attacked Darius were crucified; and he married Rūshanak.[257] He penetrated the realm of Darius and became its ruler.

Some authorities on ancient history assert that this Alexander who fought the younger Darius was a rebellious brother of his and that the older Darius had married Alexander's
[697] mother, the daughter of the Greek king, and that her name was Helen (Hali).[258] She was carried to her husband, the elder Darius, but when he found her foul of odor and perspiration, he sought a way to counter it. Authorities agreed that she was to be treated with an emulsion of a tree called *Sandar* in Persian. It was steamed and she bathed in it, and much of the foul odor was removed, but not all of it. Because of that he refrained from being with her. Finding her loathsome, he returned her to her

257. On Alexander's wife see Justi, *Iran Nb*, 262, s.v. Roxane, No. 3.

258. Alexander's mother was named Olympia. The reference here must be to Helen of Troy.

people. She had become pregnant by him, however, and gave birth while among her people, to a boy. She named him after herself and after the tree in whose effusion she had bathed in order to cure her malodorousness—Helen-Sandarus. Such is the origin of the name Alexander.

Darius the Elder died, and his son Darius the Younger took over. The Greek kings had paid annual tribute to Darius the Elder When the Greek king, Helen's father and Alexander's maternal grandfather, passed away kingship passed to his daughter's son, and Darius the Younger sent him the customary reminder, "You are late in paying us the usual tribute, which was also paid by your predecessor. Send us the tribute of your country or we shall declare war upon you." But the reply that reached him was, "I slaughtered the hen, ate its meat, and only the extremities remained. If you wish, we shall leave you in peace; but if you wish, we shall come forth against you." Thereupon, Darius loathed him and came forth to do battle with him.

When the kings met in battle, two chamberlains of Darius stabbed him, and Alexander sentenced the two chamberlains (*ḥājib*) for the assassination. They had acted on their own, and (thus) failed to secure their (own) safety. Alexander found Darius smitten and he dismounted seeing the king in the throes of death. Wiping the dust from the face of Darius, he [698]
eased his head onto his lap and told him, "It is your two chamberlains who have killed you; I would like you, O noblest, most generous King of Kings, to have been spared this fate. Enjoin me whatever you may wish." Darius then requested that Alexander should marry his daughter Rūshanak; that he should take her unto himself, and perpetuate Persian nobility, and not impose foreign rule upon the Persian nobility. Alexander accepted his testament and acted accordingly. Then the two assassins of Darius came to Alexander, who decided their fate. He said to them, "I am fulfilling your stipulation (for reward) but there was no stipulation about your lives. I am putting you to death; for it is proper that assassins of kings should not be spared unless it be under inviolable guarantee." So he had them put to death.

Some mention that the Greek king in the days of Darius the

Elder used to pay tribute to Darius. But that king died, and Alexander became the Greek king. He was a resolute, strong, and cunning man. It is said that he attacked some western king, whom he defeated, and he therefore felt emboldened to attack Darius the Younger and to stop paying the tribute his father used to pay. This enraged Darius who wrote vehement messages to Alexander. The relations between them soured, and both moved toward battle. Fully prepared, they met at the frontier, and exchanged communications and messengers. Alexander was afraid to fight Darius; he called for reconciliation. But Darius consulted his aides, who bore a grudge against Darius, and they extolled going to war.

Scholars have disagreed about the frontier and the site where
[699] they clashed. Some mention that it took place in the region of Khurāsān, near the Khazars. The opposing forces engaged in a fierce battle, so that the kings became involved. That day Alexander was on a wondrous steed called Būkfārasb.[259] It is said that a Persian attacked (Alexander); piercing the Greek lines, he struck Alexander a blow with a sword, causing fear for the king's life. Alexander admired the feat and exclaimed, "That is a Persian horseman with proverbial valor!" But the grudges held by the men of Darius were at work. There were two men of his guard from Hamadhān who had exchanged messages with Alexander. They sought to deal treacherously with Darius. Finally they stabbed him and, having inflicted a lethal blow, they fled. It is said that when the horror occurred and the news reached Alexander, he rode out with his retinue. Reaching Darius, he found him in the throes of death. Alexander spoke to him; putting the dying man's head on his lap, he wept over him, saying, "You were attacked from the rear. You were alone among enemies and your trusted men betrayed you. Ask of me whatever you desire, for I am intent on keeping close relations between us." He meant, so this source maintained, the closeness between Salam and Hīraj, the sons of Afrīdhūn.[260]

Horrified by what had happened to Darius, Alexander

259. Boucefalos means "bull-headed".
260. See *EI*^{2}, s.v. Farīdūn.

thanked God for his own safety. Darius then requested that his daughter Rūshanak be married to Alexander and be treated with consideration and respect, and that his death be avenged. Alexander agreed. Then the two men who had attacked Darius came seeking their reward. Alexander ordered that they be beheaded and crucified, and that an announcement be made, [700] "Such is the punishment of him who dares to raise a hand against his king, and is disloyal to his people." They say that Alexander carried away (many) books—the learning of the Persians on the sciences, the stars, and philosophy—after they had been translated into Aramaic and then into Greek.[261]

Some assert that at the time that Darius was slain he had two sons, Ashak and Ardashīr[262] and also a daughter, Rūshanak. The reign of Darius lasted fourteen years. Some (authorities) mention that the tribute which Alexander's father paid to the kings of Persia consisted of golden eggs. When Alexander became king, Darius sent him a demand for that payment but Alexander replied, "I have slain the hen which used to lay those eggs, and I ate its meat. So declare war!"

Alexander reigned after Darius b. Darius. I have already mentioned the view of those who say that Alexander was the brother of Darius the Younger and the son of Darius the Elder. As for the Greeks and many genealogists, they say that Alexander was the son of Philip—some say of Philip b. Metrius. It is (also) said (that he was the) son of Maṣrīm b. Hermes b. Hardas b. Mīṭūn b. Rūmī b. Lantī b. Yunān b. Japhet b. Thūbah [701]

---

261. This statement derives from the Zoroastrian tradition where it is maintained that Persian wisdom was carried away to Greece by Alexander, which explains why translations of philosophical and scientific works from Greek into Persian are merely an act of bringing what was originally Persian wisdom back to its source. A similar notion existed with regard to translations of Indian writings to Persian. On the borrowings from Greek and Indian lore into Persian, see Bailey, *Zoroastrian problems*, 81ff.

262. Ashak is the reputed ancestor of the Parthian dynasty, the dynasty of the Arsacids. Like the Sasanian dynasty, so also with regard to the Arsacids, Iranian historical traditions endeavored to connect them genealogically with their predecessors, the Achaemenids. See Justi, *Iran Nb*, 28, s.v. Aršaka, No. 9. Ardashīr is the founder of the Sasanian dynasty; although according to his official genealogy he is the son of Pāpak and possibly grandson of Sāsān (or otherwise connected to the latter), he is here made out to be the son of the last Achaemenid monarch. See Justi, op. cit., 35, s.v. Artaxšaθra, No. 15.

b. Sarḥūn b. Rūmyah b. Barbat b. Jubal b. Rūfī b. al-Aṣfar b. Eliphaz b. Esau b. Isaac b. Abraham, God's friend.[263]

After the death of Darius, Alexander annexed the empire of Darius to his own kingdom, and ruled Iraq, Asia Minor al-Rūm, Syria, and Egypt. Following the death of Darius, he reviewed his army; it is said that he found the army to consist of 1,400,000 men; of these 800,000 were of his own force, and 600,000 were from the (old) force of Darius. It is reported that on the day he ascended the throne he said, "God granted us triumph over Darius and granted us the opposite of Darius's threats." Alexander destroyed the cities, fortresses, and fire temples of the Persians. He slew their priests, and he burned their books and the archives of Darius. Appointing some of his aides as governors over the empire of Darius, he marched on toward India where he slew its king and conquered its capital. From there he marched toward China, and did there as he did in India. The whole of the earth was his, and he ruled Tibet and China. With four hundred men he entered the dark area near the North Pole, and (he entered) the area of southern sun in search of the Well of Immortality. He marched there for eighteen days, then left and returned to Iraq. Alexander appointed the diadochs (*mulūk al-ṭawā'if*), and he died on the road at Shahrazūr[264]—he was thirty-six, some say. He was carried to his mother at Alexandria.

[702] As for the Persians, they assert that Alexander's reign lasted fourteen years. The Christians assert that it lasted thirteen years and some months, and that Darius was slain at the beginning of the third year of Alexander's reign.

It is said that upon Alexander's command twelve cities were constructed, each one of them named Alexandria. One of them in Iṣbahān, called Jayy, was shaped like a serpent (*ḥayyah*). Three towns were built in Khurāsān, among them Harāt, Marw, and Samarqand.[265] In Babylonia he built a town for

---

263. This list combines elements taken from Jewish biblical sources with those whose origin is in Greek mythology.

264. A town in old Media, the Jibāl district of Islamic times. See LeStrange, *Lands*, 190f.

265. On Herāt see LeStrange, *Lands*, 407ff.; on Maru, 397ff.; on Samarqand, 463ff.

Rūshanak, the daughter of Darius, and in the Greek territory in Helakos he built a city for the Persians. He also built other cities.

When Alexander died, the realm was offered to his son Alexander, but he refused for he preferred piety and worship. They say the Greeks made Ptolemy, the son of Lagos, king. He reigned for thirty-eight years. The Greek age of the empire continued from the time of Alexander until the Romans took over. Religion and government under the Israelites in Jerusalem and its environs was not monarchic in form; then the Persians and the Romans devastated their country, and banished them from it after John the Baptist was slain.

After Ptolemy b. Lagos, Syria, Egypt and the lands to the [703] West (al-Maghrib) were ruled by Ptolemy Philadelphus for forty years. After him, Ptolemy Euergetes ruled for twenty-four years, and then Ptolemy twenty-one years, and then Ptolemy Epiphanes ruled for twenty-one years. Then Ptolemy Euergetes ruled for twenty-nine years, and Ptolemy Soter for seventeen years. Ptolemy Alexander I ruled for eleven years. After him ruled the Ptolemy who disappeared from the throne after eight years. He was succeeded by Ptolemy Dionysos who ruled for sixteen years. After him ruled Ptolemy Cleopatra for seventeen years. All these were Greeks. Each of the kings following Alexander was addressed as Ptolemy, just at the Persian rulers were each addressed as Chosroes (Kisrā).[266] All the Ptolemies were called Mufqānīs.[267]

According to what is mentioned, after Cleopatra, Syria was ruled by Rome alone. The first Roman to rule was Gaius Julius, for five years. After him, Syria was ruled by Augustus for [704] fifty-six years. In the forty-third year of his reign Jesus was born. Three hundred and three years elapsed between the rise of Alexander and the birth of Jesus.

---

266. This is historically inaccurate. Kisrā became a general term for kings of the Sasanian dynasty only in the Islamic period, as far as we can tell, and not during the reign of the Sasanians.

267. Possibly a distortion of "Macedonian". The Ptolemies were of Macedonian origins.

The Account of the Persians After the Death of Alexander

We return now to the history of the Persian empire.

Authorities on the history of the ancients disagree about the ruler of the Sawād of Iraq after Alexander, and about the number of regional princes (*mulūk al-ṭawā'if*) who ruled in Babylonia after him down to the emergence of Ardashīr Bābakān.[268] According to what I have been told, Hishām b. Muḥammad said that Seleucus Nicator and then Antiochus ruled after Alexander.[269] He said that it was Seleucus who founded the city of Antioch; also that these kings held sway over the region of al-Kūfah. They used to travel the routes of al-Jibal and the regions of al-Ahwāz and Fārs. Then a man called Ashak,[270] a son of Darius the Elder, revolted—he was born and raised in Rayy.[271] Assembling a large host, he moved against Antiochus. The latter marched against him, and they met in the area of Mosul.[272] Antiochus was slain, and Ashak seized the Sa-

268. Ardashīr ruled from ca. A.D. 226 to 240.

269. They ruled from 305 to 280 B.C. and from 280 to 211 B.C. respectively.

270. The Parthian kingdom existed from the mid-third century B.C. to the third century A.D. Ashak ruled about 247–211 B.C.

271. On al-Rayy in Media (al-Jibāl), called Rhages by the ancient Greeks, see Le Strange, *Lands*, 214ff.

272. Mosul, or, as the place is known in Arabic, al-Mawṣil, is in the medieval province of al-Jazīrah in Iraq, on the river Tigris. See LeStrange, *Lands*, 86ff.

wād. He then extended his control from Mosul to al-Rayy and Iṣbahān.[273] The other regional princes were in awe of him because of his genealogy, and they respected his record. Recognizing his superiority, they put his name first in their messages, and he put his own name first in addressing them.[274] They called him king and sent gifts to him. Yet he neither appointed nor dismissed any of them. [705]

He was succeeded by Jūdharz,[275] the son of Ashakān. He is the one who raided the Israelites the second time. According to that which has been mentioned, the cause for God inflicting him on them was that they had slain John the Baptist. Jūdharz slew many of them, and they never regained anything like their first commonwealth (*jamāʿah*). God deprived them of prophethood and visited humiliation upon them.

The Romans (Rūm) led by their supreme king attacked Fārs. He sought to avenge there the death of Antiochus, king of Babylonia, who had been slain by Ashak. The ruler of Babylonia at the time was Balāsh,[276] the father of Ardawān, whom Ardashīr b. Bābak had slain. Balāsh wrote to the regional princes informing them of the campaign planned by the Romans against their lands, and of the Roman forces which he could not confront. He wrote that should he succumb, the Romans would defeat all of them. Then the princes, each according to his ability, sent Balāsh men, arms, and money, so that he amassed four hundred thousand men, and appointed as their commander the prince of Ḥaḍr,[277] one of the princes who held

---

273. Iṣbahān is in the Jibāl area, in ancient Media. It is adjacent to the town of Jay (older Gabe). See LeStrange, *Lands*, 202ff.; *EI*², s.v. Isfahan.

274. On the style of addressing letters see J.C. Greenfield, *Irano-Judaica*, 4–11 (esp. 4–7).

275. Jūdharz is known in the Greek sources under the form Gotarzes. The first king by this name ruled ca. 91–87 B.C.; Gotarzes II ruled ca. A.D. 38–51.

276. The name occurs in the Greek sources as Vologeses, and it has the form *wlgš* in the Middle Iranian inscriptions. There were five kings by this name among the Arsacids. The last Vologeses, who preceded Artabanus V, ruled ca. A.D. 207–227. See Frye, *History*, 360. On the forms of the name see T. Nöldeke, *ZDMG*, 28 (1874), 93–102, esp. 94f.

277. The Roman name of al-Ḥaḍr was Hatra. It was an important caravan center and the place of a local Arab semi-independent state in the Parthian period, in the Jazīrah area of Iraq. See LeStrange, *Lands*, 98f.; *EI*², s.v. al-Ḥaḍr; *CHI* 3(1), 490ff., 594ff.

an area between the Sawād and the Jazīrah. This man marched at their head until he encountered the king of the Romans. He slew the king of the Romans and plundered his camp. That was an incentive for the Romans to found Constantinople and to transfer the capital from Rome to that place. It was founded by
[706] the emperor Constantine, the first to embrace Christianity.[278] He banished the remaining Israelites from Palestine (Filasṭīn) and Jordan (al-Urdunn)[279] because, as he asserted, they had slain Jesus. Constantine found the wooden cross upon which they believed Christ had been crucified, and the Romans subsequently revered it and placed it among their treasures, where it remains unto this day.[280]

Persian rule continued to break down until the rise of Ardashīr. Hishām mentions what I have stated on his authority, but he does not state the duration of the Persian empire. Other authorities on Persian history report that after Alexander the empire of Darius was ruled by those who were not of the Persian dynasty. Nevertheless, they deferred to the one who ruled the mountainous area, and they showed loyalty to him.

---

278. Valerian, who ruled A.D. 253–259, was treacherously seized at a parley, and died as captive in the hands of the Persians. Constantinople became a capital in A.D. 330. Constantine ruled A.D. 306–337.

279. The medieval boundaries do not correspond to those of modern times. Jordan (Urdunn) refers here to territories on both sides of the river. See LeStrange, *Palestine*, index, 602; *EI*², s.v. Filasṭīn.

280. It is usually connected with the name of Saint Helen (d. ca. A.D. 328), the wife of Constantius I Chlorus. It was also claimed that the cross had been found during the construction of Constantine's church on Golgotha.

The Arsacid (Ashaghān) Kings

The Arsacid kings were addressed as regional princes (*mulūk al-ṭawā'if*), and their rule lasted 266 years.[281] Ashak b. Ashaghān ruled for ten of these years. He was succeeded by Shapūr (Sābūr) son of Ashaghān who reigned for sixty years. In the forty-first year of his reign, Jesus arose in the land of Palestine. Some forty years after the ascension of Jesus, Titus, the son of Vespasian the Roman emperor, attacked Jerusalem, slew the [707]
people of the city, and took their progeny prisoners. Upon his order, the city was demolished so that no stone remained upon another.

(Then the following Arsacids ruled): Jūdharz son of Ashaghān the Elder, ten years; Bīzan, twenty-one years; Jūdharz, nineteen years; Narsī, forty years; Hurmuz, seventeen years; Ardawān, twelve years; Chosroes, forty years; Balāsh, twenty-four years; Ardawān the Younger thirteen years. Then came the reign of Ardashīr, the son of Bābak.

Others say that after Alexander, Persia was ruled by the regional princes, among whom Alexander divided the realm. In each region a prince asserted himself from the time he was ap- [708]
pointed, except in the Sawād which for fifty-four years after Alexander's death was in the hands of the Greeks (Rūm). Among

281. The actual length of Arsacid rule was about twice as long as that. See above n. 270.

the regional princes was one of royal descent appointed to al-Jibāl and Iṣbahān. Later his progeny seized the Sawād and ruled it, as well as al-Māhāt,[282] al-Jibāl and Iṣbahān, as chiefs of the other regional princes. It was customary to cite this chieftain and his sons first; therefore only they are mentioned by name in the historical accounts.

They say that Jesus was born in Jerusalem, fifty-one years after the rise of the regional rulers. Their reign lasted from Alexander to the rise of Ardashīr, a total of some 266 years. Among the princes who ruled over al-Jibāl and whose progeny succeeded in seizing the Sawād, was Ashak b. Ḥarah b. Rasībān b.
[709] Artashakh b. Hurmuz b. Sāham b. Zarīn b. Isfandiyār b. Bishtāsb. The Persians assert that Ashak was the son of Darius. Some say he was Ashak, the son of Ashakān the Great, of the progeny of Kayabiwah b. Kayqubādh, and that he reigned for ten years.

After him, there ruled (in the following order): Ashak b. Ashak b. Ashakān, twenty-one years; Shapūr (Sābūr) b. Ashak b. Ashakān, thirty years; Jūdharz the Elder b. Shapūr b. Ashakān, ten years; Bīzan b. Jūdharz, twenty-one years; Jūdharz the Younger b. Bīzan, nineteen years; Narsī (Narsah) b. Jūdharz the Younger, forty years; Hurmuz b. Balāsh b. Ashakān, seventeen years; Ardawān the Elder b. Ashakān, twelve years; Chosroes b. Ashakān, forty years; Bihāfarīd, the Arsacid, nine years; Balāsh, the Arsacid, twenty-four years. It is said that Ardawān the Younger b. Balāsh b. Fīrūz b. Hurmuz b. Balāsh b. Shapūr (Sābūr) b. Ashak b. Ashakān the Elder, whose grandfather was Kayabiwah b. Kayqubādh,[283] was the greatest of the Arsacid rulers in power and victory, and the most famous and mighty in subduing the regional princes. It is also said that he seized
[710] the district of Iṣṭakhr since it was adjacent to Iṣbahān. Then he set out for Jūr[284] and other points in Fārs which he seized.

282. Al-Māhāt is a late Iranian form (with Arabic plural ending) of what was called in earlier times Māda, i.e., Media. Geographically it is identical with Jibāl, and Iṣbahān is an important town within that district.

283. This list is summarized in Justi, *Iran Nb*, 413, parallel with other lists given in several different sources.

284. Jūr (in Persian Gōr) is the old name of what was later called Fīrūzābād, in the district of Fārs. See LeStrange, *Lands*, 255f.; *CHI* 3(2), 751.

Their rulers submitted to him, for the rulers of the regions were in awe of him. He reigned thirteen years after which Ardashīr's reign began.

Others say that after Alexander, Iraq and the area between Syria and Egypt were ruled by ninety kings over ninety entities, all submitting to the ruler in al-Mada'īn,[285] that is, the Arsacids. Among the Arsacid rulers were: Pakoros (Afqūrshāh) b. Balāsh b. Shapūr (Sābūr) b. Ashakān b. Ash the Great (al-Jabbār) b. Siyāwakhsh b. Kayqāwus the King, sixty-two years; Shapūr (Sābūr) b. Afqūr, in whose days Christ and John the Baptist lived, fifty-three years; Jūdharz b. Shapūr b. Afqūr, who attacked the Israelites to avenge the death of the Baptist, and whose reign lasted fifty-nine years; Abzān, his nephew, the son of Balāsh b. Shapūr, forty-seven years; Jūdharz b. Abzān b. Balāsh, thirty-one years; his brother Narsī b. Abzān, thirty-four years; his paternal uncle al-Hurmuzān b. Balāsh, forty-eight years; his son al-Fīrūzān b. al-Hurmuzān b. Balāsh, thirty-nine years; his son Chosroes b. al-Fīrūzān, forty-seven years; his son Ardwān b. Balāsh, the last of them, was slain after a reign of [711]
fifty-five years by Ardashīr b. Bābak.

The reign of Alexander and of the various regional princes lasted approximately 523 years.

---

285. Al-Madā'in, which literally means "the towns," is a name which continues a similar designation current in the Sasanian period (it is preserved, e.g., in Greek). The term designates a group of towns on the Tigris River. Chief among them were Ctesiphon, which served as an important center of government in the Sasanian period, and Seleucia. An important Jewish center existed in the town of Maḥoza, which formed part of the same complex. See LeStrange, *Lands*, 33ff. The relevant sources are given with detailed discussions in A. Oppenheimer, *Babylonia Judaica*, 179ff.

The Events That Occurred During the Rule of These Regional Princes

The Persians assert that sixty-five years after Alexander seized Babylonia, and fifty-one years after Arsacid rule began, Mary the daughter of ʿImrān gave birth to Jesus. But the Christians assert that Jesus was born to her 303 years after Alexander conquered Babylonia, and that John the Baptist was born six months before Jesus. They report that Mary was pregnant with Jesus when she was thirteen years old. They also report that Jesus lived thirty-two years and a few days before his ascension, and that Mary lived six more years after his ascension, altogether over fifty years. They assert that John and Jesus met in the Jordan River when Jesus was thirty years of age, and that John was slain before the ascension of Jesus.[286] Zechariah b. Berechiah, the father of Yaḥyā b. Zechariah, and ʿImrān b. Māthān, the father of Mary, were married to two sisters. One
[712] was married to Zechariah—she was the mother of John; the other was with ʿImrān b. Māthān, and she was the mother of Mary. ʿImrān b. Māthān died when the mother of Mary was

286. See Qur'ān 19, a *sūrah* which is entitled "Mary" (Maryam). It contains the story of Zechariah (Zakariyyā') and the birth of his son John the Baptist (Yaḥyā); also the immaculate conception, the birth of Jesus and his gift of speech in the cradle. Note that Mary of Sūrat Maryam (Miriam) is the sister of Aaron, the brother of Moses.

pregnant with her. When Mary was born, Zechariah provided for her after her mother's death, because her aunt, the sister of her mother, was with him. The name of Mary's mother was Hanna bt. Fāqūd b. Qabil; the name of the sister of Mary's mother, that is, the name of John's mother was Elizabeth bt. Fāqūd. Zechariah provided for Mary, and she was engaged to Joseph b. Jacob b. Māthān b. Eleazar b. Eliud b. Achim b. Zadok b. Azor b. Eliakim b. Abiud b. Zerubabbel, b. Shealtiel b. Jechonia b. Josiah b. Amon b. Manasseh, b. Hezekiah b. Ahaziah b. Jotham b. Uzziah b. Joram b. Jehosaphat b. Asa b. Abijah b. Rehoboam b. Solomon b. David.

According to Ibn Ḥumayd—Salamah—Ibn Isḥāq: As far as I could learn her lineage, Mary was the daughter of ʿImrān b. Josiah b. Amon b. Manasse b. Hezekiah b. Ahaziah b. Jotham b. Azariah b. Amaziah b. Joash b. Ahaziah b. Joram b. Jehosaphat b. Asa b. Abijah b. Rehoboam b. Solomon.

To Zechariah was born John, the son of the (great) aunt of Jesus, the son of Mary. In his youth John became a prophet and [713]
travelled. He came to Palestine, calling upon the people. John the Baptist and Jesus met, and then parted after John baptized Jesus. It is said that Jesus sent John the Baptist with twelve apostles to teach the people. Among their prohibitions was marriage to a niece.

According to Abū al-Sā'ib—Muʿāwiyah—Aʿmash—al-Minhāl—Saʿīd b. Jubayr—Ibn ʿAbbās: Jesus, son of Mary, sent the Baptist with twelve apostles to teach the people. Among their prohibitions was marriage to a niece. Their king had a niece who excited him, and he wanted to marry her. Every day he carried out some wish of hers. When her mother learned of this, she told her daughter, "If you come to the king, and he asks you what your wish is, tell him, 'my wish is that you slay the Baptist.'" When she came to him, he asked what her wish was. She said, "I wish you to slay the Baptist," whereupon he replied, "Ask me for something else." But she responded, "I shall ask you for nothing else." Thereupon he summoned the Baptist and called for a bowl.[287] Then he slew the Baptist, and

287. The story of Salome. See Matth. 14:1–11; Mark 6:16–29; Josephus, *Ant.*, Book XVIII, Ch. V, 2, does not mention the romantic aspect of the story.

a drop of the Baptist's blood fell upon the ground and kept boiling until God sent Nebuchadnezzar against the Israelites. An old woman of the Children of Israel came and showed Nebuchadnezzar that blood. God thus planted in his mind the thought to kill the Israelites over that spot until the blood came to rest; so he killed seventy-thousand of them who were of the same age, until the drop of blood came to rest.

[714] According to Mūsā b. Hārūn al-Hamdānī—ʿAmr b. Ḥammād—Asbāṭ—al-Suddī—Abū Mālik and Abū Ṣāliḥ—Ibn ʿAbbās and Murrah al-Hamdānī—Ibn Masʿūd and some companions of the Prophet: An Israelite saw in a dream that the destruction of the Temple and the Israelites was to come about through the son of a widow in Babylon—an orphaned youth called Nebuchadnezzar. They believed the vision, and it proved true. The man began to inquire about the youth (in his dream) and then came to the boy's mother while her son was gathering firewood. The youth arrived with a bundle of firewood on his head, threw it down, and sat down near the house. Then the Israelite spoke to him and gave him three dirhams, saying, "Buy food and drink with these." For a dirham he bought meat; for another, bread; and for the third, wine. They ate and drank. The next day, the same (thing) happened, and again on the third day. Then the Israelite said, "I should like you to write a guarantee of safe-conduct for me, in case you should some day become king. The youth replied, "You are poking fun at me," to which the Israelite said, "No, I am not; but it would not hurt you to shake hands over it." The mother of the young man spoke, saying to her son, "What is it to you? If it happens, so be it; if not, it won't hurt you." So he wrote a guarantee of safe-conduct for the man. The latter now said, "Suppose you come, and people around you separate us; make a sign by which you will recognize me." The youth said, "Lift your document on a pole, so that I may recognize you." Then the man gave him clothes and gifts.

[715] The king of the Israelites honored the Baptist. He favored him and consulted him, never deciding on a matter without him. But the king wanted to marry the daughter of one of his wives. He asked the Baptist about it, and the latter forbade it, saying, "I do not approve of your marrying her." Word of this

reached her mother and she hated the Baptist for forbidding the king to marry her daughter. She betook herself to the maiden when the king sat down for his wine, dressed her in fine red clothes, with perfume and jewels; and over all (this finery), a black garb. Sending her (daughter) to the king, she instructed her to give him wine to drink and to serve him; and should he desire her, she should refuse until he grants her wish. If he grants her wish, she should ask that the Baptist's head be brought to her on a platter. She acted thus, starting to serve him drink, and offering more. When he was overcome with wine, he desired her. She said, "I shall not comply until you give me what I ask of you." He said, "What are you asking of me?" She replied, "I ask of you that you send for the Baptist and that his head be brought to me on this platter." "Woe, ask me for something else," he said; whereupon she stated, "I do not want to ask for anything else."

When she refused, he sent for the Baptist; his head was brought, and the head kept talking until it was placed before the king. It was saying, "She is forbidden unto you." When the king awoke, lo and behold, the Baptist's blood was boiling. The king asked for dust to be thrown over it, but the blood rose boiling above the dust. More dust was thrown upon it, but the blood rose above it. He continued throwing dust upon it until it reached the city wall, yet the blood kept boiling. This reached Ṣayḥā'īn[288] who appealed to the people. He wanted to [716]
send an army there, and to appoint a man to lead it. Nebuchadnezzar came to him and said, "The force you sent that time was too weak. But I entered the city and heard the people talk; therefore, send me." So he sent him. Nebuchadnezzar set out and reached that place (Palestine), where they fortified themselves against him in their towns. He was thus unable to subdue them. When his situation became grave, and his men were hungry, he was on the verge of retreat.

Then an old Israelite woman came out and inquired, "Where is the commander of the army?" Brought before him, she said, "I have learned that you are about to retreat with your army,

288. The legendary Persian ruler under whom Nebuchadnezzar is supposed to have served.

without conquering this city." He said, "Yes. Our stay has been long, my men hunger, I cannot go on with the siege." She then said,"Do you suppose that if I open the city to you, you will grant my request, (that is,) kill whom I order you to kill, and stop when I ask you to do so?" "Yes," he replied to her. She then said, "In the morning, divide your army into four parts; place one part at each corner, raise your hand to heaven, and call out, 'We ask victory of You, O God, for the blood of the Baptist.' The city will surely collapse." They did accordingly and the city did collapse. Then they entered it from all sides. She now said to him, "Keep killing over this blood until it subsides." She led him to the Baptist's blood which was rising over a wall of dust. Over it he killed until the blood subsided. He killed seventy thousand men and women. When the blood calmed down, she said to him, "Stop." For if a prophet is slain, God will not be satisfied until the slayer is slain, and he who approved the slaying.[289]

[717] Then the possessor of the guarantee of safe-conduct came before him with his document. Nebuchadnezzar refrained from killing him and his family, but he destroyed the Temple, and upon his order it was strewn with corpses. He said, "Whoever threw a corpse there, will be exempt from the annual poll-tax." The Romans helped him in the destruction because the Israelites had slain the Baptist. When Nebuchadnezzar destroyed it, he led into captivity the notables and chieftains of the Israelites, among them Daniel, Eli, Azariah and Mishael, all of them children of the prophets; he also took the exilarch with him. When he arrived in Babylonia, Nebuchadnezzar found that Ṣayḥā'īn had died. He thus came to rule in his stead, and he held Daniel and his friends in the highest regard. But the Magians were envious of them, and denounced them to Nebuchadnezzar, "Daniel and his friends do not worship your God, and they do not partake of your slaughtered animals."[290] Nebuchadnezzar now summoned the exiles and questioned them.

289. The story of the boiling blood caused by the murder of the prophet Zechariah occurs in Jewish midrashic sources, but without the erotic aspect. See Ginzberg, *Legends*, IV, 304; VI, 396ff.

290. Daniel 1:8; 3:12.

They said, "Yes, we have a Lord whom we worship, and we do not eat of your slaughtered animals." Upon his order a trench was dug, and they were thrown into it, six of them; and a ferocious lion was thrown in with them to devour them. The captors said, "Let us go eat and drink." They did so and then returned, and found the captives sitting and the lion lying with his paws stretched out. The lion did not so much as scratch or wound any of them. But they discovered still another man with them. They were counted and found to be seven. The king exclaimed, "Who is this seventh man? There were only six." Then the seventh man came forth. It was an angel, and he slapped Nebuchadnezzar who turned into a wild beast for seven years.[291]

According to Abū Jaʿfar: This is related on the authority of sources both mentioned and not mentioned in the present work; namely, the report that it was Nebuchadnezzar who [718]
waged war on the Israelites after they slew the Baptist, is erroneous in the opinion of Muslim and non-Muslim experts in pre-Islamic history and lore. For they are unanimous in saying that Nebuchadnezzar waged war on the Israelites when they slew their prophet Isaiah, in the age of Jeremiah b. Hilkiah; and that according to the Jews and the Christians, 461 years separate the age of Jeremiah and the destruction of the Temple by Nebuchadnezzar from the birth of the Baptist. They state that that is clearly established in their writings and scriptures, for they count seventy years from the destruction of Jerusalem by Nebuchadnezzar to its reconstruction in the age of Cyrus son of Ahasuerus, the governor (*isbahbadh*) of Babylonia on behalf of Ardashīr Bahman b. Isfandiyār b. Bishstāsb and then on behalf of his daughter Khumānī; then eighty-eight years after the rebuilding of Jerusalem to the victory of Alexander over Khumānī, and the annexation of her empire to his; then 303 years from Alexander to the birth of the Baptist. This, they say, makes 461 years.

The Zoroastrians agree with the Christians and Jews about the period of the destruction of Jerusalem and about Nebuchadnezzar. They also agree about the story of the Israelites

291. See Ginzberg, *Legends*, IV, 300, 334, 339; VI, 423, 428.

[719] down to Alexander's victory over Jerusalem and Palestine, and the death of Darius. But they contradict them about the duration of the period between Alexander's reign and the birth of the Baptist, as they maintain that it was fifty-one years. Between the Zoroastrians and the Christians there is a controversy, as I have mentioned, about the length of the period between Alexander's reign and the birth of the Baptist.

The Christians assert that the Baptist was born six months before Jesus, and that it was an Israelite king named Herod who put him to death on account of Herodias who was the wife of Herod's brother Philip. Herod loved her, and she consented to lie with him. She had a daughter, Salome. Herod wanted to live with Herodias, his brother's wife, but the Baptist forbade it and told him that it was not permissible. Herod admired the daughter and one day she aroused him, and then asked for a favor; he agreed, and instructed one of his men to carry out her request. She then ordered the man to bring her the Baptist's head, and he complied. When Herod learned about it, he was shocked and thoroughly frightened.[292]

I have quoted Hishām b. Muḥammad al-Kalbī to present the view of the experts on pre-Islamic history and lore.

As for Ibn Isḥāq's version, we learned it from Ibn Ḥumayd—Salamah—Muḥammad b. Isḥāq: The Israelites flourished after that, meaning, after their return from Babylonia to Jerusalem.
[720] They transgressed, and God again sent messengers to them. Some of them were rejected, some slain, until the last prophets sent to them were Zechariah, John (the Baptist), the son of Zechariah, and Jesus, the son of Mary. They were descended from David. John's lineage is: Zechariah b. Iddo b. Meshullam b. Zadok b. Nachshon b. David b. Solomon b. Meshullam b. Zedekiah b. Berechiah b. Shefatiah b. Fakhor b. Shallum b. Jehoshaphat b. Asa b. Abiah b. Rehoboam b. Solomon b. David.[293]

When God took Jesus from their midst to heaven, they slew the Baptist. Some say when they killed the Baptist, God

292. See Mark 6:14–29; Matth. 14:1–12; Josephus, *Wars*, II, 911.

293. The genealogical list is drawn from a composite of Zechariah 1:1; Ezra 8:16–17; Nehemiah 3:4; 7:59. See also Matth. 1.

sent against them a Babylonian king called Khardūs.[294] He marched against them with a Babylonian host and entered Palestine. When he defeated them, he summoned one of his military chieftains, a man addressed as Nābuzarādhan the executioner, to whom he said, "I have sworn by my deity that if I defeat the people of Jerusalem, I shall kill them until their blood flows amidst my encampment, and until I find none to [721]
kill." The king commanded Nābuzarādhan to slay them until such was done.

Nābuzarādhan entered the Temple. He stood over the spot where they used to offer their sacrifice, and he found blood there that was boiling. He asked them, "O Children of Israel, why is this blood boiling? Tell me about it and do not conceal anything." They said, "It is the blood of a sacrifice which we had offered and which was not accepted from us; and therefore it is boiling, as you see. We have offered sacrifices for eight hundred years, and the sacrifice has always been accepted, except this one." He said, "You have not told me the truth." They replied, "If things were as they used to be, it would be accepted; but we have been deprived of kingship, prophecy, and inspiration, and that is why this sacrifice of ours was not accepted." Nābuzarādhan slew seven hundred seventy of their leaders on that spot, but the blood did not calm down. Upon his order seven hundred of their young men were brought and slaughtered over the blood, but it did not calm down. He ordered that seven thousand of their sons and their spouses be slain there, but the blood did not cool. When Nābuzarādhan saw that the blood was not calming down, he said to them, "O Children of Israel, woe unto you. Tell me the truth, and endure for the sake of your Lord. For a long time you have been in possession of the land, acting in it as you please. [Tell me], before the last of you is slain, male or female." When they saw the gravity of the mayhem, they told him the truth, "This is the blood of a prophet of ours who often sought to forewarn us of divine wrath. Had we been obedient to him, he would have guided us. He used to tell us about you, but we did not believe him. We killed him, and this is his blood." Nābuzarādhan then [722]

294. That is, Herod.

asked, "What was his name?" They answered, "John, the son of Zechariah." He exclaimed, "Now you have told me the truth. That is why your Lord is taking revenge upon you."

When Nābuzarādhan perceived that they had told him the truth, he prostrated himself and said to those around him, "Lower the gates of the city, remove from it those who were here of the host of Khardūs." He remained with the Israelites. Then he exclaimed, "O John, son of Zechariah, my Lord and your Lord knows the affliction suffered by your people on your account, and how many of them have been slain on your account. Be calm now, by God's grace, before I exterminate your people." Then the Baptist's blood subsided so that Nābuzarādhan stopped the killing, saying, "I believe in the God of the Children of Israel. I sincerely believe in Him; I know for sure that He is the only God. No other deity can there be beside Him. Had He any associate, heaven and earth would not hold together. It would be wrong for Him to have a son. May He be blessed, sanctified, praised, glorified, the King of Kings who reigns the seven heavens with knowledge and wisdom, strength and power; He who spread out the earth and set therein firm mountains for eternity. Thus it befits my Lord to be, and His realm to be.[295]

It was revealed to a leader of the remnant of the prophets that Nābuzarādhan was a sincere *ḥabūr*—*ḥabūr* in Hebrew is a new convert.[296] Nābuzarādhan told the Israelites, "Khardūs, the enemy of God, ordered me to slay so many of you that your blood should flow amidst his encampment. I cannot disobey him." They told him, "Do as you were ordered." Upon his
[723] command, they dug a trench. He ordered that horses, mules, asses, cattle, sheep, and camels in their possession be placed there and slaughtered, and that blood be made to flow throughout the camp. Upon his order the corpses of the people who had been slain were thrown over the slaughtered animals, so that Khardūs was certain that the trench was filled with dead Israel-

295. See Qur'ān 13:3; 15:19; 50:7. Note the Muslim view that Jesus is not the son of God.

296. Presumably Hebrew *ḥaber,* meaning "companion, friend" or "scholar". Note that Arabic *ḥabr* means a Jewish scholar.

ites. When the blood reached his camp, he sent to Nābuzarādhan the message, "Stop, their blood has reached me; I have been revenged for what they have done." Whereupon he left for Babylonia after almost annihilating the Israelites.[297] It was the last calamity that God brought upon them. God said to his prophet Muḥammad, "And we decreed for the Children of Israel in the Book . . . And we have made Gehenna a prison for the unbelievers."[298] The divine "perchance" (found in the extended passage) has come true. The first calamity was at the hand of Nebuchadnezzar and his hosts. Then God caused "the turn," and the final calamity struck them—Khardūs and his hosts. It was the greater of the two calamities, the one in which their land was destroyed, their men slain, and their women and progeny taken prisoner. God says, "To destroy utterly that which they ascended to."

---

297. See Ginzberg, *Legends*, IV, 304; VI, 397ff.

298. Qur'ān 17:4–8. The full text reads: "And We decreed for the Children of Israel in the Book: 'You shall do corruption in the earth twice, and you shall ascend exceedingly high.' So when the promise of the first of these came to pass, We sent against you servants of Ours, men of great might, and they went through the habitations, and it was a promise performed. Then We gave back to you the turn to prevail over them, and We succoured you with wealth and children, and We made you a greater host. If you do evil, it is to them likewise. Then when the promise of the second came to pass, We sent against you Our servants to discountenance you, and to enter the temple, as they entered it the first time, and to destroy utterly that which they ascended to. Perchance your Lord will have mercy upon you; but if you return, We shall return; and We have made Gehenna a prison for the unbelievers."

The Story of Jesus Son of Mary and His Mother

Mary and her cousin Joseph, the son of Jacob, were attached to the service of the sanctuary. It is said that when Mary's water and Joseph's water ran out, each of them would take the pitcher to go to the cave where they used to draw the water
[724] they liked. They would fill the pitcher, and then return to the sanctuary. When the day arrived on which the angel Gabriel met her—it was the longest and hottest day of the year—the water ran out. She said, "O Joseph, should we not go fetch water?" He said, "I have more than enough for the day, enough to last until tomorrow." She then said, "By God, I have no water left." She took her pitcher and went alone. She entered the cave, and found Gabriel there—God made him appear to her as a shapely human—and he said to her, "O Mary, God has sent me to you to give you a boy most pure." At this she exclaimed, "I take refuge in the All Merciful from you, if you fear God!" (She had thought that he was a man, a mortal.) But he said, "I am but a messenger come from your Lord." She then said, "How shall I, whom no mortal has touched, have a son; neither have I been unchaste?" He replied, "Even so. The Lord has said, 'Easy is that for Me, and We may appoint him a sign unto men and a mercy from Us; it is a thing decreed.'"[299]

---

299. Qur'ān 19:17–21. Cf. *EI*^{2} s.v. Īsa, Djibril, and *SEI* s.v. Maryam, Yaḥyā.

That is, God has decreed that it is so. When the angel spoke thus, she submitted to the divine decree, and he breathed into her bosom. Then he left her, and she filled her pitcher.

According to Muḥammad b. Sahl b. ʿAskar al-Bukhārī—Ismāʿīl b. ʿAbd al-Karīm—ʿAbd al-Ṣamad b. Maʿqil, the son of the brother of Wahb—Wahb: When God sent Gabriel to Mary, he appeared to her as a shapely man. She then said, "I take refuge in the All Merciful from you, if you fear God!" Then he [725] breathed into the opening of her garment; the breath reached her womb, and she conceived Jesus. A relative of hers was with her, Joseph the carpenter by name. Both were going to the Temple which is near Mount Zion. At the time, that Temple was one of their greatest sanctuaries. Mary and Joseph were then serving at that Temple, and service there was a great honor. They were both attending to the sanctuary, perfuming, sweeping, cleaning, and whatever was necessary. They were the most eager worshipers of the age.

Joseph was the first to censure Mary's pregnancy. He was distressed by what he saw, horrified, and knew not what to ascribe it to. When Joseph was ready to accuse her, he remembered that she was pious and innocent, that she had never absented herself from him. When he wanted to exonerate her, he observed what had happened to her. When this began to oppress him, he spoke to her. First he said to her, "A thought has occurred to me about you, and I have tried hard to still and conceal it; but it has overcome me, and I have decided to talk about it to calm my heart." She said, "Say a pleasant word;" whereupon he replied, "That is all I wanted to say; tell me, does a field grow without a seed?" She replied, "Yes." He said, "Does a tree grow without rain striking it?" She said, "Yes." "Can there be a child without intercourse?" he asked. "Yes," she replied, "Do you not know that God made the field sprout on the day of creation without any seed; rather, the seed was [726] from the field which God made sprout without seed. Do you not know that God made the tree grow without the rain, and that with the same power he produced the rain for the life of the tree, after he had created each of the two separate? Or do you think God could not make the tree grow without using water upon it? Or, were it not for the water He could not make the tree grow?"

Joseph said to her, "I do not say that. I know that it is within God's power to act as it pleases Him. He only has to say 'Be, and it is.'"[300] Mary then said to him, "Do you not know that God created Adam and his wife without male or female?" "Certainly," he replied. When she told him that, it occurred to him that what was happening to her was a divine thing, and that he should not ask her about it since he felt she was concealing it. Thereafter Joseph took care of the Temple service, and spared Mary all the work she used to perform there. He did so because he saw how delicate her body was, the yellowing of her complexion, the dark hue of her face, the growth of her abdomen, her weakness, the intent gaze. Previously, Mary was different. When the time of her confinement was close, God revealed to her, "Leave the land of your people, for if they seize you, they will revile you and kill your child."

She came to her sister who was then pregnant and to whom the birth of the Baptist had been announced. When the two met, the Baptist's mother felt that her child was bowing within her in recognition of Jesus.[301] Joseph then carried Mary to Egypt on a donkey. During the entire trip there was nothing be-
[727] tween her and the saddle.[302] Joseph travelled with her, and when they were close to Egypt, far from the land of her people, birth-pangs seized Mary which forced her to lie on the haversack of the donkey under a palm tree. It was winter, and Mary's delivery was difficult. When in pain, she took refuge under the palm tree. Angels embraced and surrounded her in ranks. When she gave birth and was in sorrow, she was told, "No, do not sorrow; see, your Lord has set below you a rivulet. Shake also to yourself the palm trunk, and there shall come tumbling upon you dates, fresh and ripe. Eat therefore, and drink, and be comforted; and if you should see any mortal, say, 'I have vowed to the All Merciful a fast, and today I will not speak to any man.'"[303]

---

300. A frequent locution in the Qur'ān. See for example 2:111; 3:52.
301. Luke 1, especially verses 41–44.
302. Matth. 2:13–15.
303. Qur'ān 19:24–27.

The dates came tumbling upon her, though it was wintertime. Wherever idols were worshiped, the idols were toppled and thrown upside down. Devils took fright but remained unaware of the cause. They rushed to Iblīs,[304] who was on his throne in the deep green sea like the throne that had been upon the water, and he veiled himself in imitation of the veils of light before the All Merciful. The devils came to him while six hours of daylight were remained. When Iblīs saw their congregation he was frightened, for since he had dispersed them he had never seen all of them together. He had seen them in small groups only. He questioned them, and they told him that something had happened upon earth, and that the idols were turned upside down. These idols were most conducive to human perdition. "We used to enter their insides, address the humans, and contrive to direct them, while the people thought [728]
that the idols were speaking to them. When this event occurred, however, it detracted from the stature of the idols, humbling and humiliating them. We fear humans will not worship them anymore. Know, that we did not come to you before crossing land and sea, and doing whatever we could, but we are still utterly ignorant about the cause of what happened."

Iblīs told them, "Truly, this is a grave matter. I know it was concealed from me. Stay here." He flew away and was absent for three hours during which time he passed by the place where Jesus was born. When he saw the angels surrounding the spot, he realized that this was where the event had occurred. Iblīs wanted to approach it from above. But the angels' heads and shoulders that reached up to heaven were over it. He then tried to reach it from under the earth but the angels' feet were firmly entrenched below—lower than Iblīs expected. Thereupon he tried to enter among them, but they shoved him away. Then he returned to his associates, and said to them, "I come to you after crossing the whole earth, east and west, land and sea, the four quarters of the world, and the upper sphere. I managed to do that in three hours." Then informing them about the birth of Christ, he said to them, "It was concealed from me. No fe-

304. That is, the Devil. See *EI*^{2}, s.v. Iblīs.

male womb has ever conceived without my knowledge, and none has given birth without my presence. I am more apt to mislead the newborn than he is to find right guidance. No prophet was ever more calamitous to me and to you than this one."

That night a group set out to go to Christ, urged by the rise of an unknown star. They had been discussing that the rise of
[729] that star was one of the signs of the birth of a child, as indicated in the Book of Daniel. They set out on the road to reach the newborn, and carried gold and frankincense and myrrh. They passed by the king of Palestine. He asked them where they were bound, and they told him. He then asked, "Why of all things this gold, frankincense, and myrrh that you bring as a gift for him?" They replied, "They befit him because gold is the noblest possession, and this prophet is the noblest of his age; myrrh heals wound and fracture, and similarly, this prophet will be raised by God to heaven, uniquely in his time." Upon hearing this, the king resolved to kill the child. He told them, "Go, and when you have found him, bring me word, and I shall follow in your footsteps." They departed, and delivered the gifts to Mary. They wanted to return to the king to bring him word of the place of Jesus, but an angel met them, saying, "Do not return to him, and do not bring him word of the child's place, for the king wanted to learn of it only to slay the child." Thus they departed by another road.[305]

Mary carried the child on the donkey, and Joseph was with her. So they went down into Egypt. This is the "height" in the verse, "We gave them refuge upon a height, where was a hollow and a spring."[306] Mary spent twelve years there, concealing the child, and nobody saw him. She did not trust anybody to be in contact with him, nor to provide for his suste-
[730] nance. She would collect the ears of grain as soon as she heard of a harvest. While carrying the cradle on one shoulder, she would carry the vessel containing the ears of corn on the other. Then Jesus turned twelve. The first miracle of his witnessed by people occurred when his mother was staying at the home of

---

305. Matth. 2.
306. Qur'ān 23:15.

an Egyptian dignitary (*dihqān*).[307] A treasure was stolen from him while only poor people were living in his house, yet he did not accuse them. Mary was saddened by that dignitary's misfortune. When Jesus noticed his mother's sadness at the misfortune of their host, he asked her, "Oh mother, would you like me to guide him to his property?" She said, "Yes, my son." He then said, "Tell him to assemble the poor men of his home;" whereupon Mary told the dignitary, and he assembled them. When they were assembled, Jesus approached two of them, one blind, the other crippled. He put the cripple on the shoulder of the blind man and said to him, "Stand up with him." The blind man said, "I am too weak." Jesus replied, "How then were you able to do that yesterday?" When they heard his words, they forced the blind man to get up with the cripple. When he stood up carrying the other, the cripple plunged to the window of the treasury. Jesus said, "This is how they cheated the landlord yesterday; the blind man used his strength, and the cripple his eyes." The cripple and the blind said, "He is right." And they returned the property to the dignitary. The dignitary replaced it in his treasury, and said, "O Mary, take half of it." But she replied, "It is against my grain to do so."[308] He said, "Give it to your son." And she replied, "He is even more scrupulous than I."[309] Soon afterward one of the dignitary's sons gave a wedding feast, and all the people of Egypt gathered there. When [731]
the feast was over, people from Palestine (Shā'm) visited him. The dignitary was not prepared for them. They came, and he had no wine to offer them. When Jesus saw him worry about it, he entered one of the dignitary's houses in which there were two rows of jars. As he walked by them, Jesus touched the tops of the jars and each jar, to the last of them, became filled with wine. He was twelve years old. Upon seeing what he had done the people were in awe of him and of the powers that God had endowed him with.

God revealed to his mother Mary, "Go up with him to Palestine." She did as he commanded, and stayed in Palestine until

307. For this term, which is of Persian origin, see *EI*², s.v. Dihḳān.
308. Text: *innī lam akhluq lidhālika.*
309. Text: *huwa aʿẓamu minnī sha'nan.*

he was thirty years old. Then inspiration came upon him at the age of thirty. His prophethood lasted three years, and then God raised him unto Himself. When Iblīs saw him on the day of the temptation, he (Iblīs) could achieve nothing. Iblīs presented himself as an old and respectable man, and with him were two obstreperous devils just like himself in appearance; they merged amid the company of men.[310]

Wahb asserted that the sick often flocked to Jesus, as many as fifty thousand at a time. Those who could reach him did so. But if one could not, Jesus would walk up to him. He would heal them by praying to God. Iblīs came to him in a dazzling, beautiful shape. When the people saw the devil, they were attracted to him, and followed him. He began to tell them of wondrous things, namely, that this man was wonderful, that he spoke in the cradle, that he revived the dead, that he proph-
[732] esied concerning the hidden, and that he healed the sick. "So this is God." But one of his companions exclaimed, "You are all wrong, old man. Shame upon what you have said. It does not befit God to reveal himself to humans. Nor does he dwell in a womb, or in the cavities of women. But this is the son of God." The third said, "How evil is what the two of you have said. Both of you are mistaken and wrong. It does not befit God to have a child. But this one is god along with Him." After they completed their talk, they disappeared. This was the last time they were seen.[311]

According to Mūsā b. Hārūn—ʿAmr b. Ḥammād—Asbāṭ—al-Suddī—Abū Mālik and Abū Ṣāliḥ—Ibn ʿAbbās and Murrah al-Hamdānī—Ibn Masʿūd—some of the Prophet's companions: Mary went out to the side of the prayer niche (*miḥrāb*), as she was menstruating, and hid behind the walls to separate herself from the people. This is indicated in the (following) verses, "When she withdrew from her people to an eastern place, and she took a veil apart from them"[312] mean-

310. See Matth. 4. Note that Iblīs adopted similar garb when he sought to assist the Quraysh in dealing with Muḥammad shortly before the Prophet's emigration from Mecca to al-Madīnah. See Ibn Hishām, *Sīrah*, I, 324.

311. Devils discuss the issues that gave rise to dissension and heresy in the early church.

312. This and the following quotes are from Qur'ān 19:16–31.

ing east of the prayer niche. When she was pure, lo and behold, she encountered a man, as it says, "Then We sent unto her Our Spirit [that is, the angel Gabriel] that presented himself to her a man without fault." When she saw him, she was frightened, and exclaimed, "I take refuge in the All Merciful from thee! If thou fearest God. . ." He said, "I am but a messenger come from thy Lord, to give thee a boy most pure." She said, "How shall I whom no mortal has touched have a son, neither have I been unchaste [that is, a harlot]." He said, "Even so, your Lord has said, 'Easy is that for Me, and We may appoint him a sign unto men and a mercy from Us; it is a thing decreed.'"

She wore a gown. He held her sleeves and breathed into the opening of her garment which was split in front. The breath en- [733]
tered her breast, and she conceived. Her sister, the wife of Zechariah, came to visit her at night. When Mary opened the door for her, the sister clung to her. The wife of Zechariah said, "Oh Mary, do you know I am with child?" Mary replied, "Do you know that I too am with child?" Zechariah's wife then said, "I felt that the child in me was bowing to the child in you," as it is written "confirming the Word of God." The wife of Zechariah gave birth to John (the Baptist). When the time arrived for Mary to give birth, she went out to the eastern side of the prayer niche. She reached the edge, "and the birthpangs surprised her by the trunk of the palm tree." As she was suffering the delivery, ashamed before the people, she exclaimed, "Would that I had died before this, and become a thing forgotten [that this, the memory of me should be forgotten, as well as any trace of me, and no eye should see me]." But Gabriel called unto her from below, "No, do not sorrow; see, your Lord has set below you a rivulet [that is, a watercourse]. Shake also to yourself the palm trunk [it was a broken-off trunk]." She shook it and, lo and behold, it was a palm tree; he produced for her a stream in the prayer niche, and dates fresh and ripe came tumbling down. He then said to her, "Eat, therefore, and drink, and be comforted; and if you should see any mortal say, 'I have vowed to the All Merciful a fast, and today I will not speak to any man.'" At that time, one fasting would not talk until evening. She was told, "Say nothing further."

When she gave birth to the child, Iblīs the devil sent to in-

[734] form the Israelites, "Mary gave birth to a child." They came angrily, and called out to her. "Then she brought the child to her folk, carrying him, and they said, 'Mary, you have surely committed a monstrous [that is, grave] thing! Sister of Aaron, thy father was not a wicked man, nor was thy mother a woman unchaste. What is it with you, sister of Aaron?'" She was descended from Aaron, the brother of Moses, so that this expression is the equivalent of saying, "Oh, brother of tribe such and such;" it indicates a family relationship. She then told them what God had commanded her to say. When they wanted her to talk further, "Mary pointed to the child [Jesus] then." But they became angry, and exclaimed, "'Her mocking at us by telling us to speak to this boy is more distressing to us than her unchastity.' They said, 'How shall we speak to one who is still in the cradle, a little child?'" But Jesus spoke to them. "He said, 'Behold, I am God's servant; God has given me the Book and made me a prophet. Blessed he has made me, wherever I may be.'"

Then the Israelites said, "Only Zechariah made her pregnant; he used to have relations with her." So they sought him, but he had fled from them. Iblīs presented himself to him in the shape of a shepherd, saying, "O Zechariah, they have caught up with you; pray to God that this tree might open up for you, and that you might enter it." He prayed to God, the tree opened up, and he entered it, but the fringe of his garment remained outside. The Israelites passed by Iblīs, and said, "O shepherd, have you seen a man here?" He replied, "Yes. He enchanted this tree; it opened up, and he entered it, and there is the fringe of his garment." They proceeded to cut the tree with saws while the man was in it. And you will not find a Jew without such a fringe on his garb.[313] When Jesus was born,
[735] every idol upon the earth fell on its face.

According to al-Muthannā—Isḥāq b. al-Ḥajjāj—Ismāʿīl b. ʿAbd al-Karīm—ʿAbd al-Ṣamad b. Maʿqil—Wahb: When Jesus son of Mary was told by God that he was about to leave this world, he became afraid of death and grieved. He summoned the apostles and prepared food for them saying, "Come to me

313. See Num. 15:38ff.

tonight. I have something to discuss with you." When they assembled at night, he served them supper. When they finished the meal, he began to wash their hands, cleansing them with his hands, and wiping their hands with his garment. But they considered it a grievous act and were displeased, whereupon Jesus said, "Indeed, he who rejects anything I do tonight, is not of mine, and I am not of his." So they waited until he had finished. Then he said, "What I have done with you tonight in serving you the meal, washing your hands with mine—this is to make you and me equal. You consider me the best of you, so do not be arrogant towards one another. Sacrifice yourselves for one another, just as I sacrifice myself for you. My request of you is that you call out to God; call out fervently to postpone my end." When they turned to pray and sought to be fervent, they fell asleep and could not pray. He began to wake them, saying, "Praised be God, could you not watch one night to help me?" They said, "By God, we do not know what happened to us; we were keeping vigil but were unable to keep awake tonight, and as soon as we attempted to pray, we were prevented from doing so." He said, "The shepherd is taken away, the flock disperses."[314]

He began to use such language announcing his death. Then [736]
he said, "The truth is that one of you shall deny me thrice before the cock-crow, and one of you shall sell me for a few coins, and he shall eat my price." They walked out and dispersed. The Jews were looking for him. They seized Simeon, one of the apostles, and said, "This one is a companion of his." But he denied it, and said, "I am not his companion." So they left him. Then another caught him, but he denied it again. Then he heard the cock crow, and wept. When morning came, one of the apostles came to the Jews, and said, "What will you give me if I lead you to Christ?" And they set for him thirty pieces of silver. He took those, and led them to him. Before that they were not sure of Christ. But now they seized him, chained him, tied him with cord, and began to lead him, saying, "You revived the dead, chased away the devil, and cured the possessed; will you not set yourself free from this cord?" They spat upon

314. Mark 14; Matth. 26; Luke 22.

him and threw thorns upon him, until they brought the wooden board upon which they wanted to crucify him. But God raised him up to Himself, and they crucified "only a likeness of that shown to them."[315] A week passed. Then his mother and the woman whom Jesus healed and cured from derangement came weeping at the place of crucifixion. But Jesus came to them and said, "Why are you weeping?" They said, "Because of you;" whereupon he replied, "God raised me up to Himself, and nothing but good has happened to me. Only a likeness was shown to them. Instruct the apostles to meet me at place such and such." They met him at that place, eleven of them, as the one who had betrayed him and led the Jews to him was missing. Jesus asked the apostles about him. They said, "He rued what he had done, and strangled himself to death."
[737] Jesus said, "Had he repented, God would have forgiven him." He asked them about John, a youth who was following them, and said, "He is with you. Go! Each of you will speak the language of a people to warn and summon them."[316]

According to Ibn Ḥumayd—Ibn Isḥāq—an impeccable authority—Wahb b. Munabbih al-Yamānī: God allowed Jesus, the son of Mary, to die at three o'clock in the day; then He took him unto Himself.

According to Ibn Ḥumayd—Salamah—Ibn Isḥāq: The Christians assert that God granted him death for seven hours of the day, and then resurrected him saying, "Descend upon Mary Magdalene on her mountain, for nobody wept for thee as she did, nor did anybody grieve for thee as she did. Let her assemble for thee the apostles, and send them forth as preachers for God, for you have not done that." God let him descend to her; the mountain was aglow with light as he descended, and she gathered the apostles. Jesus sent them out and commanded them to tell men in his name of the divine injunction. Then God raised Jesus unto Himself, gave him wings of an angel and dressed him in radiance. No longer did Jesus relish food or drink; he was flying along with the angels, around the throne.

---

315. Qur'ān 4:145.

316. Mark 14:18; 15:66–72; Matth. 26:14–15; 27:2–10; 28:16; 34; Acts 1:16–20.

He was (both) human and angelic, celestial and terrestrial. The apostles then dispersed, as commanded. The night on which he was sent down is celebrated by the Christians with frankincense.

Among the apostles, and the followers who came after them were the apostle Peter and Paul who was a follower and not an apostle;[317] they went to Rome. Andrew and Matthew were [738]
sent to the country whose people are man-eaters, a land of blacks, we think; Thomas was sent to Babylonia in the east, Philip to Qayrawān (and) Carthage, that is, North Africa. John went to Ephesus, the city of the youths of the cave, and James to Jerusalem, that is, Aelia. Bartholomew was sent to Arabia, namely, the Hijāz; Simeon to the land of the Berbers in Africa. Judas was not then an apostle, so his place was taken by Ariobus. He filled in for Judas Iscariot after the latter had perpetrated his deed.

According to Ibn Ḥumayd—Salamah—Ibn Isḥāq—ʿUmar b. ʿAbdallāh b. ʿUrwah b. al-Zubayr—Ibn Sulaym al-Anṣārī al-Zuraqī: One of our women was under a vow to appear on al-Jammāʾ, a mountain in ʿAqīq near Madīnah,[318] and I went with her. We stood on the mountain and, lo and behold, there was a huge grave with two huge stone slabs over it—one at the head, one at the feet. On them was an inscription in the ancient script (*musnad*)[319] which I could not decipher. I carried the slabs with me halfway down the mountain; they proved too heavy, however, so I threw one (down) and descended with the other. I showed it to readers of Syriac (to determine) whether they knew its script; but they did not. I showed it to [739]
psalm (*zabūr*) copyists from the Yaman and those versed in reading the *musnad* script; but they did not recognize it, either.

As I found nobody who recognized it, I threw it under a coffer we had, and there it lay for years. Then people from Māh[320] in

---

317. In Islamic terms the messengers or apostles pave the new path. Their work is continued by the *tābiʿūn*, the followers, members of the next generations, who lead the Faithful.

318. A network of mountains and valleys. See EI^2, s.v. al-ʿAḳīḳ.

319. That is, the script of ancient South Arabia.

320. Māh is the late form of the name of ancient Media. See above, n. 282, on

Persia came to us looking for pearls, and I said to them, "Do you have a script?" "Yes," they said. I brought out the stone for them and, lo and behold, they read it. It was in their script, "This is the tomb of Jesus, son of Mary, God's messenger to the people of this land." They were its people at that time. Among them he died, so they buried him on the mountaintop.

According to Ibn Ḥumayd—Salamah—Ibn Isḥāq: The rest of the apostles were assaulted, viciously exposed to the sun, tortured, and dishonorably paraded. The Roman king, who ruled over them and who was an idol-worshiper, heard this. He was told that a man among the Israelites, subject to his rule, was assaulted and slain. The man had announced to them that he was God's messenger. He performed miracles, revived the dead and healed the sick. He created a bird of clay, breathed into it, and it flew, by God's permission. He told of hidden things. The king exclaimed, "But why did you not mention this to me, about him and them? By God, had I known, I would not have let them have a free hand against him!" Then he sent for the apostles and snatched them from the hands of the Israelites. He asked the apostles about the faith of Jesus and about his fate. They told him, whereupon he embraced their faith. The king released Sergius and concealed him.[321] He took the wooden cross on which Jesus had been crucified, and he honored and preserved it because Jesus had touched it. The king thus became an enemy of the Israelites, and killed many of
[740] them. From this arose Christianity in Rome.

Some historians mentioned that Jesus was born forty-two years after Augustus had become emperor. Augustus continued to live on, and his reign lasted fifty-six years; some add a few days. The Jews assaulted Christ. The sovereign in Jerusalem at the time was Caesar, and it was on his behalf that Herod the Great reigned in Jerusalem. Messengers of the king of Persia came to him. Sent to Christ, they came to Herod by mis-

---

Māhāt. The Muslim view is that Jesus escaped crucifixion. Here it is intimated that he lived on in Arabia under Iranian rule.

321. Saint Sergius, a Roman officer, was martyred ca. A.D. 303. His shrine was popular in Rusāfat al-Shā'm and attracted Arab nomads. See Trimingham, *Christianity among the Arabs in pre-Islamic times*, London-New York 1979, 235ff.

take. They informed Herod that the king of Persia had sent them to offer Christ the gifts they carried, gifts of gold, myrrh and frankincense. They told him that they had observed that Christ's star had risen—they had learned through computation. They offered him the gifts at Bethlehem in Palestine. When Herod learned about them, he plotted against Christ, and looked for him in order to slay him. God commanded an angel to tell Joseph, who was with Mary at the sanctuary, that Herod intended to slay the child, and to instruct him to flee to Egypt with the child and its mother.

When Herod died the angel told Joseph, who was in Egypt, that Herod was dead and that his son Archelaus reigned instead—the man who had sought to slay the child was no longer alive. Joseph took the child to Nazareth in Palestine, to fulfill the word of Isaiah the prophet, "I called you out of Egypt."[322] Archelaus died, and the younger Herod became king, in whose reign the likeness of Christ was crucified. Sovereignty at the time was in the hands of Greek and Roman kings; Herod and his sons, who ruled on their behalf, had titles nevertheless—the sovereigns were titled "caesar." At the time [741]
of the crucifixion it was the younger Herod who reigned in Jerusalem on behalf of Tiberius, the son of Augustus, except in the matter of (criminal) court. This was entrusted to a Roman called Pilate, on behalf of caesar; the exilarch was Liunan son of Babbutan.[323] They mention that the man who was taken for Jesus and crucified was a Jew called Joshua, son of Pandera.[324] The reign of Tiberius lasted a little over twenty-three years, over eighteen years before the ascension of Jesus, and five thereafter.

---

322. The reference ascribed here to Isaiah is in Hosea 11:1.

323. Augustus ruled from 31 B.C. to A.D. 14; Archelaus 4 B.C. - A.D. 6; Tiberius A.D. 14–37. The Muslim author projects the institute of the exilarch into the distant past. The name of the exilarch is unclear.

324. In ancient anti-Christian lore, Jesus is the illegitimate son of a Roman named Pandera. See Morton Smith, *Jesus the Magician*, New York 1978, 26ff., 46–50, 178.

The Roman Rulers

The Roman rulers, according to the Christians, reigned over Palestine from the ascension of Christ to the age of the Prophet Muḥammad.

Abū Ja'far says: They assert that after Tiberius, Palestine and other parts of Syria were ruled by Gaius, son of Tiberius, for four years. He was succeeded by another son, Claudius, for fourteen years, following which Nero ruled for fourteen years. He slew Peter and crucified Paul head down. For four months Boṭlāius [Vittelius] ruled thereafter. Then Vespasian, father of Titus whom he sent to Jerusalem, ruled for ten years. Three years after his rise to power, forty years after the ascension of
[742] Jesus, Vespasian sent Titus to Jerusalem. Titus destroyed it and slew numerous Israelites in his wrath over the fate of Christ. The following Roman kings then ruled:

> Titus, son of Vespasian, ruled for two years; Domitian, sixteen years; Nerva, six years; Trajan, nineteen years; Hadrian, twenty-one years; Antonin, twenty-two years; Marcus and his sons, nineteen years; Commodus, thirteen years; Pertinax, six months; Severus, fourteen years; Antoninus (=Caracalla), seven years; Marciarus (=Macrinus), six years; Antoninus (=Elagabalus), four years; (Severus) Alexander, thirteen years; Ghasmiyanus (=Maxinimus),
> [743] three years; Gordian, six years; Philipp, seven years;

Decius, six years; Gallus, six years; Valerian and Gallienus, fifteen years; Claudius II, one year; Critalius, six months; Aurelian, five years; Tacit, six months; Florian, twenty-five days; Probus, six years; Carus and his two sons, two years; Diocletian, six years; Maximian, twenty years; Constantine, thirty years; Constantine, thirty years; Constantine, thirty years; Julian the Apostate, two years; Jovian, one year; Valentinian and Gratian, ten years; Valentinian II, one year; Theodosius the Great, seventeen years; Arcadius and Honorius, twenty years; Theodosius II and Valentinian, sixteen years; Marcian, seven years; Leo, sixteen years; Zeno, eighteen years; Anastasius, twenty-seven years; Justin I, seven years; Justinian I, twenty
years; Justin II, twelve years; Tiberius, six years; Maurice [744]
(Maurikios) and his son Theodosius, twenty years; Phocas, who was slain, seven and a half years; Heraclius, to whom the Messenger of God wrote an epistle, thirty years.

From the rebuilding of the Temple, after it was destroyed by Nebuchadnezzar, to the hijrah there elapsed, according to these scholars, over a thousand years. From the reign of Alexander to the hijrah there elapsed over 920 years. Of these, 303 years elapsed from the rise of Alexander to the birth of Jesus, and thirty-two years elapsed from the birth of Jesus to his ascension. From his ascension to the hijrah there elapsed 585 years and a few months.

Some authorities assert that the death of John the Baptist at the hands of the Israelites took place at the time of Ardashīr b. Bābak, after eight years of his reign, and that Nebuchadnezzar went to war in Palestine against the Jews on behalf of Shapūr (Sābūr) of the Troops b. Ardashīr b. Bābak.

According to Hishām b. Muḥammad: Among the events taking place under the petty rulers, before the rise of Ardashīr b. Bābak, was the emergence of several Arab tribes from the shores of Iraq and the settlement of some of them at Ḥīrah and Anbār.

Al-Ḥīrah and al-Anbār[325]

According to Hishām b. Muḥammad: When Nebuchadnezzar
[745] died, those Arabs whom he had settled at al-Ḥīrah when he was ordered to fight them, joined the people of al-Anbār, and the enclosure (*al-ḥayr*) remained a ruin. Thus, a long time elapsed during which no new wave (of tribesmen) from Arabia appeared. But al-Anbār had its Arab population which was joined by that of al-Ḥīrah. All of them were from Arab tribes, children of Ishmael and of Maʿadd b. ʿAdnān.[326] When the progeny of Maʿadd b. ʿAdnān, and those of the Arab tribes who were with them, multiplied and filled their land in al-Tihāmah and adjoining areas, they were dispersed by wars that occurred among them and evils that befell them. Therefore they moved out in quest of space and fertile land in the adjoining areas of the Yaman and the Syrian approaches. Some tribes that emerged settled in al-Baḥrayn, among them a group of the Azd. They had settled there in the age of ʿImrān b. ʿAmr, who was from the remnant of the progeny of ʿĀmir,[327] that is Māʾ al-Samāʾ b. Ḥārithah, that is, al-Ghiṭrīf b. Thaʿlabah b. Imrūʾ al-

---

325. See above, n. 178.

326. Ishmael (Ismāʿīl) is regarded as the ancestor of the Arabs in the Islamic tradition. ʿAdnān and his son Maʿadd are considered the ancestors of the northern Arabs. See *EI*², s.v. Ismāʿīl, ʿAdnān, Maʿadd.

327. ʿĀmir is the reputed ancestor of a South Arabian tribe by the same name. See *EI*², s.v. Djaʿda.

Qays b. Māzin b. al-Azd. Those Arabs who emerged from al-Tihāmah included Mālik and ʿAmr, the sons of Fahm b. Taymallāh b. Asad b. Wabarah b. Taghlib b. Ḥulwān b. ʿImrān b. al-Ḥāf b. Quḍāʿah, and Mālik b. Zuhayr b. ʿAmr b. Fahm b. Taymallāh b. Asad b. Wabarah with a group of their people, and al-Ḥayqār b. al-Ḥīq b. ʿUmayr b. Qanas b. Maʿadd b. ʿAdnān with all the Qanas, followed by Ghaṭafān b. ʿAmr b. al-Ṭamathān b. ʿŪdh Manāt b. Yaqdum b. Afṣā b. Duʿmī b. Ayād [746] b. Nizār b. Maʿadd b. ʿAdnān, and Zuhr b. al-Ḥārith b. al-Shalal b. Zuhr b. Ayād, and Ṣabaḥ b. Ṣabaḥ b. al-Ḥārith b. Afṣā b. Duʿmī b. Ayād. Thus a number of Arab tribes gathered in al-Baḥrayn. They became allies known as al-Tanūkh, which means "abode," and pledged themselves to assist and support one another; under the joint name of Tanūkh they became a force against other people. They bore that name as if they were some great tribe. Clans of Numārah b. Lakhm dwelled with them.

Mālik b. Zuhayr invited Jadhīmah al-Abrash[328] b. Mālik b. Fahm b. Ghānim b. Daws al-Azdī to settle with him, and he married him to his sister Lamīs bt. Zuhayr. Jadhīmah b. Mālik and all the Azd who came along settled there, and Mālik and [747] ʿAmr, the sons of Fahm, and the Azd became allies (*ḥalīf*). This (arrangement) excluded the rest of Tanūkh who were united.

The gathering and the alliance of the Arab tribes in al-Baḥrayn took place in the period of the regional princes, a period which lasted from (the time of) Alexander—who divided the countries after he slew Darius son of Darius, king of Persia—down to the victory of Ardashīr b. Bābak, the king of Fārs, over the regional princes. After that, Ardashīr was recognized as supreme authority. Thus the regional princes were called (*mulūk al-ṭawāʾif*) because each of them had only a small domain with castles and structures surrounded by a ditch. Nearby enemies were similarly established, and they would raid one another, only to retreat suddenly.

The Arabs of Baḥrayn looked towards the land of Iraq; they

---

328. A king of pre-Islamic Arab antiquity, who lived perhaps in Iraq in the third century A.D. See *EI*^{2}, s.v. Djadhīma al-Abrash. See also Nicholson, *Literary history*, 34ff.; *CHI* 3(1), 597.

were desirous of overpowering the non-Arabs in order to seize the area adjoining Arabia, or to share it with them. Taking advantage of the discord among the princes, the Arab chieftains decided to march to Iraq. All who were with them agreed to do so. The first to rise was al-Ḥīqār b. al-Hīq with a group of his people and a motley crowd of others. They found the Armānīs, who were from Babylonia and the adjoining area up to Mosul, fighting the Ardawānīs, the petty princes in the area between Niffar,[329] a town of lower Iraq, and Ubullah and the edge of the wilderness (*bādiyah*).[330] The Arabs did not submit to
[748] their rule, and pushed them out of their own land. ʿĀd used to be called Iram, and when they perished Thamūd was called Iram.[331] Later they were called Arman, and they are the remnant of Iram. They are the Nabaṭ of the Sawād. Damascus is also called Iram.[332] These tribes disappeared from the Sawād of Iraq and became remnants of tribes among the Arabs of al-Anbār. Those of al-Ḥīrah are remnants of Qanaṣ b. Maʿadd. They are related to ʿAmr b. ʿAdī b. Naṣr b. Rabīʿah b. ʿAmr b. al-Ḥārith b. Suʿūd b. Mālik b. ʿAmam b. Numārah b. Lakhm. This is the opinion of Muḍar and Ḥammād al-Rāwiyah,[333] but it is incorrect. Nothing more certain has reached us concerning Qanaṣ b. Maʿadd than Jubayr b. Muṭʿim's word that Nuʿmān was of his progeny.

Al-Anbār was so named because there were food storehouses (*anābir*) there.[334] They were called *al-ahrā'* (granaries), because the Persian king used to supply the sustenance for his men there.

Then there arose Mālik and ʿAmr, the two sons of Fahm b.

---

329. On Niffar, ancient Nippur, see LeStrange, *Lands*, 73f.; Oppenheimer, *Babylonia Judaica*, 315–319.

330. On al-Ubullah see above, n. 234.

331. On ʿĀd, Iram and Thamūd, which are names of Arab tribes in pre-Islamic times, see the relevant articles in *EI*[1] and *EI*[2].

332. Iram and Aram are similar in appearance in the Arabic script, hence probably the identification with Damascus, which was situated in the center of an Aramaic-speaking territory at the time of the Muslim conquest.

333. For Ḥammād al-Rāwiyah, an eighth century collector of Arabic verse, see *EI*[2], s.v. Ḥammād al-Rāwiya.

334. Anbār is actually a Persian word meaning storehouse, granary. See above, n. 177.

Taymallāh, and Mālik b. Zuhayr b. Fahm b. Taymallāh, and Ghaṭafān b. ʿAmr b. al-Tamthān, and Zuhr b. al-Ḥārith, and Ṣabaḥ b. Ṣabaḥ, along with those from among their tribes and allies who joined them to dwell at al-Anbār in the kingdom of the Armānīs. Then there arose Numārah b. Qays b. Numārah and al-Najdah, a tribe (*qabīlah*) of ʿAmālīq[335] claiming relationship to Kindah,[336] and Malkān b. Kindah, and Mālik and ʿAmr, the sons of Fahm, and those allied with them. They dwelled together in Niffār in the domain of the Ardawānīs. The Ardawānīs settled them at the enclosure which Nebuchadnezzar had erected for those Arab traders whom he found [749]
in his capital. This was when he was ordered to raid the Arabs in their country and to lead the troops against them. The garrison continued to be stationed at al-Anbār and Niffar, distrustful of the foreigners and distrusted by them, until the arrival of the *tubbaʿ*, that is, Asʿad Abū Karib b. Malkīkarib with his troops. Asʿad left behind those who had no strength to follow his troops, and those who were too weak to proceed with him or to return home. Thus they joined the Arabs within the enclosure and mingled with them. Kaʿb b. Juʿayl b. ʿAjrah b. Qumayr b. Thaʿlabah b. ʿAwf b. Mālik b. Bakr b. Ḥabīb b. ʿAmr b. Ghanam b. Taghlib b. Wāʾ il referred to this in the verse:

And *tubbaʿ* raided with Ḥimyar
Until, from the people of ʿAdan he arrived at al-Ḥīrah.

The *tubbaʿ* set out marching, and then returned to them. They settled (at al-Ḥīrah), and he left them to themselves, returning to the Yaman. Among them were people from all the tribes, such as the Banū Liḥyān, who were a remnant of Jurhum, the Juʿfī, Ṭayiʾ, Kalb, and Tamīm. The remnant of Jurhum was only at al-Ḥīrah. According to Ibn al-Kalbī: Liḥyān represents the remnant of Jurhum.

Many of the Tanūkh settled at al-Anbār and al-Ḥīrah, in the

---

335. The ʿAmālīq are a mythical tribe of Arabs, the designation of whom is derived from the biblical Amalek, to which many further legends and elaborate stories were added by Arab story-tellers. See *EI*², s.v. ʿAmālīḳ.

336. Kindah was a confederation of tribes of South Arabian origin that exercised rule over the Maʿadd tribes in northern Arabia and, for a time, over al-Ḥīrah. See *EI*², s.v. Kinda; *CHI* 3(2), 601f. See **GAS** II 162 f.

area between al-Ḥīrah and the bank (*ṭaff*) of the Euphrates. To the west, they settled as far as the neighborhood of al-Anbār and its surroundings. They lived in tents, small and large, but not in clay houses; nor did they have any contact with the people living in houses. Their community extended into the area between al-Anbār and al-Ḥīrah, and they were known as the Arabs of the unwalled area (*ḍāḥiyah*). The first ruler from
[750] among them in the time of the regional princes was Mālik b. Fahm who dwelled close to al-Anbār. Following his death, his brother ʿAmr b. Fahm reigned, and upon the death of ʿAmr b. Fahm, Jadhīmah al-Abrash b. Mālik b. Fahm b. Ghānim b. Daws al-Azdī became ruler.

According to Ibn al-Kalbī: Daws is the son of ʿAdnān b. ʿAbdallāh b. Naṣr b. Zahrān b. Kaʿb b. al-Ḥārith b. Kaʿb b. ʿAbdallāh b. Mālik b. Naṣr b. al-Azd b. al-Ghawth b. Mālik b. Zayd b. Kahlān b. Sabāʾ. According to Ibn al-Kalbī: It is said that Jadhīmah al-Abrash was from the proto-Arabs (*al-ʿāribah al-ūlā*) of the Banū Wabar b. Umaym b. Lūdh b. Shem b. Noah.[337] Jadhīmah was one of the brightest Arab kings, far-reaching and effective in his raids, and most resolute. He was the first to rule in Iraq. The Arabs joined him, and he raided standing armies. He was a leper. The Arabs were too awestruck to mention him by name or genealogy; they called him by his nickname out of respect. Thus they referred to Jadhīmah al-Waḍḍāḥ (the Luminous) or Jadhīmah al-Abrash (the Speckled). His dwellings were in the area between al-Ḥīrah and al-Anbār, and in Baqqah and Hīt and their environs. They were also in ʿAyn al-Tamr and the rim lands up to al-Ghumayr, al-Quṭquṭānah, and Khafiyyah and the adjoining area.[338] Tribute was paid to him, and delegations used to visit him. He raided the dwellings of Ṭasm and Jadīs, in Jaww and the environs. The Ṭasm[339] and Jadīs spoke Arabic. He encountered Ḥassān b. Tubbaʿ Asʿad Abī Karib who raided the Ṭasm and Jadīs in al-

337. On Jadhīmah see above, n. 328.

338. For Hīt and ʿAyn Tamr see LeStrange, *Lands*, 65; Yāqūt, *Muʿjam*, IV, 121, 137 (al-Qutqutānah); III, 664 (Ghumayr); II, 457 (Khafiyyah).

339. For Ṭasm and Jadīs see *EI*[1], s.v. Ṭasm. For Jaww, see text above.

Yamāmah. Jadhīmah then withdrew, returning with his men, [751]
but the *tubba*ʿ's cavalry came upon one of Jadhīmah's raiding parties and destroyed it. News of them reached Jadhīmah, who then recited:

> How often did I gaze at a high spot
> northern winds flaying my garb.
> I was with youths their defender.
> they spent the night in the raid's hardships.
> Then to the livestock spoilers I was led,
> and men were left dead by us.
> We were in their passage
> as the people's passage was brotherhood.
> I wish I knew what slew them.
> We set out at nightfall but they stayed on at night;
> They were ours.
> When one of us spoke, they shouted.
> Ours were the distant deserts
> whose black people were scattered,
> A company of the best, a witness
> that is, my people, my kinsfolk.
> I imbibed wine amidst them
> delighted, with no voices.
> Now over the generosity that was, my young girls
> might weep over me.
> I am the lord of all men,
> beside my restraining and discouraging Lord.

By "restraining" he meant He who cuts short their lives; by "discouraging" he meant God who makes them fail.

Ibn al-Kalbī says: Three lines of the poem are genuine; the rest are not.[340] In his account of expeditions and raids of the proto-Arabs, a pre-Islamic poet declared:

---

340. The authenticity of much of pre-Islamic poetry in Arabic, which was transmitted orally and was not committed to writing before the rise of Islam, was regarded as suspect by some medieval Arab scholars. It was assumed, with some plausibility, that much of it was made up in the Islamic period for a variety of reasons, not least among them the great interest in Arab antiquities that developed in the early period of Islam. The statement by Ibn al-Kalbī reflects this kind of critical attitude. See Nicholson, *Literary history*, 131ff.

Jadhīmah, in Yabrīn, his abode
[752] became possessor of the treasure of ʿĀd of old.

Jadhīmah acted as prophet and soothsayer. He had two idols, called the two Dayzans. The place of the two Dayzans at al-Ḥīrah is known. They were entreated for water, and aid against the enemy. The Iyād[341] were at the well of Ubāgh, a man of the ʿAmālīk. Jadhīmah settled at that well, and conducted raids against the Iyād. It is mentioned that Jadhīmah had a servant from the Lakhm[342] who had among his maternal uncles, men of the Iyād. His name was ʿAdī b. Naṣr b. Rabīʿah b. ʿAmr b. al-Ḥārith b. Suʿūd b. Mālik b. ʿAmam b. Numārah b. Lakhm—he was handsome and graceful. Jadhīmah raided the Iyād, so they sent men who gave the custodians of the two idols wine to drink and then stole the two idols. This is how the idols came to be possessed by the Iyād. A message was now sent to Jadhīmah, "Your idols are with us. They shun you and are attracted to us. If you will assure us that you will not raid us, we shall return them to you."

He said, "Send me ʿAdī b. Naṣr also." They did, along with the two idols. Jadhīmah left the Iyād in peace, kept ʿAdī, and put him in charge of his wine. Jadhīmah's sister Raqāsh,[343] the daughter of Mālik, noticed ʿAdī and fell in love with him. She sent for him and said, "O ʿAdī, speak to the king about your marrying me, for you are a man of lineage and status." But he said, "I dare not talk to him about the matter, nor do I wish him to marry you to me." She said, "When he sits over his wine, and his drinking companions arrive, give him pure wine to drink, but offer the company diluted wine; then when he is overcome with wine, talk to him about marrying me; he will not refuse you nor decline, and if he marries you to me, make the company witnesses."

[753] The young man acted upon her order. When the wine had taken effect, he asked the king for the girl's hand, which was

341. On the ancient Arab tribe of Iyād see *EI*^{2} s.v.

342. The Lakhm were an Arab tribe who formed a state around al-Ḥīrah, which was friendly to the Sasanians. See Rothstein, *Dynastie der Lahmiden*; S. Smith, *BSOAS*, 16 (1954), 425–468; *CHI* 3(2), 596ff.

343. *EI*^{2}, s.v. Djadhīma al-Abrash, reads this name as Riqāsh.

granted to him. ʿAdī went to her, and celebrated his wedding feast that very night. He became red-stained from the woman's perfume, and Jadhīmah, disapproving of ʿAdī's appearance, asked, "What are those traces, ʿAdī?" To which ʿAdī replied, "From the wedding." "What wedding?" asked the king. At this ʿAdī replied, "The wedding with Raqāsh." Jadhīmah then said, "Woe unto you. Who married her to you" ʿAdī answered, "The king did." Jadhīmah slapped his forehead and threw himself upon the ground in remorse and lament, while ʿAdī fled from his presence. Nobody saw any trace of him or heard of him (after that). Jadhīmah sent for Raqāsh, and said to her:

Tell me, and do not lie
did you fornicate with a noble man or an ignoble one?
Was it a slave?
then you are worthy of a slave.
Perhaps a worthless man?
then a worthless one you deserve.

She replied, "No, you gave me in marriage to an Arab who is well-known, and of noble birth. You did not consult me about my fate, and I had no power over myself." He recognized her plea and let her be. ʿAdī b. Naṣr returned to the Iyād, and stayed with them. One day he left with youths on a hunt, and one of the young men, who was from the Lihb, shot him at a spot between two mountains. He retired to a tent, and died. Raqāsh was with child, and she gave birth to a boy whom she named ʿAmr.[344] She reared him until he grew up. She then perfumed him and clothed him, and brought him to his uncle Jadhīmah. As soon as Jadhīmah saw the boy, he was taken by him, and he showered him with tender love. The boy frequently visited the king's children, and stayed with them. One day, Jadhīmah set out into the wilderness with his kin and children in a year of abundant rich herbage. Tents were set up for him in a garden with flowers and pools. The princes, and ʿAmr with them, were gathering mushrooms. Whenever they found a good mushroom, they ate it, but whenever ʿAmr found one he con- [754]

344. On ʿAmr b. ʿAdī see *EI*² s.v.

cealed it in his waistband. They raced toward Jadhīmah while ʿAmr recited:

> This is what I have gathered, and the best of it is in it [*fīhi*] when every gatherer [but myself] has his hand to his mouth [*fīhi*][345]

Jadhīmah hugged him and held him, pleased with his word and deed. The king ordered a silver trinket and a necklace made for ʿAmr; ʿAmr was the first Arab to wear a necklace, and was nicknamed ʿAmr the Necklaced (Dhū al-Ṭawq). While he was in his prime, he was lured and carried away by the jinn. Jadhīmah searched for him for a long time throughout many lands, but to no avail. Two brothers from Bulqayn, one called Mālik, the other ʿAqīl, sons of Farij b. Mālik b. Kaʿb b. al-Qayn b. Jasar b. Shayʿallāh b. Asad b. Wabarah b. Taghlib b. Ḥulwān b. ʿImrān b. al-Ḥāf b. Quḍāʿah came from Syria and sought to meet Jadhīmah for whom they had brought gifts and precious things. While they were on their way, they alighted at a house. They had a songstress with them whose name was Umm ʿAmr. She served them food, and while they were eating, there arrived a haggard, naked youth with tangled hair and long nails. Looking ill, he sat down at their side and stretched out his hand for food. The songstress gave him a leg. He ate it and then stretched out his hand toward her. She said, "Give the slave a leg, he will covet the arm." It became a proverb. Then she offered the two men some of her wine, and tied up the skin. ʿAmr b. ʿAdī said:

[755] Pass round from left to right! Why do you allow Umm ʿAmr,
me and my comrades thirst,
Yet you will not serve me this morning, Umm ʿAmr,
Am I the worst of us three?[346]

Mālik and ʿAqīl then asked, "Who are you, young man?" His answer was, "As you do not know me or my lineage, I am ʿAmr b. ʿAdī, the son of a Tanūkh woman of the Lakhm tribe; tomorrow you shall not see me at Numārah, but renounced."

---

345. Translated in Lane, *Arabic-English Lexicon*, 472 col. 3.
346. This verse is from the Muʿallaqah of ʿAmr b. Kulthūm. The translation is based on Nicholson, *Literary history*, 111.

Mālik and ʿAqīl rose to embrace him. They washed his head, cut his nails, cleansed his hair, dressed him in clothes they had, and said, "We could not present to Jadhīmah anything more precious to him or more beloved by him than his sister's son. God has returned him to Jadhīmah through us." The two set out taking ʿAmr along, and reached the gate of Jadhīmah at al-Ḥīrah. They announced to him the glad tiding, and he rejoiced greatly, but he did not recognize ʿAmr in his current state. The two brothers exclaimed, "Bless you, a man in his state will change." Jadhīmah then sent ʿAmr to his mother and he stayed with her for a few days, after which she returned him to her brother. Jadhīmah said, "I saw him on the day he disappeared, when he was wearing a necklace. Since then, till this day, he has never left my mind nor my heart." They returned the necklace to ʿAmr. But when the king looked at him, he said, "ʿAmr has outgrown the necklace." This locution has become proverbial. Jadhīmah turned to Mālik and ʿAqīl, "How about your reward?" They replied, "Our reward is to be your boon companions as long as we and you are alive." So they were the two boon companions of Jadhīmah and became proverbial in Arabic poetry. It is about them that Abū Khirāsh al- [756]
Hudhalī says:[347]

By your life, Kabīshah has not been bored by my appearance,
yet my stay with her was slight indeed.
Know you not, that long before us, they had to part
The two sincere boon companions, Mālik and ʿAqīl?

Mutammim b. Nuwayrah said:[348]

For a long time we were [inseparable] like Jadhīmah's two boon-companions
so that it was said, "Never will they part."
But after we parted, lo, Mālik and I,
despite the long companionship, we spent not a single night together."

---

347. See Hell, *Neue Hudailiten-Diwane*, II, 24, 49. Here the first line is different. The text of Hell reads, "By my life, my appearance truly upset Umaymah [*laʿamrī laqad rāʿat Umaymata ṭalʿatī*]."

348. See Nöldeke, *Beiträge zur Kenntnis der Poesie*, 100, 106.

ʿAmr b. Ẓarib[349]

The ruler of the Arabs in the Jazīrah and the fringes of Syria was ʿAmr b. Ẓarib b. Ḥassān b. Udhaynah b. al-Sumaydaʿ b. Hubār al- ʿAmlaqī—he is also called al-ʿAmlīqī. Jadhīmah gathered hosts of Arabs and marched toward ʿAmr to attack him, while ʿAmr b. Ẓarib advanced from Syria at the head of his forces. They met, and they fought a fierce engagement. ʿAmr b. Ẓarib was slain and his forces scattered; Jadhīmah with his men returned safe and sound, carrying their booty. Concerning this, al-Aʿwar b. ʿAmr b. Hunāʾah b. Mālik b. Fahm al-Azdī recited the (following) verses:

[757] It is as if ʿAmr b. Tharb had never lived as a king,
and never did banners around him flutter.
He encountered Jadhīmah with a spreading cavalry
like locusts jumping amidst flames.

---

349. On ʿAmr b. Ẓarib, see Nicholson, *Literary history*, 35.

Al-Zabbā'[350]

After 'Amr, his daughter al-Zabbā' reigned. Her name was Nā'ilah. Al-Qa'qā' b. al-Darmā' al-Kalbī referred to her in the verse:

> Do you know a home between the road
> and Nā'ilah's ancient track?

Her army consisted of remnants of the 'Amālīq and the proto-Arabs, and Tazīd and Ṣāliḥ, the two sons of Ḥulwān b. 'Imrān b. al-Ḥāf b. Quḍā'ah, and those who joined them from the tribes of Quḍā' ah. She had a sister named Zabībah. Al-Zabbā' built herself a fortress on the western bank of the Euphrates. She used to spend the winter with her sister, and the spring at Baṭn al-Najjār from where she would go to Palmyra (Tadmur). When her power was well established and she was well entrenched in her reign, she decided to attack Jadhīmah al-Abrash to avenge the death of her father. Her sister Zabībah, thoughtful, clever and cunning that she was, said to her, "O al-Zabbā', if you attack Jadhīmah, it may be a battle fraught with consequences. If you are victorious, you will have achieved your vengeance; but if you are slain, your kingdom will be

350. On al-Zabbā', see Nicholson, *Literary history*, 35ff. M. Piotrovskii discussed the legend in Paleztinskij Sbornik v. 84 (1970).

gone. War is a matter of ups and downs, and its vicissitudes cannot be avoided. Your glory still prevails over your foe and contestant; you have not yet encountered trouble or vicissi-
[758] tudes of fate, and you do not know who may be the victor, and whose turn it may be." Al-Zabbā' said to her, "You offer reflection and good advice and it is well taken." She gave up the idea of attacking Jadhīmah and she approached the matter by way of duplicity, treachery, and craftiness. She wrote to Jadhīmah inviting him to visit her and her kingdom, and to join his country with hers. She also wrote him in her letter that she felt that the reign of women tended only toward ill-repute, weak rule, and inefficient administration; that she considered nobody but him to be her peer and to be worthy of her kingdom. "Come to me, join my kingdom to yours," (she wrote), "join my country to yours and assume my power along with yours."

When al-Zabbā's letter reached Jadhīmah, and her messengers came to him, he was delighted with her invitation and excited by her offer. He assembled men of good sense and intelligence from among his trusted associates. He was at the time at al-Baqqah on the bank of the Euphrates. he presented the invitation of al-Zabbā' to them, and consulted them on the matter. They agreed he should proceed to her and take over her kingdom. Among them was a man called Qaṣīr b. Sa'd b. 'Umar b. Jadhīmah b. Qays b. Rabī b. Numārah b. Lakhm. Sa'd (his father) had married a servant of Jadhīmah, and she gave birth to
[759] Qaṣīr. Resourceful and energetic, he was an influential advisor to Jadhīmah. He opposed the advice of the other men, saying, "Feeble thought and sheer treachery." The locution became proverbial.[351] But they refuted his words and contested his thoughts. Then he said, "I see a matter that is neither odd nor even"—this too became a proverb.[352] Then he said to Jadhīmah, "Write to her that if she is sincere, let her come to you; if not, do not expose yourself to her power, and do not fall into her trap. You enraged her, because you killed her father." But Jadhīmah did not accept Qaṣīr's advice. Qaṣīr then recited:

351. *ra'y fātir wa-ghadr ḥāḍir.*
352. *innī la'arā amr laysa bi-l-khasā wa-lā al-zakā.*

I am a man whom failure will not deflect from quenching his thirst
if the gall of excess comes before the goal.[353]

Jadhīmah replied, "No, but you are a man whose opinion is cautious, not enterprising"—this too became a proverb.[354] The king now summoned his nephew ʿAmr b. ʿAdī for consultation. ʿAmr encouraged Jadhīmah to proceed, and said, "The Numārah are my people; they are with al-Zabbāʾ. If they could they would join you." Jadhīmah listened to him, rejecting Qaṣīr's counsel. Qaṣīr then said, "None follows Qaṣīr's advice." Concerning this Nahshal b. Ḥarrī b. Ḍamrah b. Jābir, of Tamīm recited:

The master, obstinate, defied me,
Just as Qaṣīr was not followed in the two Baqqahs
But when the result of my affair and his affair became clear,
And hearts turned with the failures of affairs
he wished belatedly he had followed my advice
As events followed events.

The Arabs said, "In Baqqah the affair was settled."[355] The expression then became a proverb. Jadhīmah appointed ʿAmr b. ʿAdī to be his deputy over his realm and power, and ʿAmr b. ʿAbd al-Jinn al-Jarmī to head his calvary. Then he set out with his best men, taking the route along the western side of the Euphrates. When he alighted at al-Furḍah[356] he summoned [760]
Qaṣīr and asked, "What is the prudent course?" "Prudence you left at al-Baqqah," was the reply—it became proverbial.[357] The messengers of al-Zabbāʾ received the king with gifts and pleasantries, whereupon he said, "O Qaṣīr, what think you?" The reply was, "A minor occurrence in a major affair"—this too became proverbial.[358] "The cavalry will meet you," (Qaṣīr

353. *innī imruʾ lā yamīlu al-ʿajz tarwiyatī idhā atat dūna shayʾ mirrat al-wadham.*

354. *fī al-kinn lā fī al-ḍiḥḥ.*

355. *fī Baqqah ubrima al-amr.*

356. See LeStrange, *Lands,* 107, 125.

357. *bi-Baqqah tarakta al-raʾy.*

358. *khaṭar yasīr fi khaṭb kabīr.* On this seventh century poet see GAS II 196 f.

continued). "If they march in front of you, the woman is sincere; but if they outflank you and encircle you, they mean treachery. Ride al-ʿAṣā—this was Jadhīmah's unrivalled mare—"and I, too, shall ride her and accompany you."

The king was met by the cavalry and the squadrons, and they separated him from al-ʿAṣā. But Qaṣīr jumped on the mare's back. Jadhīmah glanced at him as he was turning back on the mare, and exclaimed, "Woe to his mother! What resolution on ʿAṣā's back"—this became proverbial.[359] Then he exclaimed, "What a frustration al-ʿAṣā is carrying."[360] The mare ran until sunset, and then expired after having covered a vast distance. Qaṣīr erected a tower over the spot, called the ʿAṣā Tower. The Arabs say, "The best al-ʿAṣā did was to set an example."[361]

Jadhīmah was surrounded by horsemen and brought before al-Zabbāʾ. When she saw him, she uncovered and, lo and behold, the hair of her pudendum was plaited. She said, "O Jadhīmah, do you see the concern of a bride?"[362] This became a proverb. He said, "The limit has been reached, the moist ground has dried up, and I see a case of treachery."[363] She replied, "By my deity, we do not suffer from a lack of razors, or scarcity of surgeons, but it is a custom of men"—this too became proverbial.[364] Then she said, "I was told that royal blood is a cure against madness." She seated him on a skin and ordered a golden bowl which she prepared for him. She gave him
[761] wine to drink until he was intoxicated, and then ordered the veins in his arm to be cut. She moved the bowl toward him. She had been told that if a drop of his blood should fall outside the bowl, his blood would be avenged. Out of respect for royalty, kings were not killed by decapitation except in battle. When Jadhīmah's hands weakened, drops of his blood spilled outside the bowl, and al-Zabbāʾ said, "Do not lose any of the

359. *wayl ummihi ḥazm ʿalā ẓahr al-ʿAṣā.*

360. *yā ḍulla mā tajrī bihi al-ʿAṣā.* See Lane, *Arabic-English Lexicon* 1797, s.v. *ḍull.*

361. *khayr mā jāʾat bihi al-ʿAṣā mathal.*

362. *a-daʾb ʿarūs tarā?*

363. *balagha al-madā wa-jaffa al-tharā wa-amr qhadr arā.*

364. *mā binā min ʿadam mawāsin wa-lā qillat awāsin wa-lakinnahu shīmat mā unāsin.*

king's blood." Whereupon Jadhīmah said, "Leave blood lost by its owner"—the phrase became proverbial.[365] Jadhīmah died and al-Zabbā' sought to absorb his blood with a piece of cotton in her perfume container.

Qaṣīr left the tribe where the mare al-ʿAsā had died, and continued on his way until he came to ʿAmr b. ʿAdī who was at al-Ḥīrah. Qaṣīr then said to him, "Oblivious or avenging?"[366] The reply was, "No, avenging, marching"—and it became a proverb.[367] Qaṣīr now met up with Jadhīmah's people; they had split. One faction was with ʿAmr b. ʿAbd al-Jinn al-Jarmī; another, with ʿAmr b. ʿAdī. Qaṣīr went back and forth until he brought them together, and ʿAmr b. ʿAbd al-Jinn became reconciled with ʿAmr b. ʿAdī. The people sympathized with ʿAmr b. ʿAdī, who said about it as follows:

I called upon Ibn ʿAbd al-Jinn for peace after he
ran in the distance of imprudence, and hurried.
But when he refrained from impeding us by being obstinate
I urged him like a mother would her young ones.

ʿAmr b. ʿAbd al-Jinn replied:[368]

Verily, by blood flowing, and running hither and thither,
Which you would think to be dragon's blood
Upon the mountain top of al-ʿUzzā', or by al-Nasr
And what the monks sanctified at every temple,
The most saintly Christ son of Mary. [762]

The verse was found in this form, incomplete; the third line is likely to have read, "such and such happened." Qaṣīr now said to 'Amr b. ʿAdī, "Prepare and be ready; do not let your uncle's blood be unavenged." ʿAmr replied, "But how can I reach her when she is more inaccessible than the eagle of the air?"—this became a proverb.

---

365. *daʿū dam ḍayyaʿahu ahluhu.*

366. *a-dāthir am thā'ir?*

367. *thā'ir sā'ir.*

368. The translation is based on Lane, *Arabic-English Lexicon*, 2033. For the pre-Islamic deity al-ʿUzzā', see *SEI.* Nasr "vulture" or "eagle" was also a deity in pre-Islamic Arabia. See W. Robertson Smith, *The religion of the Semites*, 226; J. Wellhausen, *Reste arabischen Heidentums*, 23.

Al-Zabbā' asked one of her woman soothsayers about power and rule, and the woman replied, "I see your death because of a youth, vile and disloyal, ʿAmr b. ʿAdī; you will not die at his hand but at your own, on his account." Wary of ʿAmr, al-Zabbā' built a tunnel from the audience hall in which she held court to a fortress inside her city, and said, "Should something unexpected occur, I shall enter the tunnel to get to my fortress." She called in a painter, the best and most successful of her country's painters. She equipped him, treated him well, and said to him, "Go in disguise and reach ʿAmr b. ʿAdī, stay with his retinue, join them, mingle with them, make them aware of your knowledge of painting and your expertise. Then make the acquaintance of ʿAmr b. ʿAdī, and paint him seated, standing, riding, in simple garb, and fully armed, reproducing his costumes and color. If you succeed in carrying this out,
[763] come to me." The painter set out, and he arrived at ʿAmr's (camp). Proceeding according to the instructions of al-Zabbā', he carried out his task. Then he returned to her with the likenesses she wanted, so that she might recognize ʿAmr b. ʿAdī in any shape or guise and be on her guard.

Qaṣīr said to ʿAmr b. ʿAdī, "Cut off my nose, beat my back and leave her to me." To this ʿAmr replied, "I am not going to do that. This is not what you deserve from me." Qaṣīr now said, "If you would help me, you will be clear of blame"—this became a proverb.[369]

According to Ibn al-Kalbī: The father of al-Zabbā' built the tunnel for her and her sister; her sister's fortress was inside her city. ʿAmr said to Qaṣīr, "You are a man of discernment." But Qaṣīr cut off his own nose, and covered his back with wounds. So the Arabs say of a ruse, "Qaṣīr cut off his nose."[370] Al-Mutalammis refers to this in the verse:

For the sake of blood vengeance it was that
  Qaṣīr cut off his nose, and Bayhas plunged to death by sword.[371]

---

369. *khalli ʿannī idhan wa-khalāka dhamm.*

370. *jadaʿa anfahu Qaṣīr.*

371. On the pre-Islamic poet al-Mutalammis see Nicholson, *Literary history,* 107f. Bayhas lost seven brothers. To urge blood revenge, he wore the

Another version has "He desired death." 'Adī b. Zayd recited:[372]

Like Qaṣīr when he found nothing else,
Qaṣīr cut off his ears and nose for gratitude.

When Qaṣīr cut off his nose and injured his back he left, pretending that he was fleeing. He claimed that 'Amr did it all to him asserting that Qaṣīr had been plotting against his uncle Jadhīmah who was gullible about al-Zabbā'. Qaṣīr then proceeded to al-Zabbā'. [764] She was told that Qaṣīr was at the gate, and he was admitted by her order. Lo and behold, his nose had been cut off and his back carried the signs of beating. She said, "What is it that I see upon you, O Qaṣīr?" He replied, "'Amr b. 'Adī asserted that I had misled his uncle by extolling the trip to you, and that I had duped him and sided with you against him. He thus did to me what you see; I proceeded to you, as I knew that nobody would be more averse to him than you." She treated him kindly, honored him, and found in him some of the resoluteness, good sense, experience, and knowledge of royal affairs that she sought.

When he felt that she had become friendly with him and trusted him, he said to her, "I have much wealth in Iraq, including rarities, clothes, perfume. Send me to Iraq so that I may get my wealth and bring to you some of the clothes and rare garments, Iraqi varieties of perfumes and commodities. You will gain much profit and acquire objects useful to royalty, for Iraq's rarities are incomparable." He kept describing this to her in glowing terms, until she let him go and sent a caravan with him. She said, "Go to Iraq, sell what we have equipped you with there, and buy for us of their rarities in clothes and the like." Qaṣīr set out with what she gave him. He reached Iraq and came to al-Ḥīrah disguised. He was received by 'Amr b. 'Adī, to whom he told the story. Qaṣīr said, "Equip me with cloth, rarities, goods. Maybe God will deliver al-Zabbā' to us,

---

shirt instead of the trousers and vice versa. When asked about it, he said, "I wear garb for every occasion, be it pleasant or calamitous." See Nicholson, ibid.

372. A pre-Islamic Christian poet. See *GAS*, II, 778; *EI*², s.v. 'Adī b. Zayd; Nicholson, *Literary history*, 45–48.

and you will be able to exact your vengeance and slay your enemy." ʿAmr gave Qaṣīr what he needed, supplying him with all manner of clothes and other goods. Qaṣīr then returned to al-Zabbāʾ and displayed it all to her. She liked what she saw and was pleased, and her trust and confidence in him increased.
[765] She then equipped him with even more goods than on the first trip, and he again went to Iraq. He met ʿAmr b. ʿAdī and obtained from him what he thought would suit al-Zabbāʾ. He returned to Iraq on a third trip, reported to ʿAmr, and said, "Gather your trusted men and soldiers, and prepare for them sacks and haircloth"—according to Ibn al-Kalbī, Qaṣīr was the first to use sacks. "Load two men each in a sack on a camel," (he continued), "and sew the seams of the sack heads on the inside. When they are inside the city of al-Zabbāʾ, I shall station you at the gate of her tunnel; the men will come out of the sacks, shout at the city people, and kill whoever resists. If al-Zabbāʾ comes seeking the tunnel, strike her with the sword."

ʿAmr b. ʿAdī acted accordingly. He loaded the men in sacks, as suggested by Qaṣīr, and sent the camels off to al-Zabbāʾ, with men and arms. When they were close to her city, Qaṣīr came to her, announcing their arrival and the quantity of garments and rarities they were carrying to her. He asked her to come out to see the train of those camels and their load, saying, "I brought what shrieks and keeps silent"—this became a proverb.[373]

According to Ibn al-Kalbī: Qaṣīr hid during the day, and traveled at night; he was the first to do that. Al-Zabbāʾ came out and saw the camels almost collapsing under the heavy load. She said, "O Qaṣīr,

[766] What is the matter with the camels that their march is so slow?
Do they carry stone or iron?
Or solid cold lead?"

The camels entered the city until the last passed by the gatekeeper. He was a Nabatean holding an ox-goad. With it he prodded the sacks near him; the prod hit the waist of a man in

373. *jiʾtu bi-mā ṣāʿa wa-ṣamata.*

the sack and the man broke wind. The gate-keeper became frightened and exclaimed in Nabataean,[374] *"Bishta be-saqqe,"* meaning "There is mischief in the sacks"—the phase became proverbial. When the camels reached midtown, they were made to kneel down. Qaṣīr had signaled to ʿAmr the gate of the tunnel, and had shown it to him. The men got out of the sacks and threw themselves upon the people of the city, attacking them with arms. ʿAmr b. ʿAdī stood at the gate of the tunnel. Al-Zabbāʾ rushed back to get into the tunnel but noticed ʿAmr standing there. She recognized him from the picture the painter had made. She sucked her seal-ring, which contained poison, and exclaimed, "By my own hand, not by yours, O ʿAmr"—the phrase became a proverb.[375] ʿAmr countered and, striking her with his sword, he killed her. After inflicting casualties among the city's people, ʿAmr returned to Iraq.

In his ode (*qaṣīdah*), ʿAdī b. Zayd referred to the story of Jadhīmah, and of Qaṣīr and al-Zabbāʾ, and how ʿAmr b. ʿAdī killed al-Zabbāʾ:

Were the abodes changed or obliterated?
    Did they become very antiquated or did they disintegrate . . . ? [767]

Al-Mukhabbal, that is, Rabīʿah b. ʿAwf al-Saʿdi[376] recited:

O ʿAmr, I longed to join you,
    and for each longing to join there is separation.
Nay, how often have I seen time parting.
    those whose inclination is not to part.
Good luck had al-Zabbāʾ, she built herself
    abodes and fountains with tunnels,
Gentle-paced, fine-necked camels from the people of Dūmah
    carried prosperous life to her, devoid of hardship.
Until they were scattered by a shining sword,
    violence flashing like a blade.

---

374. This is in Aramaic.
375. *bi-yadī, lā bi-yadika yā ʿAmr.*
376. On the sixth-century poet, ʿAdi b. Zayd see *EI*² I 196. On the seventh-century poet al-Mukhabbal see *GAS* II, 201ff.

And Abū Ḥudhayfah, on the day he and his men were in straits,
pressed by the vortex cleft, battle turmoil at Ufāq;
With him Maʿadd and the ʿIbād and the Ṭayyiʾ,
and among the troops squadrons and companies of men.
He bestowed excellent and comely animals around him
to a troop; their bodies seemed released.
Then there came upon him an hour when he had no escape from fate;
that seemed to be on the day of his final destiny,
a gift whose vessel was turned to spill.

An Arab poet said:

We slew Faqḥal and Ibn Rāʾin and uprooted al-Zabbāʾs plant with reaping hook.
When the caravans arrived, she said, "Is it solid weight of date, or iron and stone."

[768] ʿAbd Bājir, whose name was Bahrā, was one of the proto-Arabs. They formed ten tribes (*ḥayy*): ʿĀd, Thamūd, ʿAmālīq, Ṭasm, Jadīs, Umaym, al-Mūd, Jurhum, Yaqṭan and al-Silf—al-Silf was included in the Ḥimyar:[377]

May your foot ride from the calamity.
You rode a camel [that was] not low
Upon the ʿArāqī in Ṣafā of al-Ṭawī.
If you be angry, be angry with the unwalled well,
And blame the chief, ʿAmr b. ʿAdī.

After Jadhīmah, the kingship fell to his sister's son ʿAmr b. ʿAdī b. Naṣr b. Rabīʿah b. al-Ḥārith b. Mālik b. ʿAmr b. Numārah b. Lakhm. The latter was the first Arab king to settle in al-Ḥīrah, and the first of the Arab kings in Iraq whom the people of al-Ḥīrah glorified in their writings, and to whom they are related. They are the kings of Naṣr's house. ʿAmr b. ʿAdī continued his reign until his death at the age of 120. He ruled as an autocrat who raided and seized booty. Missions waited on him throughout his long reign. However, he would not recognize

377. See *EI*^{2}, s.v. ʿĀd. Al-Mūd may be suggested by Gen. 10:26, and Umaym by Gen. 25:4. See *EI*^{2} I 450 on ʿAmr b. ʿAdī.

the regional princes of Iraq, nor did they recognize him. This continued to the rise of Ardashīr b. Bābak among the Persians. [769]

What we mentioned here about Jadhīmah and his nephew ʿAmr b. ʿAdī, flowed from our previous discussion of the kings of the Yaman whose reigns were not orderly. A chieftain among them was ruler over his province (*mikhlāf*) and region (*maḥjar*) only, not beyond that. If any of them deviated from this, or distinguished himself and went beyond this limitation by advancing well beyond his province, then it was due rather to his personality and not entrenched rule, or ancestry and progeny. It was similar to what happens to some exceptional bandit who raids district after district, surprising the people, but when pursued, he shows no stability. Such was the case of the rulers of the Yaman. One after the other would sometimes emerge from his province and region, and gain something on his march, but he would then rush home in fear of pursuit. No one would show allegiance to him, other than the people of his province, nor would they pay him taxes. ʿAmr b. ʿAdī, Jadhīmah's nephew, whose story we have recounted, became a ruler (in the same way) as his progeny did, that is, in the fashion practiced by the Arabs in the environs of Iraq and the *bādiyah* of the Hijāz.[378] They became rulers because the Persian kings employed them for this purpose, relying on them to keep the adjacent Arabs under control. This continued until Abarwīz b. Hurmuz killed al-Nuʿmān b. al-Mundhir, and transferred these functions to others. [770]

Regarding this we discussed the story of Jadhīmah and ʿAmr b. ʿAdī. We did this as we wanted to continue the complete history of the Persian kings, and to confirm (*istashhada*) what has been told about them, insofar as we are able to do so. The story of the family (*āl*) of Naṣr b. Rabīʿah,[379] and those rulers and governors who served the Persian kings in securing the frontier Arabs in the *bādiyah* of Iraq, is known and recorded among the

378. *Bādiyah* signifies countryside, wilderness, area of nomadism. See *EI*² supplement, s.v. al-bādiya. Parvīz b. Hurmuz abolished the kingdom of al-Ḥīrah in A.D. 602.

379. For Naṣr, an ancestor of a ruling family in al-Ḥīrah, see Rothstein, *Dynastie der Laḫmiden*, 39.

people of al-Ḥīrah. It is known in their churches and recorded in their writings.

According to Hishām b. Muḥammad al-Kalbī: From al-Ḥīrah's churches I used to obtain data about the Arabs, the genealogy of the family of Naṣr b. Rabīʿah, the dates of their service to the Persian emperors and the chronicle of their years. For in those churches is a record of their kingdom and all their affairs.

As for Ibn Ḥumayd, he gave us a different version concerning the offspring of Naṣr b. Rabīʿah and their migration to Iraq. His version was different from that of Hishām and from the account we received on the authority of Salamah—Ibn Isḥāq—some scholars. Ibn Ḥumayd b. Rabīʿah b. Naṣr al-Lakhmī had a vision. We shall mention it later when discussing Ethiopian power and their occupation of the Yaman. We shall also mention the interpretation of the dream by Saṭīḥ and Shiqq, and their response to his vision. Ibn Ḥumayd then mentioned in this report of his: It occurred to Rabīʿah b. Naṣr, after questioning Saṭīḥ and Shiqq and obtaining their reply, that what those two had said depended on the Ethiopians.[380] He equipped his sons and the people of his house to enable them to
[771] move to Iraq to improve their lot. Rabīʿah wrote on their behalf to a Persian called King Shapūr (Sābūr) b. Khurrazād, whereupon the king settled them in al-Ḥīrah.[381] Among the progeny of Rabīʿah b. Naṣr was al-Nuʿmān, the king of al-Ḥīrah, that is, al-Nuʿmān b. al-Mundhir b. al-Nuʿmān b. al-Mundhir b. ʿAmr b. ʿAdī b. Rabīʿah b. Naṣr.[382] This is according to the genealogy and learning of the people of the Yaman.

---

380. Rothstein, *Dynastie der Lahmiden*, 30–40, 50ff. The South Arabian version indicates that a king of the Yaman, Rābiʿah b. Naṣr, had a dream which was interpreted by two sages, Saṭīḥ and Shiqq, as referring to an Ethiopian invasion. This started a migration to the north. Hishām b. al-Kalbī indicates another tradition, that Arab royalty had migrated northwards even before the Lakhmids. The newcomers established a federation (*ḥilf*) with the indigenous population. The Lakhmid royalty was thus incorporated into the local dynasty. It would appear that these events took place in the third century A.D.

381. That is Shāpūr VII, ca. A.D. 240–272. See Nöldeke, *Geschichte*, 25, n. 7.

382. Al-Nuʿmān b. Mundhir ruled in al-Ḥīrah in the years A.D. 592–604. See the chronological table in S. Smith, *BSOAS*, 16 (1954), 425–468 (for the table, 430).

Ṭasm and Jadīs[383]

Says Abū Jaʿfar:
We shall now discuss the Ṭasm and Jadīs as their history also falls within the period of the regional princes. The extinction of the Jadīs was brought about by Ḥassān b. Tubbaʿ, as stated above in the account of the *tubba*ʿs of Ḥimyar who were contemporaries of the Persian kings.

According to Hishām b. Muḥammad, and also, Ibn Ḥumayd —Salamah—Ibn Isḥhāq and other Arab scholars: I was told that the Ṭasm and Jadīs were among the dwellers of al-Yamāmah.[384] At the time, al-Yamāmah was a most fertile and highly cultivated land, a land most prosperous, with a variety of fruit, wondrous orchards, and tall castles. They were ruled by a ruler of the Ṭasm, a wicked and tyrannical king; nothing deterred him from his capriciousness. His name was ʿAmlūq, and he mistreated and humiliated the Jadīs. One of his acts of tyranny and humiliation against them was his command that no virgin of the Jadīs should be given to her husband until she had been brought to be deflowered by the king. A man of the Jadīs, al-Aswad b. Ghifār said to the chieftains of his people, "You see the shame and humiliation we suffer. Dogs would [772]

383. See above, n. 339.
384. For al-Yamāmah in Arabia see Yāqūt, *Muʿjam*, s.v., where a detailed account of the land as well as a version of the present story is given.

loathe and resent it. Follow me, for I am calling upon you to rise to the occasion (*ʿizz al-dahr*) and reject the humiliation." They asked, "How is that?" He answered, "I shall prepare a party for the king and his people. When they come, we shall rise against them with our swords. I shall deal with him, and slay him, and each of you will turn against his dinner companion." They agreed unanimously, whereupon he prepared a party and ordered his people to unsheath their swords and hide them in the sand. He said, "When the guests arrive, strutting in their finery, pick up your swords, and attack them before they take their seats; slay the leaders, for, having slain them, the underlings will be of no account." The king arrived and was slain, as were the leaders. Then the men attacked the underlings and wiped them out. A man of the Ṭasm, Riyāḥ b. Murrah by name, fled, and came to Ḥassān b. Tubbaʿ appealing for help. Ḥassān, at the head of the Ḥimyar, set out, and when he had covered one third of the distance to al-Yamāmah, Riyāḥ said, "Bless you. I have a married sister among the Jadīs. Her name is al-Yamāmah. Nobody upon earth has better vision than she. She will notice a rider from the distance of a three-night ride. I am wary lest she warn the people of your approach. Therefore, command each and every one of your men to cut down a tree, hold it in front of him, and proceed with the tree in his hand." Ḥassān gave the command. His men complied with the command, and then he proceeded.[385]

But al-Yamāmah looked out and noticed them, so she said to the Jadīs, "The Ḥimyar are on the march." They said, "What is it that you see?" She replied, "I see a man upon a tree, biting into a shoulder, or mending his shoe." They did not believe
[773] her. Yet it was as she said. In the morning, Ḥassān struck. He wiped them out and devastated their country, razing their castles and fortresses. (The region known as) al-Yamāmah was called, at the time, Jaww and al-Qaryah. Al-Yamāmah, the daughter of Murrah, was now brought to Ḥassān, whereupon he ordered that her eyes be gouged out. They found black veins in them. He said to her, "What is this black stuff in your veins?" She replied, "It is a tiny black stone called antimony

385. See Nicholson, *Literary history*, 25.

[*ithmīd*] which I used to color the eyelids." They say she was the first person to use antimony to color the eyelids. Ḥassān then ruled that Jaww should be called al-Yamāmah.

Arab poets spoke of Ḥassān and this expedition of his. Thus al-Aʿshā said:[386]

Be like her who when her visitor could not yet be seen,
gave him from afar a frightened glance.
No woman with her vision arose
to see the truth; like the truthful soothsayer in his rhymed prose,
She turned an eye unerring
as the mirage was floating over Ra's al-Kalb and rising.
She said, 'I see a man [biting] a shoulder blade in his palm
or adjusting a shoe; woe to me, whichever he did.'
But they believed her not, and in the morning they were overwhelmed
by Ḥassān spreading trap-ropes and death.
They forced the people of Jaww from their abodes; [774]
they destroyed the tall structures, razing them to the ground.

Also Namīr b. Tawlab al-ʿUklī recited:[387]

Have you not asked about ʿĀdiyāʾ and his house,
the wine and the vinegar, the inevitable ups and downs,
And about their maiden, ʿAnz, on the evening when she perceived
and heard from afar through space.
She said, "I see a man whose palm is turning
a tree-root, while Jaww is secure, devoid of fear."
She saw the vanguard of the army and in front of it
the run of the camels to the shout for Tubbaʿ,
As if a good man of the Jaww people, at the morning drink,
were smitten by the diluted poison potion.
They were as the most prosperous you ever saw,
yet began to rob the well-equipped traveller's provision.

---

386. See Ḥusayn, *Diwan*, 153 n. 13; also *EI*², s.v. al-Aʿshā; Nicholson, *Literary history*, 123ff.

387. For this seventh-century poet see *GAS*, II, 222ff.

Said al-Yamāmah, "Carry me standing [upon the camel].
I shall be slain if you send the camel to me kneeling."

Ḥassān b. Tubbaʿ who struck down the Jadīs is Dhū Muʿāhir, who was Tubbaʿ b. Tubbaʿ Tubān Asʿad b. Abī Karib b. Malkīkarib b. Tubbaʿ b. Aqran. He was the father of Tubbaʿ b. Ḥassān
[775] who—so the people of the Yaman assert—came to Mecca and covered the Kaʿbah. The ravine of al-Maṭābikh (the Kitchens) was given this name because he had set up the kitchens there and fed the people. Ajyād (Long Necks) was called thus because his cavalry was there.[388] He came to Yathrib,[389] alighted at a house called today the ruling house, and slew a great number of Jews because of a complaint made to him by the Aws and the Khazraj about the Jews being bad neighbors. He sent his son Ḥassān to Sind, and Samir Dhū al-Janāḥ to Khurāsān, and instructed them to proceed to China. Samir passed Samarqand, besieged it until he conquered it, and slew its warriors taking captives and booty. Then he proceeded to China where he met Ḥassān. Some people of the Yaman assert that those two died there; others claim that they came back to Tubbaʿ with wealth and booty.

Among the events taking place in the period of the regional princes is the event mentioned in the Qurʾān about the young men who took refuge in the cave, those whose ears were smitten.

---

388. For these locations see Yāqūt, *Muʿjam*, IV, 561, 622, 623.
389. That is, al-Madīnah before the migration of the Prophet Muḥammad.

The Story of the Men of the Cave[390]

They were youths, as God described them in the glorious Qur'ān, who believed in the Lord. God said to his prophet Muḥammad, "Or do you think the Men of the Cave and al-Raqīm were among Our signs a wonder?"[391] Al-Raqīm is the inscription engraved on a tablet by the people to which the youths belonged, in order to tell their story. They put it on the gate of the cave to which the youths had escaped, or carved it on the rock in which they had sought refuge, or wrote it on a tablet placed in a coffer that was left nearby when the youths took to the cave. The number of the youths, they say on the authority of Ibn ʿAbbās, was seven and there was a dog with them. [776]

According to Ibn Bashshār—ʿAbd al-Raḥmān—Isrā'īl—Simāk—ʿIkrimah—Ibn ʿAbbās: "And none knows them, except a few."[392] I am of the few. They were seven.

According to Bishr—Yazīd—Saʿīd—Qatādah, Ibn ʿAbbās used to say: I am of those few whom God made an exception; they were seven, their dog was the eighth.

---

390. This is based on the Christian story of the seven sleepers. The legend arose around the fourth century persecution of the Christians, and is centered on Ephesus. It derives its Islamic name from Qur'ān 18, which is entitled "The Cave" (*al-Kahf*). The sleepers are known as *aṣḥāb al-kahf*. See *EI*², s.v. Aṣḥāb al-kahf.

391. Qur'ān 18:4.

392. Qur'ān 18:21.

Concerning the name of one of them, that is, the one empowered to buy food for them, the divine words mention that they said when they awoke from their slumber, "Now send forth one of you with this silver to the city, and let him look for which of them has the purest food, and bring you provision thereof." According to ʿAbdallāh b. Muḥammad al-Zuhrī—Sufyān—Muqātil: "Now send forth one of you with this silver for the city," refers to the one named Yamnīkhā.

According to Ibn Isḥāq—Ibn Jumayd—Salamah: His name was Yamlīkhā. Ibn Isḥāq used to say: The number of the youths was eight, their dog was accordingly the ninth of the group.

[777] According to Ibn Ḥumayd—Salamah—Ibn Isḥāq, who used to give their names saying: One of them, the oldest, who spoke to the king in the name of the group was Maksimilinā; another was Mahsimilinā; the third, Yamlīkhā; the fourth, Martūs; the fifth, Kaṣūṭūnas; the sixth, Bīrūnas; the seventh, Rasmūnas(?) the eighth, Baṭūnas; and the ninth, Qālūs. They were young.

According to Ibn Ḥumayd—Salamah—Ibn Isḥāq—ʿAbd allāh b. Abī Najīḥ—Mujāhid: I was told that some of them, because of their youth had teeth that shone like silver. They were of a people that worshiped Roman idols, but God put them on the true path to Islam. According to many of our early learned masters, their faith was the faith of Jesus.

According to Ibn Ḥumayd—al-Ḥakam b. Bashīr—ʿAmr, that
[778] is, Ibn Qays al-Mulāʾī: The Men of the Cave and al-Raqīm were the youths who practiced the religion of Jesus, the son of Mary, that is, they practiced Islam while their king was an unbeliever.

Some assert that their story and withdrawal to the cave took place before Christ, that Christ told his people about them, and that God awakened them from their sleep after Christ's ascension. That is, God awakened them during the interval (*fatrah*) between Christ and Muḥammad.[393] God knows best how it happened. Muslim scholars are agreed that it took place after Christ. No scholar vested in antiquity will deny that it happened in the period of the regional princes. At that time there

393. See EI^2, s.v. Fatra.

was a king (named) Decius, an idol-worshiper, it is said. Word reached him that the youths were opposed to his faith, and he set out to search for them. To keep their faith they fled to a mountain. I was told by Ibn Jumayd—Salamah—Ibn Isḥāq—ʿAbdallāh b. Abī Najīḥ—Mujāhid—Ibn ʿAbbās: the name of that mountain was Nīḥlūs.

According to al-Ḥasan b. Yaḥyā—ʿAbd al-Razzāq—Muʿammar—Ismāʿīl b. Sadūs—Wahb b. Munabbih: the reason for their faith, and the subsequent religious disagreement with their people was as follows. An apostle of Jesus came to the [779] city of the Men of the Cave. He sought to enter the city but was told that at the gate of the city there was an idol, and that nobody could enter unless he prostrated himself before the idol. Not wishing to enter the city, he came to a bathhouse that was close by. He worked there as a wage earner for the owner. As the latter noticed that the man was a blessing to his bathhouse, he gave him sustenance, observed him and became friendly with him. Several youths from the city became attached to the worker. The apostle began to tell them about heaven and earth, and the life to come. He spoke to them until they began to share his beliefs. He would tell the owner, "Tonight do not disturb my prayer." So it went until the son of the king came with a woman to the bathhouse. The apostle rebuked him, saying to the prince, "You are the king's son and you come with this harlot." The prince was ashamed and left, only to come another time. The apostle upbraided him again and cursed him and scolded him, but the prince disregarded it. He entered, and the woman entered with him, and both died in the bath. It was reported to the king, "The bath attendant slew thy son." The attendant was sought in vain, for he had fled. The king asked, "Who was acquainted with him?" The youths were mentioned and then sought, so they left the city. They passed by a friend in a field who was in a similar position. They mentioned that the search for them was on. The friend joined them; with him was his dog. At night they took refuge in the cave, saying, "We [780] shall spend the night here, and in the morning, God willing, you will decide what to do." But their ears were smitten. The king and his men came forth in pursuit of them, and found them inside the cave. But whenever anyone wanted to enter, he was scared away, and nobody was able to enter. Somebody said to the king, "Is it not true that if you could seize them, you would kill them?" The king replied, "Certainly." The man suggested, "Then erect a gate over the cave, and leave them inside to die of thirst and hunger." This was done.

Much time had passed since that gate was built over the cave, when a shepherd was overtaken by rain near the cave. He thought, "What if I opened this cave and let my flock in to protect it from the rain." He kept trying until he succeeded. The next morning, God returned life to their bodies and the youths awoke. They sent one from among them with silver to buy food for them, but whenever he arrived at a gate of their city, he saw something he did not recognize. Finally he came to a man, and said, "Sell me food for these coins." The man asked, "Where did you get these coins?" He said, "Yesterday, with friends, I left the city. We were overtaken by night, but in the morning they sent me [for food]." The seller said, "These coins are of the age of king so and so; but how did you get them?"

He brought the youth before the king, who was a righteous ruler. The king asked, "Where did you get these silver coins?" The youth replied, "My friends and I left the city yesterday, and night overtook us in such and such cave; then [in the morning] my friends ordered me to buy food for them." The king now asked, "Where are your friends?" And the youth replied, "In the cave." They went with him and came to the gate of the cave, whereupon the youth said, "Let me go in to my friends first." When they saw him approach, both he and they "were smitten upon their ears." Anybody who (tried to)
[781] enter was frightened away, and people were unable to go in. So they built a church there and made it a sanctuary for prayer.

According to al-Ḥasan b. Yaḥyā—ʿAbd al-Razzāq—Muʿammar—Qatādah—ʿIkrimah: The men of the cave were Roman princes for whom God had provided the true faith (Islām). They stood alone in their faith, dissenting from their people until they reached the cave, where God struck them upon their ears. They spent ages there (in the cave) while their community (*ummah*) perished and a righteous (Muslim) community took its place, whose king was a true believer (Muslim).

There was disagreement concerning spirit and body. Some

maintained that all would be revived in body and spirit; others asserted that they would be revived in spirit while the bodies would be consumed by the earth, and would disintegrate. The king was exasperated by the dispute. He got up, put on haircloth, sat on dust, and prayed to God, "Oh, Lord, You see the dispute of these men; send them a sign to make it clear." God sent the men of the cave, and they sent one of their number to buy food for them. He entered the marketplace, but he did not recognize the faces, although he knew the streets. He saw faith manifest in the city. Walking furtively, he came to a man who sold food, but when the seller saw the silver coins, he did not recognize them.

The seller remarked, "I thought they were the light quarters, that is, the small change." The youth said, "Is not your king such and such?" "But no," said the seller, "Our king is so and so." And so it went on until they came before the king. The king interrogated the youth, who told him about his friends. The king then sent for the men involved in the dispute. He assembled them and said, "You disagreed concerning spirit and body. Now the Almighty has sent you a sign. Here is a man of [782]
the people of the late king [anonymous]." The youth said, "Let us go to my friends." The king and his men set out on the road and reached the cave. The youth said, "Let me enter to join my friends." But when he saw them, God smote upon his ears and their ears. The king and his men were kept waiting. Finally, they entered and beheld perfect bodies but with no life in them. The king exclaimed, "This is a God-sent sign unto you."

According to Qatādah: While on a raid, Ibn ʿAbbās and Ḥabīb b. Maslamah passed by the cave and, lo and behold, there were bones in it. A man said, "These are the bones of the men of the cave." Ibn ʿAbbās replied, "Their bones disappeared over three hundred years ago."

Jonah Son of Amittai[394]

According to Abū Ja'far: In the period of the regional princes belongs the story of Jonah, son of Amittai. He is said to have been from a town in the region of Mosul, called Nineveh. His people worshiped idols, so God sent Jonah to them with an injunction against this worship and a command to repent, to turn to God from their unbelief, and to believe in but one God. What happened to him and to those to whom he was sent is told in the Qur'ān. It says, "Why was there never a city that believed, and profited from its belief, except the people of Jonah? When they believed, We removed from them the chastisement of degradation in this present life, and We gave unto them enjoyment for a time."[395] It also says, "And Dhū al-Nūn, when he went forth enraged and thought that We would have no
[783] power over him; then he called out in the darkness, 'There is no God but Thou. Glory be to Thee! I have done evil!' So We answered him and delivered him out of grief; even so do We deliver the believers."[396]

The early scholars of the community of our Prophet Muḥam-

394. Yūnus b. Mattā is the biblical Jonah. For Jewish legends of Jonah, see Ginzberg, *Legends*, IV, 245–253; VI, 348, 352. For the Qur'ānic account see *SEI*, s.v. Yūnus. In the Qur'ān Jonah is also called Dhū al-Nūn or Ṣāḥib al-Ḥūt, that is, "the Whale Man."

395. Qur'ān 10:97f.

396. Qur'ān 21:87ff.

mad differed about how Jonah had defied the Lord, thinking the Lord would have no power over him, and about the time of the event. Some maintained that the reference was to the time before he called upon the people to whom he was sent, and before he gave them the Lord's message. The point is that the prophet was commanded to proceed to the people to whom he was sent when divine chastisement was in store for them, to announce to them how the Lord kept chastisement from them so that they might repent their evil practices hateful to the Lord. The prophet asked to be excused from the mission but the Lord did not grant a respite, so the prophet was angry with the Lord for hurrying him to execute His command, and for rejecting the request for a respite.

Those Who Held This View

According to al-Ḥārith—al-Ḥasan al-Ashyab—Abū Hilāl Muḥammad b. Sulaym—Shahr b. Ḥawshab: Jonah was visited by the angel Gabriel who told him, "Go to the people of Nineveh and warn them that chastisement is imminent." Jonah then said, "I shall seek a riding beast." Gabriel replied, "The command is too urgent." Now Jonah said, "I shall look for footwear." Gabriel again replied, "The command is too urgent." Angrily Jonah proceeded to the ship and boarded it, but it stalled, moving neither forward nor backward.

Then they drew lots, and the lot fell to Jonah. The whale (*al-ḥūt*) came wagging its tail. It was divinely announced, "Whale, O Whale! We shall not make Jonah into your sustenance! Rather We make you a retreat for him, a sanctuary." The whale swallowed Jonah, and proceeded with him from that spot to Ubullah. From there it proceeded up the Tigris, until it [784]
deposited Jonah at Nineveh.

According to al-Ḥārith—Al-Ḥasan—Abū Hilāl—Shahr b. Hawshab—Ibn ʿAbbās: The mission of Jonah took place after the whale had ejected him. Others say that it took place after he called upon those to whom he had been sent to follow the divine instruction, and after he had delivered to them the Lord's message. He threatened them with the onset of the divine chastisement at an appointed time; but he departed as they did not repent, nor did they consider obeying God and believing in Him. But when divine chastisement cast its shadow upon the people, it enveloped them as described in the Qur'ān. Then they repented, and turned to God; and God lifted the chastisement. Jonah heard of their deliverance, and the lifting of the chastisement with which he had threatened them. Angered thereby, he said, "I threatened them but my threat was belied." He left, angry with the Lord, and refused to return to them, for they had denounced him as a liar.

Those Who Held This View

According to Ibn Ḥumayd—Salamah—Ibn Isḥāq—Yazīd b. Ziyād—ʿAbdallāh b. Abī Salamah—Saʿīd b. Jubayr—Ibn ʿAbbās: God sent Jonah to the people of his town, but they rejected his message and ignored it. When they acted thus, God
[785] revealed to him, "I shall send upon them chastisement on such and such day; so leave them then." Jonah announced to his people the divine chastisement in store for them. They said, "Observe him; if he leaves you, then by God, his threat will come true." On the eve of chastisement, the people set out warily behind Jonah. They left the city for an open space and separated the animals from their young ones. Then they cried out to God for help. They appealed to Him to annul his decision, and he granted them that annulment. Jonah was expecting news about the city and its people. A passer-by told him what the people of the city had done. "What did the people of the city do?" asked Jonah. The passer-by replied, "This is what they did. As soon as their prophet left them, they understood that he spoke the truth when he threatened them with the chastisement; so they left their city for an open space, and separated all the mothers from their young ones, and cried out to God for help. They repented, their repentance was accepted, and chastisement was averted." Upon hearing this, Jonah said angrily, "By God, I shall never return to them as a liar. I threatened them with chastisement on a certain day, then it was averted from them." He departed, angry with the Lord, and fell into the devil's snare.

According to al-Muthannā b. Ibrāhīm—Isḥāq b. al-Ḥajjāj—ʿAbdallāh b. Abī Jaʿfar—his father—al-Rabīʿ: I heard from a man who knew the Qur'ān by heart in the days of 'Umar b. al-Khaṭṭāb.[397] He was telling about the people of Jonah and how Jonah warned his people and was not believed. (According to him) Jonah told them chastisement would strike them, and (then he) left them. When they saw this and (understood) that chastisement enveloped them, they left their dwellings and ascended to an elevated spot. They prayed fervently to the Lord, calling out to him in sincere supplication, so that he might defer chastisement from them and return unto them their messenger. That is why it says, "Why was there never a city that believed, and profited from its belief, except the people of Jonah, when they believed? We removed from them the chastisement of degradation in this present life, and We gave unto them enjoyment for a time."[398] In no city overcome by chastisement was the chastisement revoked, except in the case of the people of Jonah. But Jonah did not see it that way; he bore a grudge against the Lord and left angrily. Thinking that the Lord would not be able to reach him, Jonah embarked on a ship. The people of the ship were struck by a wind-swept storm and said, "It is on account of the transgression of one of you." Jonah, recognizing that it was his fault, said, "It is my transgression; throw me into the sea." They refused, until after they cast lots, and Jonah "cast lots and was of the condemned."[399] He told them, "I informed you that this was my fault." But they refused to throw him into the sea until they cast lots for the third time. He was condemned again. When he saw that, he threw himself into the sea, at night. [786]

The whale swallowed him, "then he called out in the darkness [recognizing his sin]: 'There is no God but Thou, Glory be to Thee! I have done evil.'"[400] He had done righteous work previously, and God revealed about him, "Now, had he not been of those who glorify God, he would have tarried in its belly until the day they shall be raised."[401] The point is that

397. That is, the second Islamic caliph, who ruled in the years A.D. 634–644.

398. Qur'ān 10:97f.

399. Qur'ān 37:141.

400. Qur'ān 21:87.

401. Qur'ān 37:143–144.

the righteous deed raises man when he stumbles. (As it is written:) "And We cast him upon the wilderness and he was sick."[402] Jonah was cast on the seashore, and God caused a tree of gourds to grow. It is said the tree of gourds was a pump-
[787] kin which dripped milk until his strength returned unto him. Then one day he returned to the tree, and found it had dried up. He grieved and wept over it. But he was reproved and told, "You have grieved and wept over a tree, but you have not grieved over a hundred thousand or more whose death you have sought."

Then God extricated him from error, and made him one of the righteous. Jonah was commanded to go to his people and announce that God had forgiven them. Setting out for them, he encountered a shepherd whom he asked about his people, their situation and how they were. The shepherd told him they were well, and hoped that their prophet would return unto them. Jonah then said to him, "Say to them, 'I have met Jonah.'" The shepherd responded, "I cannot do so without a witness," whereupon Jonah pointed to a goat of the shepherd's flock, and said, "This one will witness for thee that thou hast met Jonah." At this, the shepherd asked, "What else?" Jonah responded, "And this spot where thou art will witness for thee that thou hast met Jonah." The shepherd asked again, "What else?" Jonah now replied, "And this tree will witness for thee that thou hast met Jonah, and that the shepherd has returned to his people."

The shepherd announced to the people that he had met Jonah, but they did not believe him and plotted evil against him. He exclaimed, "Do not assault me until morning." When he awoke the next day, he led them to the spot where he had encountered Jonah. The shepherd appealed to the earth, and it announced to them that the shepherd had met Jonah. He asked the goat, and it told them that the shepherd had met Jonah. They appealed to the tree, and it told them that the shepherd had met Jonah. Later on, Jonah came to them. It says,[403]

402. Qur'ān 37:145.
403. Qur'ān 37:147–148.

"Then We sent him unto a hundred thousand or more, and they believed; so We gave them enjoyment for a while."

According to al-Ḥusayn b. ʿAmr b. Muḥammad al-ʿAnqarī —his father Isrāʾ īl—Abū Isḥāq—ʿAmr b. Maymūn al-Awdī [788]
—Ibn Masʿūd, who related to us at the treasury: Jonah had threatened his people with chastisement, and told them it would come upon them within three days. They separated every mother from her progeny, and then left. The people came to God and asked for His forgiveness, whereupon God withheld chastisement from them. Jonah went out early expecting chastisement but saw nothing. A liar without clear proof used to be put to death. Jonah therefore left in anger "and shouted in the darkness."[404] This refers to the darkness of the belly of the whale, the darkness of the night, and the darkness of the sea.

According to Ibn Ḥumayd—Salamah—Ibn Isḥāq—one who told him—ʿAbdallāh b. Rāfiʿ, the *mawlā* of the Prophet's spouse Umm Salamah—Abū Hurayrah: The Prophet said, "When God wanted Jonah to be detained in the whale's belly, God urged (*awḥā*) the whale, 'Take him, but do not scratch his flesh and do not break his bones.' The whale picked up Jonah and plunged to its dwelling in the sea. When it reached the bottom of the sea, Jonah heard a sound. He said to himself, 'What is that?' Then while Jonah was in the whale's belly God revealed to him, 'This is the sea fauna glorifying God.'"

Then Jonah, in the whale's belly, glorified God. The angels heard his glorification of God, and exclaimed, "Oh, Lord, we hear a faint voice in a strange land." God said, "That is my servant Jonah. He disobeyed Me, so I detained him in the whale's belly at sea." They exclaimed, "The righteous servant from whom every day and night a righteous deed rose to Thee?" God replied, "Yes." At this, they interceded for Jonah. The whale was thus ordered to cast him upon the shore. As God said,[405]
"And he was sick." His sickness, which is described in the [789]
Qurʾān, was like that of a newborn child. When the whale cast him upon the shore, his flesh and bones were bare.

According to Ibn Ḥumayd—Salamah—Ibn Isḥāq—Yazīd b.

---

404. Qurʾān 37:87.
405. Qurʾān 37:145.

Ziyād—ʿAbdallāh b. Abī Salamah—Saʿīd b. Jubayr—Ibn ʿAbbās: Out it went, that is, the whale (with Jonah), until it ejected Jonah onto the shore, and cast him up as if he were a newborn child fully preserved.

According to Yūnus—Ibn Wahb—Abū Ṣakhr—Ibn Qusayṭ—Abū Hurayrah: He was ejected naked, and God made a vegetable cover (*yaqtīnah*) to grow upon him. We said, "O Abū Hurayrah, what was that vegetable cover?" He replied, "The gourd tree." God prepared for it female antelopes and other animals that eat the grass of the earth or the soft sod. They would stray over it and quench its thirst with their milk every evening and morning until it grew.

The Sending by God of His Three Envoys

An event which also occurred in the days of the regional princes was (the arrival of the three envoys sent by God and) [790] mentioned in the divine revelation "Spin a parable for them—the inhabitants of the city, when the messengers came to it. When We sent unto them two men, they declared them liars, so We sent a third as reinforcement." They said, "We are assuredly messengers unto you."[406] Such are the verses in which their story is told in scripture.

But the early authorities differ about their story. Some say these three, whom God mentioned in these verses and whose story He told therein, were prophets and messengers. He had sent (them) to the Roman king Antiochus, and the city in which this king dwelled and to which God sent these envoys was Antioch.

Those Who Held This View

Concerning the story of the man of Sūrah YaSin (in the Qur'ān), according to Ibn Ḥumayd—Salamah—Muḥammad b. Isḥāq—from Ka'b al-Aḥbār and Wahb b. Munabbih al-Yamanī: There was a man of Antioch. Ḥabīb was his name, and he was a

406. The story is based on a legend of Christian origins. See *EI*[1], s.v. Yāsīn; *EI*[2], s.v. Anṭākiyā. For the Qur'ānic story see 36:13ff.

silk-maker. A sickly man, he early contracted leprosy. His home was near the farthest city gate. He was a believer and an alms-giver. The man used to take his earnings in the evening, so they say, and divide them in two piles; one he would use to feed his family, the other he would give away in alms. Neither his sickness, nor his work, nor his weakness concerned him, as his heart was pure and his character upright. In the city of Antioch, in which he lived, was one of the pharaohs, Antiochus, the son of Antiochus, an idol-worshiping polytheist.
[791] God sent the three envoys: Ṣādiq, Ṣadūq, and Shalūm. First, God sent to him and the people of his city two of the envoys, but the people declared them liars. Then God sent the third as reinforcement. Others say: no, they were of the apostles of Jesus, the son of Mary. They were not God's messengers but rather the messengers of Jesus. But as the mission by Jesus was upon the command of the Almighty, the mission was an extension of God's mission. So it says, "When We sent unto them two men, they declared them liars; so We sent a third as reinforcement."

Those Who Held This View

According to Bishr b. Muʿādh—Yazīd b. Zurayʿ—Saʿīd—Qatādah regarding the following passage: "Spin a parable for them—the inhabitants of the city, when the messengers came to it. When We sent unto them two men, they declared them liars; so We sent a third as reinforcement. They said, 'We are assuredly messengers unto you.'"[407] It was mentioned to us that Jesus, the son of Mary, sent two of the apostles to Antioch, a Roman city; but they were declared liars, so he sent a third as reinforcement. They said, "We are assuredly messengers," etc.

Returning to the version of Ibn Isḥāq: When the messengers appealed (to the king) calling upon him, in God's name, that is, when they carried out their divine order and denounced the city's religion and beliefs, the inhabitants said,[408] "We augur ill of you. If you do not desist, we will stone you, and a painful

407. Qur'ān 36:13–14.
408. Qur'ān 36:17–18.

chastisement will be inflicted upon you by us." The messengers told them, "Your augury is with you," that is, your deeds. "If you are reminded? But you are a prodigal people." When the king and the people decided to kill the envoys, the news reached Ḥabīb while he was at the farthest gate of the city. He [792]
came running to them, reminding them of God, and calling upon them to follow the messengers. He said,[409] "My people, follow the messengers! Follow those who ask no reward from you, those that are rightly-guided." That is, while they are advising you they will not ask for your possessions in return for their message of guidance to you, so follow them and you will be rightly-guided.

According to Bishr b. Muʿādh—Yazīd—Saʿīd—Qatādah: When he—meaning Ḥabīb—reached the messengers, he said, "do you ask a reward for this?" They said, "No." Then he said, "My people, follow the messengers, follow those who ask no reward from you, those that are rightly-guided."

Returning to the version of Ibn Isḥāq: He then appealed to them to desist from their idol-worship, disclosing to them his faith, and to worship the Lord; and he told them that only God had the power to make him profit or hurt him. Then he said, "And why should I not serve Him who created me, and unto whom you [too] shall be returned? What shall I take, apart from Him? . . . Behold, I believe your Lord; therefore hear me," that is, I believe in the Lord you deny, listen to my word. When he said that to them, they attacked him in unison and killed him. Because of his weakness and sickness they considered him of no consequence, and none came to his defense.[410]

According to Ibn Ḥumayd—Salamah—Ibn Isḥāq—one of his companions—ʿAbdallāh b. Masʿūd: They trampled him with their feet until his intestines came out through his back. God said to him, "Enter Paradise!"[411] He entered it while alive and prospering, as God removed worldly sickness, sadness, and disease. As he attained God's mercy, Paradise, and favor, he exclaimed, "Ah, would that my people had knowledge [793]

409. Qur'ān 36:21–24.
410. Ibid.
411. Qur'ān 36:25.

that My Lord has forgiven me, and that he has placed me among the honored."[412]

God was so angry that they considered him of no consequence that He left none of the people alive; He brought revenge upon them speedily for having considered Ḥabīb easy prey. God said, "And We did not send down upon his people, after him, any host out of heaven; nor would We do so." That is, He dismissed acting through any heavenly mediator, meaning the matter was slight for Him. "It was only one Cry and lo and behold, they were silent and still." Thus God brought perdition upon that king and the people of Antioch. They became extinct from the face of earth, without a (surviving) remnant.[413]

According to Ibn Ḥumayd—Salamah—Ibn Isḥāq—al-Ḥasān b. ʿUmārah—al-Ḥakam b. ʿUtaybah—Miqsam Abū al-Qāsim, the *mawlā* of ʿAbdallāh b. al-Ḥārith b. Nawfal—Mujāhid—ʿAbdallāh b. ʿAbbās, who used to say: The name of the man of the Sūrah YaSin in the Qur'ān was Ḥabīb; his leprosy was well advanced.

According to Ibn Bashshār—Mu'ammal—Sufyān—ʿĀṣim al-Aḥwal—Abū Makhlad: The name of the man in Sūrah YaSin of the Qur'ān was Ḥabīb b. Marī.

---

412. Qur'ān 36:36.
413. Qur'ān 36:27–28.

The Story of Samson[414]

Among the stories from the time of the regional princes is (that of Samson). He was an inhabitant of one of the Roman cities (*qaryah*), who had been rightly-guided by God for his integrity. However, his people were idol worshipers. This is what happened to him and them, as told by Ibn Ḥumayd—Salamah—Ibn Isḥāq—al-Mughīrah b. Abī Labīd—Wahb b. Munabbih al-Yamanī: Samson was a righteous man (Muslim) among them, and his mother made him a Nazarite. He was a man from one of their cities where the people were idolatrous unbelievers. His abode was a few miles away. Samson would raid them alone, fighting them in God's name, satisfying his needs at their expense while killing, taking captive, and seizing possessions. He would meet them with only the jawbone of a camel. If they engaged one another in combat and he became tired and thirsty, sweet water would burst from the stone at Lehi.[415] He would then drink of it to quench his thirst, and he thus regained his strength. Neither iron nor anything else could bind him. In such fashion, he kept fighting them in God's name. Raiding them, he obtained from them what he needed. [794]

They could do nothing against him until they said, "We will

414. See Judges 13–16.

415. In Judges 15:19, this is a place name; in 15:15, it means the jawbone (of an ass).

not get at him except through his wife." They came to his wife, offered her a reward, and she said, "Yes, I shall tie him for you." They gave her a strong rope, and said, "When he is asleep, tie his hand to his neck, so that we may come and take him." When he was asleep, she tied his hand to his neck with that rope. But when he awoke, he pulled it with his hand, and it fell off his neck. He said to her, "Why did you do this?" Said she, "To try thus your strength. I have never seen anybody like you." Then she sent them a message, "I tied him with the rope,
[795] but it was in vain." So they sent an iron ring. They said, "When he is asleep, snap it on his neck." While he slept she put it on his neck, then snapped it. But when he awoke, he pulled it, and it fell from his hand and neck. He said to her, "Why did you do it?" She replied, "To test your strength; I have seen nobody like you, O Samson. Is there nothing in the world [with which] to vanquish you?" "No, except one thing," he said. She asked, "What is it?" He replied, "I am not going to tell you," but she continued to nag him about it. He had much hair, (and finally) he told her, "My mother made me a Nazarite, and I will never be vanquished nor seized except through my hair." When he fell asleep, she tied his hand and his neck with the hair on his head. This fastened him. She sent for the people and they came and seized him. They lopped off his nose and ears, gouged out his eyes, and placed him before the people amidst the pillars of the minaret. Their king and people were watching the minaret in order to observe Samson and to see what would be done to him. As he stood there, amidst their jeering, Samson prayed to God to give him strength against them. He was commanded to hold on to two pillars of the minaret, above which were the king and the men with him, and to pull at the pillars. This he did. God had restored to him his sight and the amputated parts of his body, and the minaret came crashing down on the king and the people standing there. They all perished.

The Story of Jirjīs[416]

They say that Jirjīs was a righteous servant of God among the people of Palestine, and that he lived at the time of the last apostles of Jesus. He was a merchant who profited from his trade, a man of independent means who assisted the unfortunate. He supplied himself for a journey to a king in Mosul, so [796]
we were told by Ibn Ḥumayd—Salamah—Ibn Isḥāq—Wahb b. Munabbih and other learned men. In Mosul, Dacianus (Dadhāna) was king over all of Syria. He was a fierce tyrant over whom only God could prevail. Jirjīs was a righteous man of the people of Palestine. He was a believer who was concealing his faith among a group of like-minded righteous people who concealed their faith. They had known the last of the apostles,

416. For the story of the martyrdom of saint George, a Roman officer martyred under a cruel pagan ruler (Diocletian) early in the fourth century, see *EI*², s.v. Djirdjīs. The martyr is identified with Elijah and al-Khaḍir in the Islamic tale. Various pre-Islamic elements came to be incorporated into the story. The oldest versions are: (1) The Greek text (from southern Palestine); see Casson and Hettich, *Excavations at Nessana*, II, 123–142, with extensive bibliography; (2) The Syriac version; see Brooks, "Acts of Saint George," *Le Muséon* 38 (1925), 67–115; (3) The Latin text; see Cumont, "Légende de St. Georges"; (4) The Coptic and Ethiopic versions; see Wallis Budge, *George of Lydda*. See also Delahaye, *Légendes qrecques*, 45–46. The Arabic versions are discussed by Wallis Budge, op. cit., 26–66. A Muslim Arab version was published by Cheikho in *Al-Machriq* 10 (1907), 414–420. In this version Jirjīs is called a prophet.

heard them speak, and learned from them. Jirjīs was a very rich man, a great merchant and benefactor. Sometimes he would donate his wealth for charitable purposes until nothing of it remained and he would become poor; but then he would strike it rich again and his wealth would increase manifold. Such was his material position. He would desire wealth, acquire it, and amass it for charitable purposes. Were it not for that, he would have preferred poverty to riches. He was apprehensive of the rule of the unbelievers, fearful that they might hurt him on account of his faith, or that they might tempt him away from it.

He set out for the king of Mosul, carrying money which he intended to present to him, in order that the king should not empower any princes to rule under him. Jirjīs arrived as the king was holding court in the presence of the dignitaries and princes of his people. A large fire, and various other forms of torture, had been prepared to torture those opposed to him. Upon his order a statue called Apollo had been erected, and the people had to pass before it. Whoever did not bow to it was then cast into the fire and put through various tortures. When
[797] Jirjīs saw what was happening, he was horrified, and distressed. He thought of martyrdom, but God inspired in him anger and resistance. He thought of the money he had intended to present to the king. Instead, he divided it among his coreligionists until nothing was left. He did not want to oppose the king with money; he preferred to do it personally. His anger and resentment at their acme, he approached the king saying, "Know, that you are a slave owned by a master, and that you yourself own nothing directly or indirectly, and that above you is a Lord Who owns you and others. This Lord created and sustained you; he makes you live and die; he harms you and benefits you; and yet you propose to imitate what is created by Him? God said unto man, 'Be,' and he was.[417] Deaf, dumb, speechless and sightless, [an idol] can neither hurt nor benefit. It cannot help you at all to dispense with God. You decorate it with gold and silver and make it a temptation unto man. You worship it,

417. Qur'ān 3:15 and elsewhere. The next phrase is influenced by Qur'ān 2:17.

not God, and you force humans to worship it. You call it the Lord."

Jirjīs addressed the king in this fashion about the greatness and glory of God, and he denounced the idol and the senseless worship thereof. The king's answer was to ask him who he was and from where he came. Jirjīs replied, "I am a servant of God, and the son of a servant of God. I am a son of His community [*ummah*], the lowliest of His servants, and the most needy of His aid. I was created of dust and to dust I shall return." He told the king what had brought him, and called upon the former to worship God and to repudiate idol-worship. The king summoned Jirjīs to worship the statue that he worshiped, saying, "If your Lord were the King of Kings, as you say, His effect would be visible upon you, as my impact is visible upon my people's princes around me." Jirjīs replied by glorifying divine [798]
rule, and in the course of his speech, he said, "Where would you place Tranquillinus, a dignitary of your people under your rule? And how would you compare him to Elijah under divine rule? Elijah was originally human; he ate food, and walked in the market, but limitless divine favor unto him continued. He was granted wings and dressed in light, so that he became human and angelic, terrestrial and celestial, and he floated with the angels. Tell me, how would you compare Magnentius, a dignitary of your people, with Christ, the son of Mary? For God chose him and his mother above the men of the world, and made them a sign for the believers [*al-muʿtabirīn*]."[418]

Then he spoke of Christ and how God favored him with miracles. He also said, "And tell me, how would you compare the mother of this good spirit, whom God has chosen as His word, cleansing her body for His spirit, and making her the head of His women servants? To whom would you compare her and the divine favor she was granted? To Jezebel[419] and her fate under your rule? For she was of your faction [*shīʿah*] and reli-

418. That is, those who duly consider, or observe.

419. See I Kings 21; II Kings 9:21–37. See this comparison in the encomium on Saint George, the Bishop of Ancyra. The text is translated by Wallis Budge in *George of Lydda*. For the Greek prototype, see Krumbacher, *Der heilige Georg*, 18–26.

gious community [*millah*], and God made her safe at the home
[799] of the great man of her realm. That is, until the dogs attacked her at her home and tore her flesh and lapped her blood, and the foxes and hyenas pulled her limbs. How would you compare her and her fate to Mary, the daughter of ʿImrān, and her rank in the kingdom of God?"

The king said to him, "But you are talking to us about matters of which we do not know. Bring to me the two men whom you have mentioned, so that I may see them, and consider them. I do not know of such things occurring in humans." Then Jirjīs said to him, "The denial comes to you from her heedlessness of God. As to the two men, you will not see them nor will they see you, unless you act like them and reach their abodes." The king replied, "We pardoned you and your lies became clear to us, for you boasted of deeds you were able to perform and could not verify what you said."

The king then offered Jirjīs the choice of being punished or bowing to Apollo, for which he would be rewarded. At this Jirjīs said "If Apollo is he who raised heaven and multiplied upon it bodies by God's power, you are right and your suggestion is correct; but if not, then off with you, accursed filth." When the king heard Jirjīs curse him and his deity, he was mightily enraged. He called for a wooden board which was set up for torture. The iron rake was passed over Jirjīs to tear his body and maul his flesh and skin and veins, while vinegar and mustard were sprinkled over him. When the king saw that this did not kill Jirjīs, he ordered six iron nails heated until they were aglow, and upon the king's order, Jirjīs's head was penetrated with a nail so that his brains oozed out. Now when the
[800] king saw that Jirjīs was still alive, he ordered a copper cauldron to be heated until it was aglow, and Jirjīs was placed in it. It was covered over him, and Jirjīs remained in it until it cooled off. When the king saw that Jirjīs was still alive, he called to him, "Do you not feel the pain of this torture?" At this Jirjīs replied, "Did I not tell you that there is a Lord over you, and he is closer to you than you yourself?" Then the king said, "Yes, you told me." Whereupon Jirjīs remarked, "It is He who has lifted your torture and enabled me to endure it, that it be a proof against you."

As he said it, the king felt sick, and was afraid for himself and his realm; he decided to keep Jirjīs in prison forever. But the notables of the people said, "If you leave him free to address the people, he will soon turn them against you; rather, order that he be tortured in prison to keep him from addressing the people." Upon the king's order he was thrown on the ground in prison, four iron poles held his feet and hands, and a marble column was put over his back. Seven men attempted to carry that column but could not remove it; then fourteen men failed. Finally, eighteen men did succeed. That day Jirjīs remained pegged (to the ground) under the stone. When night came, God sent an angel to him. This was the first time he was supported by an angel, and the first time inspiration visited him. The angel removed the stone from him, removed the pegs from his hands and feet, fed him and gave him to drink, gave him glad tidings and comforted him. In the morning he took Jirjīs out of the prison, and said to him, "Stay with your enemy and struggle with him mightily in the cause of God, for God says to you, 'Be of good cheer, endure, for I shall put you to the test at the hand of this enemy of Mine. For seven years he will [801]
torture you and during those years he will kill you four times. In each case I shall return your life to you, but at the fourth killing I shall accept your soul and award you your reward.'"

The others did not notice and, lo and behold, Jirjīs appeared over them, calling upon them to turn to God. The king exclaimed, "Is it Jirjīs?" "Yes," said Jirjīs. He asked, "Who released you from the prison?" "He Whose power is beyond your power," Jirjīs answered. When Jirjīs said that to the king, the latter became filled with ire and ordered various tortures. At the sight of these, Jirjīs felt fear and terror. He began to rebuke himself in a loud voice, and the people heard. When he finished rebuking himself, they stretched him between two wooden boards, put a sword over him at his throat, and then sawed his head off, so that it fell at his feet—his body was in two pieces. Then they started cutting those two parts of his body into smaller pieces. There were seven ferocious lions in a pit—they were one kind of torture—and his body was thrown to them. As he fell toward them, God commanded the lions to lower their heads and necks; the lions stood on their talons, thus protecting him from harm. That day he remained dead; it was the first death he experienced. As night fell, God collected his dismembered body, rebuilt it, returned it to life, and sent an angel to take him out of the bottom of the pit. The angel was to feed him, let him drink, and bring him glad tidings and comfort him. In the morning, the angel said to him, "O Jirjīs." "Here I am," replied Jirjīs; whereupon the angel said, "Know, that the power that created man out of dust, took you out of the bottom of the pit. Stay with your enemy, fight him mightily for the sake of God, and endure death patiently."

[802] The people were taken unaware when Jirjīs appeared while they were occupied with a joyful celebration of his alleged death. When they saw him coming toward them, they exclaimed, "How this man resembles Jirjīs; as if it were he." The king said, "No hiding for Jirjīs; that is indeed he! Do you not notice his unruffled manner, his lack of awe?" Jirjīs responded, "Certainly, it is I. What evil people! You killed and mutilated [me] but God was truly kinder and more merciful than you. He revived me, returning to me my life. Turn to this mighty Lord who showed you His deeds." When he told them that, they said to one another, "A sorcerer, he enchanted your hands and eyes, to keep them away from himself." They assembled the sorcerers that were in their land. When they arrived, the king said to their leader, "Suggest to me your greatest sorcery that will dispel my anxiety." The sorcerer said, "Call for an ox." When this was brought, he blew into one of its ears and it split in two. Then he blew into the other ear and, lo and behold, there were two oxen. Then he ordered sowing and ploughing, and the field was sown. It grew crops that ripened and were harvested. He then treaded, winnowed, and milled, and he kneaded, baked and ate; all this within an hour,[420] as you see.[421]

The king asked, "Can you transform him into an animal?" The sorcerer replied, "Which animal?" The king said, "A dog." The sorcerer then called out, "Order a goblet of water." When

420. Text: *wa-akala dhālika,* "and he ate this." Perhaps read instead: *wa-kull dhālika,* "and all this within . . ."

421. Perhaps: as they were looking on (wa-hum yarauna).

it was brought, the sorcerer blew upon it; then he said to the king, "Invite him to drink it." So Jirjīs drank it all. The sorcerer asked, "What do you feel?" He replied, "I feel quite well, as I [803] was thirsty, and by divine kindness I was given this drink, and strengthened thereby against you." When he said this, the sorcerer approached the king, and said, "Know, O King, that if you were contending with a man like yourself you could prevail over him; but you are contending with the Master of heaven, who is King beyond contention."

A poor woman heard of Jirjīs and the wondrous things he was doing. She came to him when he was at the height of his suffering, saying, "O Jirjīs, I am a poor woman. I have neither money nor provisions, except an ox with which I used to plough, but he died. I came to you that you might have pity on me, and pray to God to revive my ox. The eyes of Jirjīs welled up with tears, and he prayed to God to revive her ox; he gave her a stick and told her, "Go to your ox, strike him with this stick, and say to him, 'Live, God willing.'" She said, "O Jirjīs, my ox died some days ago, and beasts of prey tore him to pieces; and it will take me some days before I reach home." Jirjīs replied, "Even if you should find only a single tooth of his to strike with the stick, he will rise, God willing." She left and reached the spot where the ox had fallen. The first things she noticed were one of his horns and the hair of his tail. She put them together, struck them with the stick she was given, and uttered the words as instructed. Lo and behold, her ox was alive, and she put it to work. The news of it spread.

When the sorcerer spoke to the king of what he did, one of the king's men, the most powerful after the king, said, "Listen to me, O people, I shall tell you." They responded, "Yes." Then he spoke thus, "You have attributed sorcery to this man, and [804] you have asserted that he has, by sorcery, kept your hands and eyes away from himself. He has shown you that you tortured him, but it did not touch him; you slew him, yet he did not die. Have you ever seen a sorcerer able to ward off death or revive the dead?" He then related to them what Jirjīs had done, and what they had done to him, as well as the story of the woman and the ox. He remonstrated against them citing these events, whereupon they said to him, "Your speech is that of a man who has been receptive to him." He replied, "Since I have seen what I have seen of his deeds, his case has seemed wondrous to me." They replied, "Perhaps he has seduced you." At this, he declared, "Indeed, I believe, and I testify before God that I do not share your worship."

The king and his companions attacked him with daggers and cut out his tongue. Soon he was dead. They said, "The pest affected him, and God hastened his end before he spoke." When the people heard of his death, it horrified them, and they suppressed the story. But when Jirjīs saw that they were suppressing it, he came out and disclosed it, repeating to them the speech of the slain man. Four thousand men followed Jirjīs as he related the story of the dead man. They said, "He was right. How wonderful it is what he said! God will have mercy upon him!" The king now acted against them. He detained them, and he kept torturing, killing and mutilating them, until he destroyed them all. Then he turned to Jirjīs and said, "Why do you not call upon your Lord to revive these companions of yours who were slain because of you?" Jirjīs replied, "What they chose to do was for their bliss."

One of their dignitaries called Majlitis said, " You asserted, Jirjīs, that it is your God who creates and then recreates. Let me ask something of you. If your God makes it happen, I shall believe in you, I shall proclaim you truthful, and I shall save you from my people. As you see, there are fourteen platforms below us, and a table between us upon which there are goblets
[805] and plates, all made of dry wood from various trees. Well then, pray to your Lord to recreate these vessels and platforms and the table as He originally created them, so that they again become green plants which we should recognize each by its color, foliage, flower and fruit."

Jirjīs answered him, "You have asked for a thing that is extremely difficult for me or for you but is a slight matter for God." He prayed to the Lord and, lo and behold, instantly those platforms and all those vessels turned into green trees, rooted in the ground, covered with bark, branches, foliage, flowers and fruits, so that each tree could be recognized by name, color, flower and fruit. When they beheld this, Majlitis, who had requested it, turned upon Jirjīs and said, "I shall devise a torture for this sorcerer in a way that will deprive him of his ruse." He took copper, made of it a huge hollow image of an ox, filled it with naphtha, lead sulfur, and arsenic. Then he also put Jirjīs into the copper ox, lit a fire under the figure, and kept adding fuel to the flame until the figure was all aglow and everything in it had melted entirely. Jirjīs died inside. God then sent a stormy wind that filled the skies with dark clouds, constant thunder and lightning, and continuous thunderbolts. God sent whirlwinds that filled their land with smoke and darkness. Everything from heaven to earth was blackened and darkened, and for days the people were perplexed in that darkness, unable to distinguish between day and night.

God sent (the angel) Michael to carry off the figure with Jirjīs in it. When the angel removed it, he struck the ground with it, with a blow so powerful that it frightened all the people of Syria, all of whom heard it simultaneously and they prostrated themselves, dumbfounded by the powerful shock. The figure broke, and Jirjīs walked out of it alive. As he stood talking to [806] them the darkness disappeared, and all that is between heaven and earth lit up. Their souls returned to them. One of the men, Traqbalina by name, said to him, "Jirjīs, we do not know if it is you or your Lord who performs these wonders. If it is He who does so, pray to Him to revive our dead; for in these graves you see are some of our dead, some of whom we know, and others who died before our time. Pray to Him to revive them, so that they might be as they were and we might talk to them. We might recognize those we know; he whom we do not recognize, might tell us his story."

Jirjīs answered him, "You know that God grants you this pardon and shows you these miracles only to complete the proofs of his [manifest existence] for you. He does this so you might incur His wrath [later]." Then upon his order the graves were unearthed; there were bones, mortal remains and rot. He began praying, and instantly there sat seventeen persons: nine men, five women, and three boys. One of the men was very old. Jirjīs addressed him, "Old man, what is your name?" The man answered, "My name is Yūbīl." Jirjīs then asked, "When did you die?" "At such and such time," he replied. They calculated he had died four hundred years earlier. When the king and his company saw this, they said, No manner of torture has been left untried, except hunger and thirst. Torture Jirjīs with these.

They betook themselves to a well-guarded house of a very old and poor woman who had a son, blind, mute, and crippled. They imprisoned Jirjīs in her house. Neither food nor drink
[807] could reach him. When he suffered from hunger he said to the old woman, "Do you have any food or drink?" She answered, "No. By Him in whose name an oath is made, we have not had food since such and such time. I shall go out and ask for something for you." Then Jirjīs said to her, "Do you know God?" "Yes," she replied. He now asked, "Do you worship Him?" She said, "No." Jirjīs then summoned her to God. She accepted his words and left seeking something for him. In her house there was a dry wooden pillar supporting the wood (structure) of the house. He began praying, and in no time that pillar flourished to produce all kinds of known edible fruit, such as *liyyā*ʾ and beans. Abū Jaʿfar relates: *Liyyā*ʾ is a Syrian plant with an edible pit; the back of the pillar extended as a branch (*far*ʿ) over the house to give it and the place around it shade.[422]

The old woman came and found him enjoying his abundant food. When she saw from afar what had happened to her home, she exclaimed, "I believe in Him who fed you in the house of hunger. Pray to this great Lord to cure my son." Jirjīs said to her, "Bring him close to me." She did, whereupon he spit in the boy's eyes, and he saw. Jirjīs breathed in his ears, and he heard. At this, she said, "Release his tongue and feet, may God have mercy on you." Jirjīs said to her, "Hold him, it is a great day for him."

The king went out for a stroll in his city. When he saw the tree, he said to his retinue, "I see a tree where I did not know one to be before." They said, "This tree grew for the sorcerer whom you wanted to punish with hunger. He is, however, sated by this tree with whatever he desires; the poor woman
[808] has been fed, and he has cured her son. Upon the king's order the house was destroyed and the tree was to be cut down.

422. A kind of very white chickpea growing in Syria, and perhaps in the Ḥijāz.

When they attempted to cut it down, (however,) God dried it up and it returned to its former state; so they left it. The king ordered that Jirjīs be thrown to the ground face down, and pegged to four poles. A column of clay was rapidly loaded over him with daggers and knifeblades inserted under it. Then he called for forty oxen. They trampled over it all. Jirjīs, under this burden, was torn in three pieces. The king then ordered that one be burned in fire until it turned into ashes, and he sent men to scatter those ashes over the sea. But immediately they heard a heavenly voice, "Sea, God commands you to guard what is in you of this blessed body, for I wish to return it to its former state." God then sent the winds to extract and collect the ashes from the sea, so that they turn into a heap, as they were before the scattering. All this while those who scattered the ashes were still standing there. They saw the ashes rise, and from these Jirjīs emerged, shaking the dust off his head. The men then returned Jirjīs. When they reached the king, they told him of the voice that had brought Jirjīs back to life and the wind that collected the ashes. The king said to Jirjīs, "Would you like something that would be good for me and you? Were it not that the people might say that you defeated me and vanquished me, I would follow you and believe in you. Prostrate yourself before Apollo just once, or sacrifice to him just one sheep, then I shall do something to please you."

When Jirjīs heard these words of the king, he was seized with the desire to be brought before the idol so that he could destroy
it. Jirjīs hoped that once the idol was destroyed, the king would [809]
despair of it and would believe him. So Jirjīs resorted to deception and said, "Yes, if you wish, but let me come before your idol to prostrate myself before it, and sacrifice to it." The king rejoiced. He got up and kissed Jirjīs's hand, his feet, and his head. Then he said, "I suggest that you spend the day and the night at my home, on my couch, among my family, so that you might have a respite from suffering torture, and so that the people might see how you honor me." He vacated his home for Jirjīs, removing those who were in it. Jirjīs stayed there until evening; then he rose to pray and read the psalms—he had an exquisite voice. When the king's spouse heard him, she listened. Jirjīs had not been aware that she was behind him and

had joined him in weeping. He then appealed to her to embrace the faith, and she became a believer. Then he ordered her to conceal her faith. In the morning, he went to the shrine of the idols to worship them.

The old woman in whose home he had been imprisoned was told, "Do you know that Jirjīs has been seduced and has succumbed to worldly temptation, that the king made him covet his realm, and that he and Jirjīs went to the shrine of his idol to worship?" The old woman went out among others, carrying her son on her shoulder, chiding Jirjīs while the people were paying no attention to her. When Jirjīs entered the shrine amidst the people, he noticed the old woman with her son on her shoulder next to himself. He called the old woman's son by his name, and the boy spoke in reply, though he had never spoken before; then the boy rushed off his mother's shoulder and walked on his feet, upright, though he had never before touched the ground with his feet. When he stood before Jirjīs,
[810] the latter said, "Now pray for me to these idols."

The idols were then on platforms of gold, seventy-one of them—the people worshiped the sun and the moon too. The boy asked Jirjīs, "What shall I say to the idols?" Jirjīs replied, "Tell them that Jirjīs asks you and suggests to you, in the name of God, to come to him." As the boy told them that, they began to roll down toward Jirjīs. When they reached him, he struck the ground with his foot; they caved in, along with the platform, and Satan (Iblīs) emerged from the body of one of the idols, running and fleeing from the ignominy. As he passed Jirjīs, the latter seized him by his forelock, so that Satan's head and neck bowed. Jirjīs then addressed him, "Tell me, filthy spirit, accursed creation, what urges you to destroy yourself and others while you know that you and your host will go to hell." Satan replied, "If I had the choice between everything lit up by the sun, as well as that which is in the darkness of the night, a choice between this and destroying and misleading mankind, or even a single human but for one moment, I would choose that moment above all else. The passion for that seizes me, and the pleasure is like that enjoyed by all creatures. Do you not know, Jirjīs, that God made all angels bow to your father Adam, and that Gabriel and Michael and Israfil and all the

angels closest to God and the celestial host did so while I refused; for I said, 'I shall not bow to this creature as I am better than he is.' "[423] When Satan said this, Jirjīs released him. Since then Satan has not entered the inside of any idol, out of fear of [811]
collapse; nor will he ever do so, people say.

The king said, "Jirjīs, you have deceived and misled me, and destroyed my deities." Jirjīs replied, "I have done so intentionally so that you might consider and realize that had they been deities, as you say, they would have been out of my reach; but how can you believe in deities that cannot escape my reach, while I am but a bleak creature and possess only what my Lord has endowed me with." When Jirjīs said this, the king's spouse addressed them, declaring her faith and repudiating their religion, while enumerating before them the deeds of Jirjīs and the signs he had shown them. She said to them, "What are you expecting from this man if not a prayer which will make the earth under you cave in and destroy you, even as your idols perished. By God, O people, it is about your lives." The king then said to her, "Woe upon you, Alexandra! How quickly has this sorcerer misled you in one night, while I have withstood him for seven years with no impact on me." She replied, "Have you not seen how God makes him victorious over you? How God imposes his power over you? How he triumphs in the dispute with you in every respect?"

By the king's command, she was carried to the wooden board on which Jirjīs had been hung, and she was hung upon it. She was tortured with the iron combs from which Jirjīs had suffered. When she felt the pain of the torture she exclaimed, "Pray to your Lord, Jirjīs, to alleviate my pain." He said to her, "Look above you!" As she did so, she laughed. He said to her, "What makes you laugh?" She answered, "I see two angels above me, and a crown with the jewels of Paradise. They are awaiting my soul's expiration, and as soon as it expires they will crown it." Then they carried her soul up to Paradise. When God took her soul, Jirjīs began to pray. He said, "O God, You have honored me with this tribulation, to grant me the virtues of the martyrs. O God, this is my last day, the day

423. See *EI*[2], s.v. Djabrā'īl, Isrāfīl; *SEI*, s.v. Malā'ika, Mīkāl.

which you have promised me would be a rest from this world's tribulation. O God, I ask You not to accept my soul, and not to remove me from this place before You bring upon the arrogant people Your blows and vengeance which they cannot withstand. This would console me and delight me, for they have mistreated and tortured me. O God, I also ask of You that, if after me any herald of Yours should, amidst tribulation and grief, remember me and ask You [something] in my name, You should comfort him, have mercy on him, be responsive to him, and accept my intercession for him."

As he finished this prayer, God rained fire upon them. In pain, they turned on Jirjīs and struck him with swords. Then God granted him the fourth death, as promised. When the city and all within it was burnt down and turned to ashes, God carried it from the face of the earth. He overturned it, and for a long time thereafter malodorous smoke issued from under it. Anybody who inhaled it fell gravely ill. It resulted in a variety of diseases, each unlike the other.

Those who believed in Jirjīs, and were slain with him numbered thirty-four thousand in addition to the king's spouse, may God have mercy on her.

Bibliography of Cited Works

Qur'ān quotations and references follow A. J. Arberry's *The Koran Interpreted* London 1955 (reprints; paperback).

Alī, Jawād, "Mawārid Ta'rīkh al-Ṭabarī" in *Majallat al-Majma' al-'Ilmī al 'Irāqī*, 1–2. Baghdad, 1950.

Altheim, F., *Weltgeschichte Asiens im griechischen Zeitalter*. Halle (Salle), 1947–48.

Altheim, F., und Stiehl, R., *Die Araber in der alten Welt*. Berlin, 1964–69.

———, ———, *Christentum am Roten Meer*. Berlin, 1971.

———, ———, *Geschichte Mittelasiens im Altertum*. Berlin, 1970.

al-A'shā, *Dīwān al-A'shā al-Kabīr*. Ed. M. M. Husayn. Beirut, 1972.

Bailey, H. W., *Zoroastrian problems in the ninth century*. Oxford, 1943.

Bal'amī, *Ta'rīkh-e Bal'amí*. Ed., M. Taqī Bahār Melik al-Sho'arā. 2 vol. Tehran, 1341.

Bidez, J., and Cumont, F., *Les Mages hellenisés*. Paris, 1938.

Blau, O., "Altarabische Sprachstudien," *ZDMG*, 27 (1873). pp. 295–363.

Boyce, M., *History of Zoroastrianism* (Handb. d. Orientalistik). Leiden, 1975.

Brooks, E. W., "Act of Saint George," *Le Muséon*, 1925. pp. 67–115.

Budge, W., *George of Lydda*. London, 1930.

Butler's Lives of the Saints. Eds., Herbert Thurston and Donald Attwater. Vol. II. London, 1956.

BSOAS = Bulletin of the School of Oriental and African Studies. London.
CHI = *The Cambridge History of Iran*, IIIa–IIIb. Ed., E. Yarshater, Cambridge, 1983.
Cary, G., *The medieval Alexander.* Cambridge, 1956.
Casson, L. and Hettich, E. L., *Excavations at Nessana.* Vol. II. Princeton, 1950.
Cheikho, L., "Athar jadīd li- aʿmāl al-qiddīs jirjīs al-shahīd." *al-Mashriq,* 1907. pp. 414–420.
Christensen, A. *L'Iran sous les Sassanides.* 2nd ed. Copenhagen, 1944.
———, *Les Kayanides* (Det Kgl. Danske Videnskabernes Selskab. Historisk-Filologiske Meddelelser, XIX, 2). Copenhagen, 1931.
———, *Les types du premier homme et du premier roi dans l'histoire legendaire des Iraniens.* I, Stockholm, 1918. II, Leiden, 1934.
Cumont, F., "La plus ancienne légende de St. Georges." *Revue de l'histoire des religions,* 1936.
Darmesteter, J., *Études Iraniennes* II. Paris, 1883.
Delehaye, Hippolyte, *Les Legendes grecques des saints militaires.* Paris, 1909; New York, 1975.
Dozy, R., *Dictionnaire detaillé des vêtements chez les Arabes.* repr. Beirut, 1963.
———, *Supplement aux dictionnaires arabes.* 2 vols. 2nd ed. Leiden, 1927.
Encyclopaedia Iranica. London, 1982.
EI = *Encyclopaedia of Islam* (1st ed.)
EI² = *Encyclopaedia of Islam*, 2nd ed. (see *SEI*)
Encyclopaedia Judaica. Jerusalem, 1971.
Firdawsi, *Shāhnāmah*
Friedlaender, I., *Die Chadirlegende und der Alexanderroman.* Leipzig-Berlin, 1913.
Frye, R., *The History of ancient Iran* (Handbuch der Altertumswissenschaft). Munich, 1984.
GAS: See Sezgin
Gehman, H. S. (ed.), *New Westminster Dictionary of the Bible.* Philadelphia, 1970.
Gignoux, Ph. "L'organisation administrative sasanide: le cas du marzbān." *Jerusalem Studies in Arabic and Islam* IV (1984). pp. 1–29.
Ginzberg, Louis, *The Legends of the Jews.* 7 vols. Philadelphia, 1909–38.
Gnoli, G., *Richerche storiche sul Sistan antico.* Istituto Italiano per il Media ed Estremo Oriente, Reports and Memoirs, X. Rome, 1967.

De Goeje, M. J., *Glossarium* in the edition of *Annales quos scripsit . . . Tabari* Vol. 14. Leiden, 1901.
Greenfield, J. C., "Some notes on the Arsham letters," in *Irano-Judaica*, ed. by S. Shaked. Jerusalem, 1982.
Hell, J., *Neue Hudailiten-Diwane*. Vol. II. Leipzig, 1933.
Henning, W. B., *Zoroaster, politician or witch doctor?* London, 1951.
Herzfeld, E., *Zoroaster and his world*. Princeton, 1947. Reprint. New York, 1974.
Hirshberg, H. Z., *Yisra'el Ba'arab*. Tel Aviv, 1946.
Ibn Hishām, *Kitāb Sīrat Rasūl Allāh*. Ed., F. Wüstenfeld. Göttingen, 1858–60.
Irano-Judaica, ed. by S. Shaked, Jerusalem, 1982.
Jackson, A. V. W., Zoroaster. New York, 1901.
Jastrow, M., *A dictionary of the Targumim, the Talmud . . . and Midrashic literature*. Reprinted, New York, 1950.
JCOI = Journal of the K. R. Cama Oriental Institute, Bombay.
Josephus, *Antiquities of the Jews*.
JSAI = Jerusalem Studies in Arabic and Islam.
Justi, F., *Der Bundehesch*. Leipzig, 1868.
———, *Iranisches Namenbuch*. Marburg, 1895; Hildesheim, 1963.
Khoury, R. G., *Wahb b. Munabbih*. Wiesbaden, 1972.
Kolesnikov, V., "O termine marzban v sasanidskom Irane," *Palestinskii Sbornik*. 27(90), pp. 49–56. Leningrad, 1981.
Krumbacher, Karl, *Der Heilige Georg in der griechischen Überlieferung*. Abh. d.k. Bayerischen Ak.d. Wiss. philos.-philol. u. hist. klasse xxxv N.3. München, 1911.
Lane, E. G., *Arabic-English Lexicon*. 8 vols. London, 1863–93.
Lassner, J., *Islamic Revolution and historical memory*. American Oriental Series, Vol. 66. New Haven, 1986.
Le Strange, G., *The Lands of the eastern caliphate*. Cambridge, 1905.
Margoliouth, D. S., *The relations between Arabs and Israelites prior to the rise of Islam*. London, 1924.
Markwart, J., "Beiträge zur Geschichte und Sage von Eran." *ZDMG* 49 (1895), pp. 628–672.
———, *Wehrot und Arang*. Ed. H. H. Schaeder. Leiden, 1938.
Mayrhofer, M., *Iranisches Personennamenbuch*. Wien, 1977.
———, *Onomastica Persepolitana*. Wien, 1973.
Montgomery, J., *Arabia and the Bible*. Philadelphia, 1934.
Muhammad Ḥusayn b. Khalaf, *Burhān-e Qāṭiʿ*. Ed. M. Muʿīn. 2nd ed., 5 vols. Tehran, 1342.
Nagel, T., *Alexander der Grosse in der frühislamischen Volksliteratur*. Waldorf-Hessen, 1978.

Neusner, J., "Baruch b. Neriah and Zoroaster," *Journal of Biblical Research*, Vol. 32 (1964).
Nicholson, R. A., *A literary history of the Arabs*. Cambridge, 1907.
Nöldeke, Th., "Beiträge zur Geschichte des Alexanderromans." *Denkschriften d.k. Akad. d. Wiss.* Wien, Vol. 38, 1890.
———, *Beiträge zur Kenntnis der Poesie der alten Araber*. Hannover, 1864.
———, *Geschichte der Perser und Araber zur Zeit der Sasaniden*. Leiden, 1879.
———, *Das iranische Nationalepos*. 2nd ed. Berlin, 1920.
———, *Persische Studien* II in Sitzungsberichte der k. Akademie der Wissenschaften in Wien, Phil.-hist. Classe. Bd. CXXVI, xii. Wien, 1892.
———, "Zur orientalischen Geographie," *ZDMG* 28 (1874) pp. 93–102.
Nyberg, H. S., "Sassanid Mazdaism according to Moslem sources," *Journal of the J.K.R. Cama Oriental Institute*, 39 (1958), pp. 1–63.
Oppenheimer, A., *Babylonia Judaica in the Talmudic period* (Beihefte zum Tübinger Atlas des Vorderen Orients, Reihe B, N 97). Wiesbaden, 1983.
Pfister, F., *Alexander der Grosse in den Offenbarungen der Griechen, Juden, Mohammedaner und Christen*. Berlin, 1956.
Pigulevskaia, N. V., *Araby u granits Vizantii i Irana*. Moscow-Leningrad, 1964.
Piotrovskii, M., "The Arabic version of the story of Zabba" in *Palestinskii Sbornik*. Vol. 84 (1970).
Rosenthal, F., "The influence of the biblical tradition in Muslim historiography," in B. Lewis and P. M. Holt (eds.) *Historians of the Middle East*, pp. 35–45. London, 1962.
Rothstein, G., *Die Dynastie der Lahmiden in al-Hira*. Berlin, 1899. Reprint: Hildesheim, 1968.
Sezgin, F., *Geschichte des arabischen Schrifttums*. Leiden, 1967.
Shahid, I., *Byzantium and the Arabs in the fourth century*. Washington, D.C. 1984.
Shaked, Sh., "Esoteric Trends in Zoroastrianism," *Proceed. of the Israel Academy of Sciences and Humanities* III (1969) pp. 175–221.
———, "From Iran to Islam: on some symbols of royalty," *Jerusalem Studies in Arabic and Islam* VII (1985).
———, *Wisdom of the Sasanian sages* (Denkard VI) Boulder, 1979.
SEI = The Shorter Encyclopaedia of Islam.
Smith, M., *Jesus the magician*. New York, 1978.

Smith, S., "Events in Arabia in the sixth century A.D." *BSOAS* 16 (1954) pp. 425–468.
Speyer, H., *Die biblischen Erzählungen im Qoran*. Repr. Hildesheim, 1961.
Spiegel, Fr., *Eranische Altertumskunde*. Vols. I–III. Leipzig, 1871–78.
Torrey, C. C., *The Jewish foundations of Islam*. New York, 1933. Repr. 1967.
Trimingham, J. S., *Christianity among the Arabs in pre-Islamic times*. New York, 1979.
Wellhausen, J., *Reste arabischen Heidentums*. 2nd. ed. Berlin, 1892.
Wikander, S., *Feuerpriester in Kleinasien und Iran*. Lund, 1946.
Wissowa, G. (ed.), *Paulys Realencyclopaedie der classischen Altertumswissenschaft*. Stuttgart, 1984.
Yāqūt, *Muʿjam al-buldān*. Ed. F. Wüstenfeld. Leipzig, 1866–73.
Yasif, E., *Sippure Ben Sira*. Jerusalem, 1985.
Zarncke, F. "Georgslegende aus dem 9. Jahrh.," *Berichte d.k. Sächs. Ges. d. Wiss.*, 1875.
ZDMG = Zeitschrift der Deutschen Morgenländischen Gesellschaft.
ZerrīnKūb, Abd al-Ḥusayn, *Do Qarn-e Sukūt*. Tehran, 1976.

Index

N

O

P

Q